COMING TO CARE

The work and family lives of workers caring for vulnerable children

Julia Brannen, June Statham, Ann Mooney and
Michaela Brockmann

First published in Great Britain in 2007 by

The Policy Press
University of Bristol
Fourth Floor
Beacon House
Queen's Road
Bristol BS8 1QU
UK

Tel +44 (0)117 331 4054
Fax +44 (0)117 331 4093
e-mail tpp-info@bristol.ac.uk
www.policypress.org.uk

British Library Cataloguing in Publication Data
A catalogue record for this book is available from the British Library.

Library of Congress Cataloging-in-Publication Data
A catalog record for this book has been requested.

ISBN 978 1 86134 850 0 hardcover

Cover design by Qube Design Associates, Bristol.
Printed and bound in Great Britain by MPG Books, Bodmin.

Contents

List of tables and boxes

Tables

Boxes

Acknowledgements

This study was commissioned by the Department of Health in 2002 and funded by the Department of Health and the Department for Education and Skills until 2005. We are very grateful for this support. We also wish to express our gratitude to the many persons who made it possible to carry out this study of childcare workers: the local authorities, especially those working in children's services, the managers and organisers of childcare services run by local authorities, and the independent and private sectors. Thanks are also due to Stephanie Jones for her assistance with the telephone survey. Last, but most important, are the childcare workers who took part in the study. We thank them for providing such valuable insights into their work and family lives. We are also grateful for the comments provided by the peer reviewers.

ONE

Setting the scene

The people who work with children are central to keeping
them safe and helping them to get the most out of life. (HM
Government, 2003, p 10)

Introduction

This book is about the work and family lives of people who provide
care for 'vulnerable' children and young people. This includes children
who are looked after by the state in either foster families or residential
children's homes, and children living in their own families but receiving
additional support from social services. Such workers form part of the
'social care workforce', a term that is difficult to pin down and define
(Eborall, 2005; Moss et al, 2006). It has been argued that the concept of
social care transcends many conceptual dichotomies: between the public
and private; between formal and informal settings; between paid and
unpaid carers; between the state and the family; and between the care
of children and of adults (Daly and Lewis, 1999). The Commission for
Social Care Inspection, which has a duty to report annually on the state
of social care services in England, covers within its remit both services
for adults (such as care homes and domiciliary care services for older
people, services for adults with learning or physical disabilities, and social
work and mental health services for adults) and services for children
(including social work, child protection, early years, children's homes,
and fostering and adoption services). In 2004/05, the total social care
workforce was estimated to number around 1.6 million people, with
13% of them working in children's services. The majority of workers
(85%) were female, and nearly two thirds were employed in the private
and voluntary sector (CSCI, 2005a).

The children's workforce has received particular attention from
central government in recent years, partly as a result of childcare
scandals that have focused attention on failures among those working
with vulnerable children (Laming, 2003). The *Every Child Matters:
Change for Children* programme (HM Government, 2003) has made
'workforce reform' a key area for action. Subsequent developments
have included the publication of a Children's Workforce Strategy,

which aims to 'build a world-class workforce for children and young people' (HM Government, 2005a), and the creation of a Children's Workforce Development Council in 2005 to take this work forward. A key aspect of the Workforce Strategy, discussed in more detail on page 4, is developing greater integration between the different types of work with children and greater flexibility for workers to move between them.

Against this background, the current study focuses on four groups of workers:

- residential social workers working in children's homes;
- family support workers, working either in social work teams or family centres;
- foster carers working either for a local authority or an independent fostering agency; and
- childminders working with children placed and paid for by social services, often known as 'community' or 'sponsored' childminders.

All provide care for children who are referred to by policy makers as 'vulnerable', 'disadvantaged' or 'in need'. Such terminology risks characterising children as passive and dependent, in need of protection rather than as active agents in their own lives with a right to additional services (Moss et al, 2000; Brannen and Moss, 2003). However, we have used the term 'vulnerable children' in this book in order to situate the study within the current UK policy framework.

The study adopts a time perspective. Focusing on the past, it examines what motivated care workers to care, why and when they entered the childcare workforce, and what developing a 'career' in childcare work may mean in practice over the course of these workers' lives. Focusing on the present, it examines how care workers in different settings understand their work, how they experience the conditions of the work, and how they manage their care work and unpaid care within family life in the context of the policies available and the management practices of their workplaces. With a lens on the future, it examines carers' work intentions and whether they stay or leave their work and their reasons for such decisions. (For a detailed description of the study's aims see Chapter Two.)

The research and English policy background

There are several reasons why this study is particularly timely in terms of policy.

Rising demand, decreasing supply

First, the demand for care workers is increasing at the same time as demographic and economic trends are reducing the pool of people from which such labour has traditionally been drawn. There is a growing need for workers to care for children who cannot live with their parents or relatives and to provide support for children who are in need. Yet there are more opportunities in the labour market for those who in the past have taken up childcare work. The Social Services Inspectorate has pointed to a 'buoyant economy with full employment and many attractive employment alternatives to the care sector, along with high housing costs in some areas' as significant barriers to increasing the supply of social care workers (SSI, 2001, para 5.5). Furthermore, those who choose to become childminders, nursery nurses and foster carers generally have a below average level of formal education (Cameron et al, 2001; Mooney et al, 2001; Sinclair et al, 2004). As education levels have risen, particularly among women, the pool from which these workers have traditionally been drawn is shrinking.

Problems in recruitment and retention

These influences have already been felt in the significant problems that are being experienced in recruiting and retaining the social care workforce (CSCI, 2005a; HM Government, 2005a). Vacancy rates in social care are about twice as high as the average for all private and public sector businesses in England, and the problem is particularly acute among workers with vulnerable children. Much of the attention has focused on children's social workers, where vacancy and turnover rates are both reported to be around 12% nationally (Eborall, 2005), and are especially high in London where agency workers are frequently employed. However, other types of care work with children face equal problems. Residential social workers in children's homes had a vacancy rate of 13% and a turnover rate of 14% in 2004 (Eborall, 2005), and managers of children's homes typically report difficulties with recruiting and retaining staff (Mainey, 2003). Few local authorities are able to recruit sufficient foster carers to enable them to offer a choice of placements to match children's needs (CSCI, 2005b; Sinclair, 2005).

Staffing difficulties are evident too in the early years childcare sector, with numbers of registered childminders declining (Mooney et al, 2001) and an increased demand created by the government's 10-year childcare strategy (Rolfe et al, 2003). Childminders who are both suitable and willing to provide care for children referred by social workers can be particularly difficult to find, especially in the disadvantaged areas where the need for this kind of support for families is often highest (Statham et al, 2000).

Developing the children's workforce

A third reason for the study being particularly timely is the current emphasis on promoting greater flexibility within and between childcare workforces (HM Government, 2005a). A 'common core' of skills and knowledge is intended to apply to all those working with children and young people, whatever their level, occupation or setting (HM Government, 2005b). This is already being used by some providers to inform their training delivery (Harrison, 2006). It will form part of an integrated qualifications framework for the children's workforce, to be in place by 2010, which will facilitate movement across different work streams and job roles. Specialist, job-specific skills and understandings will still be required for different roles, but the aim is that a shared body of skills will support the development of a more integrated workforce:

> We need to identify what is common about the work we do together and create a flexible workforce that wants to stay working with children, one that sees a long-term career in the workforce – a career that could mean doing different types of work over time but building on skills as social care workers and social workers. (Harrison, 2006, pp 17–18)

The inclusion in our study of four separate groups of worker with vulnerable children allowed us to explore different types of pathways into and through childcare work (Chapters Three to Five) and workers' views about moving between different types of care work (Chapter Eight). Previous research has provided some 'objective' evidence of workers moving between care sectors and types of care work, possibly in search of better working conditions, particularly better remuneration. But none has explored how care workers make sense of their trajectories over time and perceive the future. Evidence on movement includes one study that found that two thirds of day nursery staff had moved within the childcare and early years field (Cameron et al, 2001). In a survey of former childminders, one third had moved to other childcare-related jobs, and a further third thought they might do so in the future (Mooney et al, 2001). Almost a quarter (23%) of all fosters carers in one survey were working or had worked in a child-related occupation (Bebbington and Miles, 1990), and a study of carers offering short breaks to families with a child in need found that over two thirds had extensive previous experience of working with children (Aldgate and Bradley, 1999). In a Scottish study, two fifths of female foster carers were working or had worked in the social care sector (Triseliotis et al, 2000). A better understanding of conditions that shape care workers' 'careers' and the way that they make sense of their work and their lives could help to target recruitment and retention initiatives more accurately, and inform government strategy for developing the children's workforce.

Increased use of the independent sector

Fourthly, care work with children is likely to be increasingly conducted through partnerships between the independent sector (private or community) and the public sector, leading to a range of different kinds of conditions in which care work is carried out. Local authority children's services are expected to work closely with a range of service providers, and developments such as children's centres and extended schools will create new settings and ways of working with vulnerable children and their families. Although the majority of foster carers still work for local authorities, increasing numbers are moving to independent fostering agencies because of the greater financial rewards, training and support that such agencies are often able to offer (Sellick and Connolly, 2002). Among children's homes, almost 60% are privately owned with a further 6% owned by voluntary providers (CSCI, 2005a). Ten years earlier, in 1995, almost two thirds of children's homes were run by local authorities (DH, 2001), so this represents a significant shift from public to private provision. The shift has implications for workers' employment conditions since, unlike fostering (where independent fostering agencies generally provide better pay and support than do local authorities), staff in private children's homes tend to be less well rewarded and protected than their counterparts in the public sector (Eborall, 2003).

Attention to work–life issues

Finally, one aspect of employer provision that is seen as increasingly relevant to issues of recruitment and retention is work–life policies and practices – how far workers are able to manage their informal caring responsibilities in the context of their paid work. Indeed, problems with recruitment and retention have emerged as the key trigger to the introduction of work–life policies (Dex and Scheibl, 2002). Concerns about care workers' own care responsibilities are increasingly expressed in the context of the more general conditions of workers' employment conditions such as pay, hours and flexibility. There are particular issues for home-based childcare workers where work impinges directly on their families, as in the case of foster carers and childminders. For foster carers, the problems reported include the sometimes stressful and demanding nature of the work, the conflicts created by time pressures, antisocial hours, lack of opportunity for career development, and the relative isolation (Sinclair, 2005). Childminders have to set boundaries between being a worker, mother and wife, between their own and other people's children and between home, family and clients (Mooney et al, 2001). Residential care workers may need to provide overnight care, and spend long shifts away from their own homes. It is important to know more about the views, practices and policies of those who employ and manage care workers, and about the strategies used by care workers in managing the work–family interface in the context of the particular occupation, in order to understand how they could be assisted to reconcile work with their caring responsibilities outside work. Agency workers and those working in private children's homes may be in a weaker position in terms of accessing family-friendly policies than those who work directly for local authorities, unless the service agreement between council and service provider sets out specific expectations in this area.

Why these workers?

The selection of our four groups of childcare workers was guided by both theoretical and policy considerations. They provide a number of contrasts, for example in the site of care, the likely lifecourse stage of the carer, the age and needs of the children cared for and the employment status of the worker (Table 1.1, p 9). The care provided by childminders and foster carers takes place within the home of the carer, usually within family settings, whereas residential care and family support work is provided in institutional settings, or at least outside the carer's home. So for some childcare workers, their homes and the site of paid care coincide, while for others they do not. While a particular kind of caring work may be preferred precisely because it fits with the care needs of the carer's own families, as is the case for many childminders and foster carers, nonetheless for those whose workplace is also their home, issues of boundary management of the work–family interface are likely to be particularly acute.

There is also evidence that these four types of work attract people at different stages of their lives, reinforcing the need for a lifecourse approach (see p 10). Childminding, for example, tends to be undertaken by women when their own children are young (Mooney et al, 2001), while foster care may be started when carers and their children are older. Indeed the ageing of the foster care workforce combined with difficulties in recruiting new carers has created concerns over the ability of councils to offer a choice of appropriate placements (Fostering Network, 2004; Morgan, 2005). Employment status and the extent to which care is commodified also differ between the four groups. Residential social work and family support work involve paid employment by a local authority (council) or private agency, while foster care in most cases is not regarded as paid employment. A national minimum standard introduced in April 2007 stipulates the minimum allowances that a foster carer should be paid to cover the cost of caring for a child placed with them, but it has been argued that this does not reflect the true cost to the carer (Fostering Network, 2006). Community childminders are usually self-employed and receive a fee for each child placed with them by social services.

A final factor guiding our selection of types of childcare worker for this study is that although some of these groups have been relatively extensively researched, for example foster carers (Sinclair, 2005 in England and Triseliotis et al, 2000 in Scotland) and residential social workers (DH, 1998), others such as community childminders and family support workers have received far less attention despite their important role in the provision of services for children in need.

Working with vulnerable children: similarities and differences

The childcare work of the four groups shares some common features, for example relatively low rates of pay and – until recently at least – few requirements for formal qualifications. However, there is also considerable diversity not only between the four categories of childcare work, but also between workers with the same job title. Foster carers, for example, may care on a long-term basis for a single child, specialise in 'therapeutic' placements for children or young people with particularly challenging behaviour, provide short-term or respite placements, or offer both short- and long-term care at the same time. Community childminders may provide daytime care for a child who is neglected or ill-treated at home, overnight or weekend care so that a parent can have a break, or continuous care for up to 28 days. Residential children's homes differ in size and focus. The residential social workers in our study worked in a variety of settings, including a short-term assessment unit with a rapid turnover of children, a unit specialising in the care of particularly difficult or challenging young people, a home for disabled children, and a long-term unit that was home to children for a number of years. Family support workers in the study were either based in family support teams, or attached to different social work teams such as leaving care, family placement or duty and assessment teams. Over the course of the research, some family support workers began spending part of their week working from a community base such as a school or doctor's surgery, reflecting the changes introduced by *Every Child Matters* (HM Government, 2003) (although some had worked in community-based family centres in the past under former policy initiatives, before being reorganised into social work teams).

In broad terms, however, the work of each group can be categorised in relation to a number of variables that are likely to impact on the experience of providing care, and possibly on the ease with which workers move between different types of childcare work (Table 1.1). These include the age group with whom the carer works, the extent of the child's needs, whether the child is looked after (by the state) or supported within their own family of origin, whether the work involves parents or just children/young people, the location where care work takes place, and the time period over which care is provided.

Residential social workers in our study typically worked with older children and young people exhibiting a high level of need and challenging behaviour. Foster carers covered the whole age range, although the preferred age range for those responding to the Postal Survey was 5 to 11, and the majority (62%) offered both short-term and long-term care. Both community childminders and family support workers provided short periods of support to children who remained the responsibility of their parents, and were more likely than the other two groups to work also with members of the child's family.

Family support workers had the most varied role, working with different age groups and with different social work teams. Among the case studies of workers explored in depth, one was attached to a leaving

Table 1.1: Dimensions of care work for the four care worker groups

	Residential social worker	Family support worker	Foster carer	Community childminder
Age of child/ client	Mostly adolescents	Parents, young children and adolescents	Young children or adolescents	Young children
Child's level of need/ difficulty	High	Medium/high	Medium/high	Low/medium
Child's legal status	Looked after	With parents/in the community	Looked after	With parents
Work with parents too	Rarely	Yes	Some contact	Varies
Time spent with client	Full-time care but provided on shift basis	Short, task-focused care	Full-time care on 24/7 basis	Daytime care, occasionally overnight or weekend
Location of care	Institution (but 'home like')	Parent's home or community setting	Carer's home	Carer's home
Worker's employment status	Employed (public and private sector)	Employed (mostly public sector)	Paid an allowance to cover expenses	Self-employed

care team, helping young people who had left care to access housing, welfare benefits and educational provision. Another worked just nine hours a week, mostly doing task-focused work with teenagers but also supervising contact visits between parents and their looked-after children, attending review meetings and court hearings. The work of a third, who was based in a family support team, involved no direct contact with children or parents but instead supporting social workers by finding and arranging placements with family and friends in order to prevent children needing to be taken into care. Two other case study family support workers were attached to reception and assessment teams in different authorities, and much of their work was with younger children and their parents.

Theoretical frameworks

This study is underpinned by a number of theoretical lenses. The first is a lifecourse perspective, which draws attention to the way lives are lived progressively over time and are embedded in social contexts in particular historical periods (Mills, 1959; Elder, 1985; Hareven and Masaoka, 1988). The notion of 'lifecourse' has particular relevance in this study and refers to the linear progression of time but not a single pathway. In sociological discourse the term is allied to the concept of 'career' (Everett Hughes, 1958). According to Elder (1978), the lifecourse comprises a number of interconnected careers or pathways relating to work, parenthood, friendship, sexuality and so on. (The concept of 'career' here means something rather different from the notion of vertical progression up occupational ladders or that which is increasingly part of the vernacular, as we shall describe in Chapter Five.) These career lines or pathways can intersect at different points in time or proceed in parallel. The concept also has an agentic aspect in that people drive their own lifecourse along different tramlines and sequence different lifecourse phases in different ways. Such a conceptual approach enables us to understand how childcare workers work out their pathways into and through childcare work in the context of what else is going on in their lives and in the context of the opportunity structures available to them such as those provided by education and training and the employers they work for. It also enables us to explore how care workers manage the intersection between their work and family pathways, in particular responsibilities for their own children's care and the care of vulnerable children.

Allied to the agentic aspect of the lifecourse careers and the ways in which people create their own lives over time is the notion of identity and the past as 'something to be worked through' with consequences for the self. In Chapter Five we discuss the ways in which childcare workers construct their identities over time and how these constructions and reconstructed identities are reflected in the ways in which they narrate the stories of their lives.

A third and central theoretical concern relates to the ethic of care and how and why childcare workers come to care about and for vulnerable children. Care is much more than work, as Joan Tronto (1993) has suggested. It involves an 'ethics of responsibility' raising key moral questions as who should take responsibility for care, what caring is done and by whom. In Tronto's terms, care is about being a citizen. 'Citizens are people engaged in relations of care with one another' (Tronto, 2004, p 92). Caring is a *moral* decision, in this case to care for vulnerable children, and consists of four ethical elements: attentiveness, responsibility, competence and responsiveness (Tronto, 1993).

Tronto's concept is reflected in the notion of care commitments and responsibilities as 'negotiated' in Finch and Mason's study of family obligations (Finch and Mason, 1993). In this interpretation, care has many aspects and is a process created in practice. A care ethic is created over time and through negotiation and social interaction, sometimes explicit but sometimes not, rather than consisting of the application of fixed rules or norms concerning the obligation to care. There are three aspects. First, the process is relational in the sense that responsibilities are a product of interaction between individuals over time (Finch and Mason, 1993, p 168). Second, it is context specific: negotiations are embedded in concrete, particular and local situations and informed by knowledge of this context and of the other actors. Third, it involves negotiation with oneself as people construct and confirm their identities as moral beings in wanting and deciding to care, in exchanges of support, and the processes through which support is negotiated (Finch and Mason, 1993, p 170).

Negotiating care responsibilities therefore recognises both individual agency and the structural context: actions decided on the basis of what seems 'right' under given social conditions. Such actions contain a complex mix of ethical, relational and contextual considerations. Deciding to enter a caring profession or as a parent to care for one's own family members in particular ways requires taking account of and weighing up many considerations – including normative beliefs, personal and family circumstances, preferences, educational and employment resources – to arrive at particular, situated decisions. Deciding to care for vulnerable children is negotiated: through dialogue with oneself and with others (Chapter Three); through interpreting and assessing different considerations, including contextual or situational constraints and opportunities (Chapter Four); through the construction of self-identities over time (Chapter Five); and through the way that care workers understand the care work they do (Chapter Six).

The way childcare workers negotiated an ethic of care was only glimpsed by us as researchers through what they said to us in their interviews. How do we know that this is what really happened in their lives? The answer is that we cannot know, nor can any methodology presume to capture the 'reality' of how an ethic of care was arrived at. We cannot expect to recreate the processes by which people 'come to care'. This process is highly complex and takes place over time as people experience care from significant others, learn to care for other people, and take responsibility for caring. However, the ways in which people created their accounts during the research interview, and the contextual sense that we as analysts made of our informants' accounts, provide some clues about what aspects of human experience are important in developing an ethic of care. While the term 'care' is used in this book to refer to many different aspects, we have focused in particular on the temporal and the spatial: how care links people's lives both over the lifecourse and in everyday time (see also McKie et al, 2002).

Structure of the book

The rest of the book is organised into nine chapters. Chapter Two describes the study's research questions, its multi-phase research design and its use of a mix of methods, together with a description of the characteristics of the participants and the local authorities where the study was carried out. Chapters Three to Five focus on the past and draw largely upon the biographical interview material in which four groups of childcare workers recounted their stories of care work and their family lives. Chapter Three addresses the disposition or orientation to care: how the research participants accounted for their care ethic in telling the stories of their lives. Chapter Four carries the story forward and identifies the points in care workers' lives when they entered childcare work and the different contextual 'triggers' for their occupational decisions. Chapter Five explores how far care workers created 'careers' in childcare work in terms of the meanings they attributed to the concept and the factors that influenced the notion of 'having a career'. It explores how far care workers shaped their identities and how the notion of a career identity was arrived at – or not.

In Chapter Six we turn to the present and examine how care workers currently make sense of the work they do and identify a number of themes. The chapter examines the different kinds of knowledge that care workers draw upon in the course of their work in the context of the resources available to them (training and qualifications and their own experiences) and analyses a number of cases in depth. Chapter Seven also has a present focus in examining how the four groups experience their work currently including the rewards of the work, and how they experience the working conditions. Similarly, Chapter Nine focuses on how workers currently manage – in this chapter their work–family lives: the spillover effects of work and family life and the strategies they adopt to manage their different care responsibilities on an everyday basis.

Chapter Eight turns to the future and, drawing on the survey material and its subsequent follow-up after 12 months, examines care workers' intentions about staying in their jobs and how far these intentions match their practice a year later. It looks at the reasons care workers give for staying and leaving the work and identifies the problems of making judgements about the future on the basis of asking people about intentions and plans in the present. In this chapter we also consider what might help to recruit and keep people in childcare work, and at the evidence for movement between different types of childcare work. Finally, Chapter Ten summarises the main conclusions from the study, and draws out implications for policy, practice and theory.

TWO

The study

Introduction

This chapter describes the study's research questions, how its research design addressed these questions, the different phases of the study, the variety of different methods used and the characteristics of the childcare workers who participated.

The study's research questions

The main research questions addressed by the study are:

- What shaped an ethic of care among different groups working with vulnerable children, in particular residential care workers, family support workers, foster carers and community childminders?
- What contextual factors prompted childcare workers to enter these occupations during the lifecourse?
- How did childcare workers shape their childcare 'careers' and their identities over time?
- How do different groups of childcare workers currently understand their work?
- How do they currently experience their working conditions?
- Over a year, how much job change took place among these four groups? Why did they leave these childcare occupations and why did they stay?
- How do childcare workers manage their work and family responsibilities?

In this study we took a step back in time by using a lifecourse approach (Chapter One) in order to understand what attracted workers into care work in the first place, how their interest in caring and care work developed over the lifecourse and how their careers in childcare unfolded and unfold over time – past, present and future. One approach was to use biographical methods with small groups of the four types of worker. We also embedded the biographical method within a mixed methods and prospective research design. We carried out a survey of four larger groups of childcare workers drawn from several English local authorities (mainly in southern England but including one in northern England) and followed up these groups one year later. These surveys provided a pool for selecting the biographical case studies and extensive data on different types of childcare workers in sufficient numbers; they also enabled us to study care workers at two points in time. For we sought not only to understand childcare workers' lives in the past and present but to explore movement in and out of childcare work in a *prospective* way. Both the intensive and extensive data together were collected to examine how care workers made sense of the work they did with vulnerable children, their experiences of their work and workplaces, and how they managed care responsibilities inside and outside the family.

Research design and methods

The design was *iterative*, encompassing four phases that flowed from one another, providing samples and sampling criteria for the next phases and also providing data to feed into the overall analysis. The study was *comparative* in design, covering four groups of childcare workers: residential social workers working in children's homes; family support workers either working in family centres or within social work teams; foster carers working either for a local authority or an independent fostering agency; and childminders working with children placed and paid for by social services, referred to as community childminders.

The groups were selected *theoretically*. First, on the basis of their type of *workplace* – two were home-based workers and two were institutionally based – since we thought that the different groups would face different challenges in care work and in managing their work–family lives. Second, the four groups also reflected workers with different *lifecourse* characteristics, as described in Chapter One. A third basis for theorising difference concerned work *orientation* and *financial remuneration*. Unlike residential social work and family support work, many foster carers do not regard fostering as employment (see Nutt, 2006 for a review) as it is only partially reimbursed and calculated in terms of the child's needs rather than the labour of the carer. By contrast, childminders typically combine a work orientation with a family orientation, often choosing this employment as a convenient way of fitting around their young children's needs (Mooney, 2003).

We adopted a *multi-method* approach that combined both quantitative and qualitative methods but also used different types of qualitative approach. How the analysis of the different datasets worked out in practice and how they were combined are discussed in Chapter Ten. The study design was also *prospective*: two surveys were conducted within a year of one another (referred to as the Postal Survey and the follow-up Telephone Survey) with the same set of respondents in which most questions were structured and pre-coded. This phase was followed by a series of biographical case study interviews with selected workers from the four groups drawn from the first survey. Semi-structured interviews with managers of the workers in the areas in which the surveys and case studies were undertaken were also conducted. The variety of methods gave us different types of data and provided different layers and levels of understanding. As we shall see, while we have drawn upon all four sources of data, some chapters have drawn mainly upon the biographical interviews. We turn now to each dataset and its sampling base.

Postal Survey

For each of the four groups of workers a Postal Survey was undertaken in late 2003 and early 2004. This sought to generate contextual information and attitude data about the four worker groups and enable us to identify cases for the case studies. Questions covered demographic characteristics, current and previous employment, understanding of, satisfaction with and commitment to care work, future employment intentions, and managing work and family responsibilities. Wherever possible, questions across the four groups remained the same and most were closed although respondents were invited to make comments at the end. The data were entered into an SPSS database and descriptive analyses were undertaken including the characteristics of and differences between the four groups of workers, for example concerning work satisfaction, and commitment to their work.

We sought to find the Postal Survey sample from two authorities who had agreed to help: a London local authority and a large shire authority in the South of England. These two authorities were selected to provide a number of contrasts: they differed in terms of size, along urban/rural dimensions, and in the extent of public, voluntary and private provision in the residential sector. In practice, neither authority could provide sufficient numbers of family support workers and community childminders and we therefore sought the cooperation of additional authorities for these two groups. Box A1 in the Appendix provides contextual information about the authorities and organisations from which the majority of our care workers were drawn.

Our aim was to sample 150 workers within each of the four groups across the public, voluntary and private sectors as appropriate and this number, or close to it, was achieved for all workers apart from community childminders, who proved the most difficult to find (Table 2.1). Authorities were not easily able to identify this group unless there was an organised scheme and many of the 10 authorities approached had no such scheme and could not help. For data protection reasons, we asked employers[1] to distribute the questionnaire on our behalf with respondents returning their questionnaires directly to the research team.

Altogether, 547 questionnaires were distributed and 305 returned giving a response rate of 56%, although there were differences between type of worker and sector (Table 2.1). The 83 residential social workers were drawn from nine homes (three in the public sector all in the same authority, three in the voluntary sector and three in the private sector). Managers of the nine homes were asked to complete a questionnaire that collected information about the home, the recruitment and retention of staff and helping staff to manage work and family responsibilities (contextual information about the homes can be found in Box A2 in the Appendix). The 84 family support workers were drawn from across three authorities, although 75% were from one authority (Authority C in Box A1 in the Appendix). Approximately half of the 74 foster carers were from an independent fostering agency and the remainder were from the two local authorities we were working with.

Table 2.1: Response rates by worker, sector and for the total sample

Care workers and sectors	Questionnaires		
	Delivered (*n*)	Returned (*n*)	Response rate (%)
Residential social worker			
Local authority	47	27	57
Voluntary	46	18	39
Private	50	38	76
Subtotal	143	83	58
Family support worker			
Local authority	152	84	55
Foster carer			
Local authority	80	38	48
Foster agency	70	36	51
Subtotal	150	74	49
Community childminder	102	64	63
Total	547	305	56

The 64 community childminders were drawn from five authorities although 42% came from one authority (Authority D in Box A1 in the Appendix).

Biographical interviews

Twenty-four cases were selected from the Postal Survey, six from each of the four groups. We adopted a biographical method in order to understand how individual care workers developed an ethic of care, and entered and developed their employment careers in relation to the whole of their lives. However, the method we used was combined with another more commonly used approach – the semi-structured interview (see also Brannen et al, 2004a for the development of this combined method).

The point of a biographical-narrative interview approach is to encourage the interviewee to give their own story as it relates to the context and events *at the time* (in our terms a narrative) without much interviewer framing, preface or interruption (Wengraf, 2001). This type of interview approach eschews 'why questions' and thereby avoids *pushing* the informant into intellectualisation and post hoc rationalisation. The method requires a particular training in which the interviewer learns to listen and refrain from intervention. In adopting this approach we started with an invitation to each care worker to tell their life story and to bear in mind that the study was about their work and family lives (Wengraf, 2001). Participants were told that they could start wherever they wanted and would not be interrupted. Some interviewees took some time to give their narrative while others gave theirs in a matter of minutes. Next, the interviewer posed a number of narrative follow-up questions once the informant indicated they had nothing more to add and was careful to keep to the original sequencing and ordering of the life story, again trying to avoid 'why questions'. Interviewers were guided in their selection of these questions by key events and experiences mentioned by informants that either or both parties judged relevant or important in the unfolding life trajectories.

The emphasis upon 'narration' – meaning here recounting past events as if they were happening in the present – serves to bring the interviewee into a closer relationship to the past that is the focus of interest, and to generate memories that are not always readily accessible to informant or researcher in conventional interviewing approaches. The narrative form allows interviewees to weave their own connections and tell their own stories (Nilsen, 1996) and provides them and the researcher with a sense of *gestalt* in which to represent lived lives

(Wengraf, 2001). On the other hand, invited to tell the story of their work and family lives, care workers were guided by the focus of the study – how and why they came to care for vulnerable children, and thus were predisposed to give an 'account' of why they had gone into care work.

The method has another virtue. It brings into the research frame all the interview evidence relevant to understanding a person's life: their own perspectives and understandings and the 'facts' of their lives that are plotted afterwards by the researcher as chronologies of biographical events. Indeed for analytic reasons the 'facts' of the 'lived life' are kept conceptually distinct from the 'told story' in order to understand how people both direct their own lives and also how their lives are shaped by the contexts and events that surround them (Wengraf, 2001). Moreover, the researcher is also required to bring into the analytic frame evidence available from other sources related to the structural context or the normative climate of a particular historical time (Brannen et al, 2004a). For what is left unspoken by an interviewee or left out by a researcher in designing their study may be as important as what is included.

We also used a semi-structured approach in the second part of the interview in order to cover particular questions not covered in the biographical interview and to ensure comparability of data on some key issues, for example interviewees' views on training. Researchers could pose these questions in whatever order they chose with as much probing as they judged appropriate. This conventional semi-structured style ensured data that directly addressed the study's research questions. Interviewees were also invited during this part of the interview to give an account of a recent typical working day. This was designed to illuminate how a particular type of childcare work is experienced.

The semi-structured interview poses some major problems, as Hollway and Jefferson (2000) suggest. One is that the researcher poses a direct question and so introduces her own frame of relevance, as could have been the case in this study about why workers wanted to care for vulnerable children. In posing such questions, we must expect interviewees to provide credible answers and explanations and so risk interviewees constructing connections in response to the question. The approach also risks foreclosing on the person's own narrative that might have been forthcoming had the interviewer allowed this. A related problem arises in the analysis of the data, that is, when the *gestalt* of the interview is broken by the researcher disaggregating the account into thematic segments of discourse. These are then divorced from the integrity of the individual case – of a life lived in context.

Such risks are lessened when a semi-structured approach is preceded by a biographical–narrative approach.

The combination of biographical and semi-structured interview approaches provided childcare workers with an opportunity to tell a story in their own terms while ensuring that the same set of issues were covered in each interview. Such issues included: how they came to be interested and involved in caring; the formative and other influences that led them into care work; and how care work fitted into their family lives and identities. The fluidity of the approach is well suited to addressing the complexities of individual lives as they are lived over time and across different spatial contexts: formal and informal care and work, and family.

Three researchers undertook the interviews: all were white and female. Most of the interviews took place in the interviewee's home and took on average about three hours. All the interviews were tape recorded using digital equipment and transcribed. All interviewees signed a consent form indicating their copyright wishes regarding the use of these recordings and transcripts. Immediately following the interview the researcher wrote up their recollection and impressions of the interview, and so providing an opportunity for reflexivity about the researcher's involvement with the interviewee and in the interview encounter. Once the transcript was available, the researcher who had undertaken the interview wrote a full summary (around 12 single-line spaced pages) organising the material under a number of pre-specified themes that provided a basis for the analysis (computer software was not used). These were discussed in research team meetings, which provided further opportunities to develop analytical concepts and reflexivity about each other's interviews. The main themes for organising the material were:

- the interview encounter, including the response to the invitation to give a biographical narrative;
- a chronology of the life history with dates and information on biographical events and changes of jobs and their timing;
- memories of childhood;
- ways of managing work–family lives and effects of care work on family life and vice versa;
- care narratives including the origin of a care ethic;
- understandings of care and experiences in this type of work;
- meanings of career, relevance of training and perceived skills for the job;
- plans for the future;

- views on the idea of a core worker and on issues of recruitment and retention.

Case selection

Cases for the biographical interviews were selected on a number of criteria. First, in view of the study's focus on the significance of a lifecourse phase for care work, lifecourse phase was an important criterion. However, we also wanted to investigate how having children affected their care work careers and understandings of care work. Since few care workers had young children of their own we focused on those with children still at home and those currently in the 'empty nest' phase who had brought up their own children. We therefore excluded those who were not parents. Second, gender was also important; even though care work is a highly gendered occupation we wanted to include some male care workers. Third, we wanted to include carers from minority ethnic groups in order to reflect the workforce in the areas studied but also because there is evidence to suggest that their orientations towards and practice in combining care work and parenthood may differ (Cameron et al, 2001). Fourth, it was necessary to reflect different employers and to include those employed by the local authority and those in the voluntary and private sectors. A fifth criterion related to the policy aims of the study concerning the future intentions of care workers and the issue of loss of care workers from the sector. The Postal Survey included questions that might indicate a range of intentions and enable us to explore these intentions in the biographical case studies and the follow-up Telephone Survey. We therefore tried to select cases according to a range of criteria that might prove theoretically fruitful in the analysis.

For foster carers and community childminders we applied additional criteria. We chose not to include those who had not cared for a child placed and paid for by the local authority or foster agency for over six months since we wanted to elicit recent as well as past experiences of care work. We sought also to include some lone parents. Unlike residential social workers and family support workers, very few of whom were currently lone parents, around one in five of the foster carers and community childminders in the Postal Survey fell into this group.

Additionally, in the case of foster carers working together with a partner we established in our initial phone contact who was the main carer. For five out of six cases, this was the person who had completed the questionnaire in the Postal Survey (three female foster carers and two male carers completed questionnaires). Because we wanted to include the perspectives of partners who were also registered as carers, we requested interviewees to ask their partners if they would be interviewed. We interviewed two of the four possible partners in the group: the partner of the male foster carer refused and in another couple, who had only recently started living together, the partner had only just been approved and had little experience of fostering.

Thus the sample was not intended to be statistically representative. The aim was to examine a range of different experiences in terms of gender, ethnicity, employer and physical location while focusing upon carers who currently or in the past had raised their own children and to extrapolate in theoretical terms from these cases.

From the Postal Survey sample of 305, 193 respondents agreed to further contact. Having excluded 44 who were not parents, this left 149 from which to select biographical case studies: 25 residential social workers, 43[2] family support workers, 33 foster carers and 48 community childminders. To achieve our sample of 24 we contacted 39. We had five refusals (two family support workers, a residential social worker and two community childminders). Two foster carers and eight community childminders did not meet our selection criteria: either they had not had a placement in the last six months (five), or they had stopped the work (three) or were taking a break (two). Table 2.2 shows the demographic characteristics for the 24 cases and the pools from which they were drawn, while Table A1 in the Appendix provides demographic and employment details for each individual case and the pseudonyms we have used for them in the book.

Telephone Survey

In order to address questions about loss to and movement within the childcare workforce, approximately a year after the Postal Survey (in 2005) we added a prospective element to the study and carried out short structured telephone interviews with those who had agreed to further contact. The aim was to establish how many were still doing the same type of work, how many had left, their reasons for moving on and what they had gone on to do. Those who were still in the same type of work were asked if they had thought about leaving and, if so, what had made them stay. The data were entered into an SPSS database and merged with the Postal Survey data so that in addition to looking at turnover and movement within care work, we could look at both whether demographic characteristics and satisfaction with the work

Table 2.2: Characteristics of the cases selected for the biographical case studies (n)

Characteristics	Type of worker									
	Residential social worker		Family support worker		Foster carer		Community childminder		All	
	Pool	Cases	Pool	Cases	Pool	Cases	Pool	Cases	Pool	Cases
Gender										
Female	20	4	42	6	28	5	48	6	138	21
Male	4	2	1	0	5	1	0	0	10	3
Ethnicity										
White	21	5	42	5	22	4	46	5	132	19
British/other minority	3	1	1	1	11	2	2	1	17	5
Mean age	42	42	45	38	48	48	44	44	45	43
Children										
At least one under 5	4	1	1	1	3	1	6	2	14	5
Aged 5-18+	12	4	21	3	20	3	29	2	82	12
Aged 18+ only	7	1	20	2	9	2	12	12	48	7

Note: Missing cases account for 'gender' and 'children' not totalling 149.

affected turnover and how intentions about the future compared to actual behavior a year later.

Of the 305 Postal Survey respondents, 88% responded to the question asking if they were willing to be contacted again, of whom almost three quarters agreed. However, if we treat those not answering this question as refusals, the number agreeing is just under two thirds (63%) (Table 2.3). Comparing those who agreed to further contact to those who refused or did not answer the question, there was little difference in terms of age, ethnicity, parenting status and time in the job, but a slightly higher proportion of refusals were received from those who worked part time (34% compared to 23% of full-timers). Proportionally, more community childminders were willing to be contacted compared to the other groups (77% versus 64% residential social workers, 61% family support workers, and 54% foster carers). This is no doubt attributable to the way in which community childminders were found through their scheme coordinator for the Postal Survey.

Table 2.3: Agreement to be contacted again

	Type of worker				
	Residential social worker (n=83)	Family support worker (n=84)	Foster carer (n=74)	Community childminder (n=64)	All (n=305)
	%	%	%	%	%
Yes	64	61	54	77	63
No/Missing	36	39	46	23	37

Some respondents did not provide contact details despite saying they were willing to be contacted. Excluding these and the 24 case studies, the potential sample for the Telephone Survey follow-up was 149, of whom 129 were interviewed (Table 2.4) representing a response rate of 87%. Only five of those contacted refused to take part, mostly due to lack of time or ill-health. The remaining shortfall was accounted for by 10 cases where telephone numbers were unobtainable (half being residential social workers) and in five cases being unable to make contact despite repeated attempts at different times of the day and week.

Manager interviews

In order to explore workplace policies and management practice concerning issues of recruitment, retention, training and work–life balance, during 2004 we interviewed 16 managers across the public, private and voluntary sectors. These included assistant directors for children and families, managers in human resources, and managers with

Table 2.4: Telephone follow-up survey sample (N)

	Type of worker				
	Residential social worker	Family support worker	Foster carer	Community childminder	All
Willing to be contacted (Postal Survey)	53	51	40	49	193
Sample for Telephone Survey	42	38	28	41	149
Achieved follow-up sample	34[a]	36[a]	24	35	129

Note: [a] Includes information provided by third party (3 residential social workers, 1 family support worker)

individual responsibility for one or more of our groups of workers such as community childminding coordinators or family service managers for family support (Box A3 in Appendix). Before the interview, managers were sent a topic guide covering the areas we wished to explore. Interviews were semi-structured and took about an hour. The majority were face to face, taking place at the interviewee's workplace, but with some managers the interview was conducted over the telephone.

Information was collected about the manager's responsibilities and how they came into the work, the training and career opportunities for this workforce, the current difficulties and potential solutions to recruitment and retention, and how workers were helped in managing their work and family responsibilities. All interviews were tape recorded and transcribed. Following the interview, the interviewer wrote notes about the interview and, once the transcript was available, a full summary was produced, organised under key topic areas of interest. The next stage involved a thematic analysis that covered the following: training and support, recruitment and retention, opportunities for progression in care work and movement between different types of care work, and employer policies and management practice on work–life issues.

Care workers' characteristics: the Postal Survey

Using data from the Postal Survey, we now turn to look at the characteristics of the care workers who responded. Where appropriate, we make a number of comparisons: for example, between our sample of care workers and the care workforce as a whole, and with other studies of these particular groups of workers.

Ethnicity and gender

The childcare workforce is characterised by a high proportion of female workers, the great majority of whom are of white ethnic origin (Simon et al, 2003). Unsurprisingly, therefore, our survey sample is predominately female and white (Tables 2.5 and 2.6) and replicates the findings of larger studies of these groups of workers (Triseliotis et al, 2000; Mooney et al, 2001; Mainey, 2003; Sinclair et al, 2004; Eborall, 2005). However, a third of the survey foster carers were from minority ethnic groups, which differs significantly from other studies of foster carers (for example Sinclair et al, 2004). Although the foster care population has become more diverse in terms of age, ethnicity and marital status (Kirton et al, 2003), the Postal Survey sample is still not representative of the wider community. Half of the foster carers in our

Table 2.5: Gender by type of worker

Gender	Type of worker				
	Residential social worker (n=82)	Family support worker (n=84)	Foster carer (n=74)	Community childminder (n=64)	All (n=304)
	%	%	%	%	%
Female	84	93	89	100	91
Male	16	7	11	0	9

Note: 1 missing case.

study were drawn from the London authority and this may account for the larger number of foster carers from minority ethnic groups.

Age

According to Simon et al (2003) the care workforce, with the exception of nursery nurses, has an age profile of between 37 and 45 years, which compares with a mean age of 39 for all female workers and 36 for jobs with a high percentage of female employees.[3] The mean age for our sample was 42, but residential social workers were on average younger (aged 36) and foster carers older (aged 46) (Table 2.7). More than a third of residential social workers compared to none of the foster carers were under the age of 30 (Table 2.8). Our sample of residential social workers is somewhat younger when compared to other studies (for example, Mainey, 2003) although Petrie et al (2007) report a mean age of 38, whereas the average age of our sample of foster carers is similar to other studies of this group (Triseliotis et al, 2000; Sinclair et al, 2004).

Table 2.6: Ethnicity by type of worker

Ethnicity	Type of worker				
	Residential social worker (n=82)	Family support worker (n=84)	Foster carer (n=69)	Community childminder (n=63)	All (n=298)
	%	%	%	%	%
White	88	98	67	95	87
Black	9	2	25	0	9
Mixed	2	0	7	3	3
Asian	0	0	2	2	1
Other	1	0	0	0	0

Note: 7 missing cases.

Table 2.7: Mean age by type of worker

	Type of worker				
	Residential social worker (n=80)	Family support worker (n=82)	Foster carer (n=72)	Community childminder (n=62)	All (n=296)
Mean age in years	36	43	46	44	42

Note: 9 missing cases.

Adults and children in the family

Forty per cent of the survey sample were living with children,[4] which compares to 48% for the care workforce generally and 38% for all female workers (Simon et al, 2003), and two thirds were living with a spouse or partner. There were differences between the four groups (Table 2.9). Residential social workers were more likely to be living alone, with friends or with parents, due no doubt to their younger age profile. There were more lone-parent households among community childminders and foster carers. The incidence of lone-parent households is higher than in other studies of these groups of workers (Mooney et al, 2001: Sinclair et al, 2004) and this may be due to sampling. Foster carers, for example, were recruited from one of the two authorities and an independent fostering agency with high proportions of carers from minority ethnic backgrounds. One study found that foster carers from minority ethnic backgrounds were more likely to reside in lone-adult households (Sinclair et al, 2004).

Table 2.8: Age distribution within each group of worker

Age	Type of worker				
	Residential social worker (n=80)	Family support worker (n=82)	Foster carer (n=72)	Community childminder (n=62)	All (n=296)
Years	%	%	%	%	%
20-29	39	11	0	5	15
30-39	23	31	18	27	25
40-49	21	32	49	42	35
50-59	16	27	28	26	24
60+	1	0	6	0	2

Notes: 9 missing cases.
Percentages do not always total 100 due to rounding.

Table 2.9: Household composition by type of worker

	Type of worker				
	Residential social worker (*n*=82)	Family support worker (*n*-83)	Foster carer (*n*=70)	Community childminder (*n*=64)	All (*n*=299)
	%	%	%	%	%
Alone	16	10	14	2	11
With friends	11	2	0	0	4
With parents	10	8	1	0	5
With spouse/ partner	33	28	21	22	26
With partner and own/stepchildren	27	41	39	55	40
Alone with own/stepchildren	2	7	21	22	12
Other	1	4	3	0	2

Notes: 6 missing cases.
Percentages do not always total 100 due to rounding.

Approximately three quarters of all workers in the survey were parents, although over half of the residential social workers were not (Table 2.10) and they made up almost two thirds of those without children. More than a third of residential social workers were under the age of 30 and with an average age of 27 for women in the population having a first child, this may explain why there are fewer parents in this group. Alternatively, the unsocial hours and shift working for residential work may deter parents from seeking such work.

Looking at the ages of the children of those who were parents, around two thirds had at least one 'dependent child',[5] but few parents had a

Table 2.10: Parenting status by type of worker

	Type of worker				
	Residential social worker (*n*=83)	Family support worker (*n*=84)	Foster carer (*n*=73)	Community childminder (*n*=64)	All (*n*=304)
	%	%	%	%	%
Parent	50	83	88	98	78
Childless	51	17	12	2	22

Notes: 1 missing case.
Percentages do not always total 100 due to rounding.

child under five (Table 2.11). Almost half the family support workers compared to a quarter of community childminders and around a third respectively of residential social workers and foster carers had no dependent children. Why are family support workers less likely to have dependent children than other groups of workers? A likely explanation is that they enter this work when they and their children are older. Having computed a variable calculating the age at which respondents reported starting working in their respective occupation,[6] we see significant differences between the four groups of workers. In contrast to residential social workers and community childminders, foster carers were more likely to be aged 40 or over when they started fostering with family support workers following behind them in age terms (Table 2.12).

Household income

Care work is generally characterised by low pay although workers in the public and voluntary sector tend on average to earn more than those in the private sector, with pay highest in London (Eborall, 2005). The average earnings of social workers[7] are well below the average earnings of most other professionals (Eborall, 2005) and home workers such as childminders comprise some of the lowest paid workers in the

Table 2.11: Age distribution of children by type of worker

Ages of children	Type of worker				
	Residential social worker (n=38)	Family support worker (n=69)	Foster carer (n=62)	Community childminder (n=63)	All (n=232)
	%	%	%	%	%
At least 1 child < 5 years	13	4	10	14	10
Children aged 5-17 years only	21	36	33	32	32
Children aged 5-18+ years	29	10	23	29	22
Children aged 18+ years only	37	49	36	25	37

Notes: 6 missing cases.
Percentages do not always total 100 due to rounding.

Table 2.12: Age started in occupation by type of worker

Age	Type of worker				
	Residential social worker (n=80)	Family support worker (n=82)	Foster carer (n=72)	Community childminder (n=62)	All (n=296)
	%	%	%	%	%
< 30	55	21	7	29	28
30-39	25	37	35	53	37
40-49	16	34	46	16	28
50+	4	9	13	2	7

Notes: 9 missing cases.
Percentages do not always total 100 due to rounding.

labour force (Felstead and Jewson, 2000). Foster care tends not to be seen as work and less than half of carers are paid a fee for the work they do, with the money intended to be spent on the children's care. Of those who are paid a fee, three quarters are paid less than £200 a week and nearly 40% receive less than £100 per week (Fostering Network, 2006).

Within our sample of care workers, almost half lived in households with a gross annual income reported to be less than £23,000 and more than a quarter were in households with a gross annual income of less than £15,000.[8] Looking across the four groups, proportionally more foster carers and community childminders were in households with a gross annual income of less than £15,000 (Table 2.13), but this is likely to be due to the number of lone parents and adults in solo households within these two groups. Significantly higher proportions of those living alone, with friends or who were lone parents were in households with a lower gross annual income (Table 2.14). There is little recent comparable data on household income for these groups of workers, but a large postal survey of over 1,000 foster carers found that 37% reported an income over and above that received from fostering of less than £15,000 and 17% reported no additional income (Kirton et al, 2003).

Other paid work

Just under a quarter of all workers had other paid employment in addition to their care work, although foster carers were more likely to have other work (43%) than residential social workers (17%),

Table 2.13: Gross annual household income by type of worker

Annual household income	Type of worker				
	Residential social worker (n=73)	Family support worker (n=73)	Foster carer (n=62)	Community childminder (n=53)	All (n=261)
	%	%	%	%	%
Less than £15,000	25	14	36	38	27
£15,000-£22,999	22	23	18	28	23
£23,000-£29,999	27	27	19	8	22
£30,000-£39,999	15	25	8	15	16
Over £40,000	11	11	19	11	13

Notes: 44 missing cases.
Percentages do not always total 100 due to rounding.

Table 2.14: Household composition by gross annual household income

Household composition	Annual household income			Total
	<£22,999 (n=129)	£23,000-£29,999 (n=56)	>£30,000 (n=76)	(n=261)
	%	%	%	n
Alone	78	13	9	32
With friends	82	9	9	11
With parents	50	21	36	14
With spouse/partner	33	37	30	63
With partner and own/stepchildren	31	21	48	100
Alone with own/stepchildren	91	9	0	35
Other	83	17	0	6
% of total	49	22	29	100

Notes: 44 missing cases.
Percentages do not always total 100 due to rounding.

community childminders (14%) or family support workers (13%). Sinclair et al (2004) report a similar figure (39%) among main foster carers with other paid work and similar proportions in either full- or part-time work (in the Postal Survey approximately 15% and 25% respectively of all foster carers). Within the Postal Survey foster carer sample were 41 couples, most of whom were fostering together. Of these, 18 (44%) were dual-earner households, 20 (49%) were single-earner households and three (7%) were households where neither adult was employed. This may support the suggestion that the traditional single (male) earner model with the (female) foster carer having no other employment is in decline (Sinclair et al, 2004).

Foster carers were more likely to be in paid work if they had no children currently placed with them. Seventy one per cent of those without a placement had other paid work, compared to 35% who had a child placed with them. Almost a quarter (23%) did not have a current placement, a higher proportion than that reported in other research (Sinclair et al, 2004).

Educational level

Comparing the educational level of the care workforce as a whole with all women workers, the two are at a similar level. However, when compared with nursing and education both the social care and childcare workforces have a lower level of education. At the end of the 1990s, just over a third (35%) of social care workers and just under a quarter (23%) of childcare workers were qualified to National Vocational Qualification (NVQ) Level 3 or above compared to just over a third (37%) of all women workers, over three quarters (78%) of nursing workers and the majority of education workers (86%)[9] (Simon et al, 2003).

The care workers in the Postal Survey were not highly qualified in terms of formal qualifications, a finding supported by other research involving these groups (for example, Mooney et al, 2001; Mainey, 2003; Sinclair et al, 2004). Of those with a qualification, approximately four-fifths of the sample, the most common qualification obtained was the General Certificate in Secondary Education (GCSE) obtained at age 16 (Table 2.15). Few had a degree or higher qualification although more foster carers had such qualifications. Although Sinclair et al (2004) reported lower educational qualifications among foster carers they found significant differences between the seven authorities in their study. Whereas the average qualified to degree level was 13%, the range was between 7% and 25% across their seven authorities. Furthermore, their data on education were collected from the family link workers and not from the foster carers themselves.

Almost a fifth (17%) reported no qualification and the numbers within this group were higher among the home-based workers compared to the institutional-based workers. Community childminders tended to have lower levels of education than residential social workers and family support workers. However, among foster carers there appear to be two groups: those with few or no qualifications and those with a higher-level qualification (Table 2.16).

Table 2.15: Educational and professional qualifications by type of worker for those with a qualification

Qualification	Type of worker				
	Residential social worker (n=74)	Family support worker (n=77)	Foster carer (n=54)	Community childminder (n=47)	All (n=252)
	%	%	%	%	%
O levels/GCSEs	84	81	82	70	80
A levels	37	33	35	19	32
University or higher degree	15	16	28	9	17
BTEC/NNEB/ NVQ L3 caring for children/ young people	45	44	20	49	40
Professional social work qualification	7	3	7	2	5
Teaching qualification	3	0	15	0	4
Nursing qualification	1	3	7	2	3
Management qualification	7	4	11	0	6
Other qualification for working with children	22	23	11	21	20
Other qualification	20	29	33	9	23

Note: Respondents could give more than one response; therefore, percentages do not total 100.

Table 2.16: Highest educational qualification by type of worker

Qualification	Type of worker				
	Residential social worker (n=83)	Family support worker (n=84)	Foster carer (n=74)	Community childminder (n=64)	All (n=305)
	%	%	%	%	%
None	11	8	27	27	17
O Level/GCSE	34	40	22	36	33
A Level	22	16	12	11	16
Degree or professional	22	21	34	6	21
Other (eg NVQ)	12	16	5	20	13

Note: Percentages do not always total 100 due to rounding.

Half of the sample had a qualification related to care work or social work, such as a professional qualification in social work, teaching or nursing or an NVQ Level 3 in the care of children and young people or its equivalent (Table 2.17). Only around a third (37%) of foster carers had a care work qualification compared to almost a half of community childminders (47%) and more than a half of residential social workers (55%) and family support workers (55%).

There is evidence that the numbers with a relevant qualification are rising as greater emphasis is placed on vocational training. For example, among childminders only 21% had a relevant qualification in 1999 (Mooney et al, 2001), but this had risen to 64% in 2003, although only 16% held a Level 3 qualification (DfES, 2004) and community childminders in particular are more likely to have a relevant qualification compared to childminders in general (Statham et al, 2000). With respect to the other groups of workers in our study,

Table 2.17: Relevant childcare or social care qualification

Relevant qualification	Type of worker				
	Residential social worker (n=83)	Family support worker (n=84)	Foster carer (n=74)	Community childminder (n=64)	All (n=305)
	%	%	%	%	%
Yes	55	55	37	47	49
No	45	45	65	53	51

Note: Percentages do not always total 100 due to rounding

it was apparent that providers of residential care were striving to meet the government's requirement for 80% of residential social workers to be qualified at NVQ Level 3; several unqualified workers interviewed were on waiting lists to do an NVQ at this level.

Conclusion

One strength of the study design has been the use of qualitative and quantitative methods to provide different types of data and different levels of understanding. The Postal Survey sought to generate contextual information about the four groups of workers and their views of care work and enabled us to identify cases for the biographical sample, including potential leavers. The biographical case study interviews captured individuals' life stories in all their depth and uniqueness and were thought to be particularly insightful into how care workers developed an ethic of care, entered and became attached to childcare work. The interviews conducted with different tiers of management in local authorities, children's services and care homes aimed to shed light on the organisational level that set the parameters for care work and its conditions. In particular, they sought to explore policy and practice concerning recruitment, retention, training and policies and practice concerning work–family balance. The follow-up Telephone Survey sought to generate understandings of care workers' reasons for entering and remaining in childcare work in a way that we could compare care workers' decisions to leave or stay in the work in relation to their earlier intentions. The two surveys provided valuable information against which to set the biographical interview data in context, while the latter explored areas of interest in greater depth not possible in surveys.

When compared to other studies, only the foster carers in our sample were unrepresentative with about half having a higher level of formal education, many being from minority ethnic groups and currently living in lone-parent or solo households, reflecting the characteristics of one of the study areas. Overall, the sample was predominately female and white. The average age of the sample was 42 although residential social workers were on average younger and foster carers older. The age at which carers entered the care work varied: residential social workers and community childminders were younger and foster carers and family support workers were older, suggesting that different types of care work attract people at different lifecourse phases.

Two thirds of the Postal Survey sample were currently living with a partner and there were more lone-parent households among home-based workers. The majority were parents with the exception of residential social workers. Few had a preschool-aged child, suggesting that work with vulnerable children and families may be difficult to combine with the care of their own young children. Gross annual household incomes were on average low, reflecting in part the lone-parent status of some and the low pay associated with the work. Foster carers were more likely to have other paid work, particularly if they had no child placed with them. The study also suggests that in couple households the principle of homogeny applied, with care workers having partners in similarly low levels of education and low remunerated occupations. Half of the sample had a relevant qualification for care work, although only around a third of foster carers.

Notes

[1] For community childminders we asked scheme coordinators to distribute the questionnaire.

[2] Two men, who had children aged 5-17, but who lived alone, were also excluded on the assumption that they may not have been involved in the day-to-day upbringing of their children.

[3] Hairdressers, beauticians, sales workers and clerical staff.

[4] Includes stepchildren, but not foster children. Figures for care workforce and all female workers are for co-resident children.

[5] Defined as under the age of 18.

[6] Based on years as a childminder and not years as a community childminder.

[7] Includes social workers employed by all types of employer, but not residential social workers.

[8] Gross annual income is likely to include income from fostering.

[9] Based on secondary analysis of the Labour Force Survey 1997-99 and the latest date for which such analysis is available.

THREE

The origins of a care ethic in care workers' childhoods

Introduction

Negotiating an ethic of care cannot be witnessed directly but may be glimpsed in people's life histories and life stories and the ways in which informants present themselves and their lives. This chapter starts at the beginning of our story of care workers' lives and addresses the question: to which periods or moments in their lives do childcare workers *first* attribute developing an ethic of care? When and where do they consider their commitment to caring for others originated? As the chapter will show, for most, their stories about care and the care ethic began in childhood, while for one care worker his entry into the world of work was given significance in early adulthood. A minority did not make reference to an ethic of care developing in childhood or early adulthood. Rather, it seems an ethic of care arose in the context of their fortuitous entry into care work, which they attributed to particular events and circumstances, to be discussed in Chapter Four.

It is unsurprising that childcare workers regarded childhood as an important period in their lives since they subsequently chose to work with children who had been neglected or abused. Childhood is a time in which we learn what care *is* from the position of receiving care. It is a formative period in which care is experienced intensively from our parents and from a variety of significant others. It is also a critical time for the individual's psychological development. The idea that children's relationship with parents is important and affects the quality of their relationships with others in later life is key to many theories of psychological development (Freud, 1949; Erikson, 1950). The development of an ethic of care is seen by development theorists to depend upon the nature of care received and the process of identification with primary carers so that being loved develops and extends the resources of the loved one in order that they can come to love others (Hollway, 2006).

The process of learning to care can work in another way also: the feeling of being unloved as a child by a parent may produce a determination or resolution in that person *not* to reproduce unloving relationships with one's own children and with others. In short, over time individuals identify with or reject the models of care that their parents and other family members offer them (Kellerhals et al, 2002).

While children are the recipients of care from parents and others they are also active in practising an ethic of care *during* childhood (Brannen et al, 2000). Children learn to care both for and about others in the course of everyday life. Some studies of young carers suggest that caring is a burden upon children when they take on more care than is normatively expected for their age group, that is in a particular society or social milieu – such as a 10-year-old taking responsibility for a sick parent or taking on care of younger siblings – often with negative effects on children's education, although this negative view has been questioned (Becker et al, 1998). However, such findings have to be set against the fact that all children develop orientations towards others and routinely exercise care in important ways as part of their everyday lives (Brannen et al, 2000).

A useful conceptual distinction in understanding the practice of care is that of 'sentient activity': identifying with and understanding the feelings and needs of others so that a person may respond to these appropriately (Mason, 1996). This concept matches Tronto's (1993) first element of her conceptualisation of a care ethic, namely attentiveness to the need for care. Children not only contribute in a range of practical ways to family life but also exercise emotional intelligence – putting themselves in others' shoes, being sensitive to how others feel, and responding to them in caring ways. In short, children develop caring competences and caring identities that *prepare* them for caring responsibilities later in adulthood.

This chapter examines the case study informants' accounts and experiences of childhood, suggesting that childhood is a key reference point for many care workers in beginning their life stories. It examines the narratives that care workers give in explaining their ethic of care. Such interpretations that locate an ethic of care in childhood are unsurprising given that we invited care workers in this study to reflect upon the whole of their lives and also because such reflections take place from the vantage point of present time and informants' current experiences as *childcare* workers. Accounts of the past have to be understood in the context of the present (Nilsen, 1997). In interpreting informants' accounts we also took into account the questions that we as interviewers posed such as 'When did you first feel you wanted to work with children?' Such questions provoked the process of making connections – between past experience and present motivations to care. As in the following chapters, it is important to understand how the research context, in this case biographical interviews, shaped informants' responses.

Stories of childhood – good, bad and undisclosed

Childhood is a natural place to begin a life story. It is also an obvious place to begin in a research project concerned to explore pathways into childcare work. But before we turn to these narratives of childhood and the connections childcare workers made to the development of an ethic of care, we may ask: what socioeconomic conditions were these workers born into? Most of the 24 case study childcare workers grew up in working-class families, some in deprived communities. In part this is due to sampling, especially in our selection of community childminders, all of whom were recruited in inner-city areas of two large conurbations with relatively high levels of deprivation. However, some of those recruited lived in a shire county and were from working-class armed forces families.

A happy childhood offers a less powerful narrative in rhetorical terms than does an unhappy one, as novels concerned with childhood have suggested. However, the accounts that care workers gave reflect a spectrum of experience from positive, neutral to negative descriptions of their childhoods, even if a significant number suggested very distressing experiences. Only one worker (a man) did not refer to childhood at all (see Table 3.1).

Those who described positive childhoods reported growing up in supportive close-knit families and talked about the benefits of having loving and caring parents. For example, a foster carer described her childhood as 'very happy' and her family as 'very very close', while a male residential social worker referred to the ways his parents' values and beliefs had given him a 'good rounded look on life'. Negative stories were about lack of care from parents, including some extreme experiences relating to parents' alcoholism and violence. Two care workers had spent time in care themselves. One spent the first 12 years of her life in a children's home while two others were brought up by their grandmothers for significant periods of time.

Some negative stories of childhood were about the reparation of bad relationships with parents while other stories suggested that the experiences were still affecting them. Andrea Adamson's account was of the first kind. Andrea was a 33-year-old white residential social worker. She began her life story in childhood and described how she had pined for her father when, aged eight, her mother had remarried.

In her opening remarks she referred to her parents' divorce and how she felt as a child when her mother remarried. While she still remembered feeling unloved by her father and resentful of her stepfather – "I was saying this the other day actually to a friend, she's going through a rough patch at the moment and I was saying how I remember feeling as a child" – she recalled how aged 18 she discovered that she was loved after all. By contrast, a residential social worker gave a very long account of her relationship with her father and made it very clear that even after all these years (she was now in her fifties) "it still hurt(s)".

Some childcare workers also reported that they had 'blocked out' bad childhood experiences, an explanation that we as interviewers respected in the questions that we posed later in the interviews (see also Brannen 2004a). For example, a community childminder, the eldest of five children, only hinted at her own bad childhood experiences when describing the condition of a vulnerable child brought into her care: [the child] "wasn't fed, wasn't clothed, wasn't changed. Hadn't had her nappy changed for about eight weeks. You know I've been there when we were younger, you know I've done all this before". The comments "I've been there" and "done all this before" suggest that this community childminder took responsibility for caring for her neglected siblings. This was confirmed when she made a passing reference to having always had children to care for even as a child: "I brought our kids up, even you know like my mother's kids and that, and so I've always had them". Much later in the interview, in talking about the differences between caring for her own children and the vulnerable children in her care, she commented: "my kids haven't been in that state. I might have been, my kids haven't".

Making connections

Some care workers made the connection between their own childhoods and a care ethic in the opening lines of their interviews when we invited them to give an account of their lives; others made a connection later in the interview when the interviewer followed up themes in the informants' initial narratives, and then again later in the interview when she asked a series of semi-structured questions. Yet other interviewees made no connections in their interviews between their childhoods and developing a care ethic. Some rejected the idea that childhood had influenced their decisions to go into caring work (see Table 3.1). Teresa Thomas, a white 56-year-old community childminder was one of five children. She grew up in London in a working-class family. Her opening narrative focused upon her mother having been a childminder when she was a child. However, Teresa insisted that she remembered rejecting childminding as an occupation, when aged 15 or 16, a social worker had suggested this to her. On the other hand, she recalled how as a child and young person she was used to having children around her since her mother did fostering. In her mid-twenties, Teresa went into childminding, a decision she described as a "fluke" that took place after she had her own children (see Chapter Four) but later in her interview she attributed a change in her feelings about caring to becoming a mother "you just don't know what it's like before you have your own child".

Several interviewees (five women and one man) attributed a care ethic to having been brought up by caring parents, while others, all women, dwelt on the fact that as children they had always been "around other children", "very fond of children" or involved in caring. Here a supportive or caring childhood is a justification for becoming caring persons. Within this narrative there are two main sub-narratives among those who remembered wanting as children to do caring: (a) those

Table 3.1: Narratives attributing origins of a care ethic by type of account of childhood

Narratives	Positive account of childhood	Negative account of childhood	No evaluation/ no account of childhood
(1) Care ethic attributed to a desire in childhood/adolescence to:			
• do care work	4		2
• be a good mother	2	3	
(2) Care ethic attributed to unhappy childhood experience: creating understanding of children in care and identification with an unloved child		6	
(3) Care ethic attributed to early adulthood			1[a]
(4) Care ethic not linked to formative years (see Chapter Four)		1	6[b]

Notes:
[a] A male childcare worker who was the only one not to refer to childhood.
[b] These workers reported no early care ethic and gave circumstantial reasons for entering care work.

who as young people remembered wanting to go into paid caring *work* (although some did not act on their desires until later in life); and (b) those who remembered wanting as children to be good mothers.

Wanting to do caring work from a young age

Caring occupations are typically aspired to and taken up by girls. Such career choices are gendered; they are shaped both by socialisation within families, schools and the wider society but also by the structuring of the labour market, which creates particular types of job opportunities for men and women. Girls typically have been attracted to caring professions and caring occupations (for childcare workers in general see, for example, Cameron et al 2002). Kathleen Roberts, a female community childminder of mixed race, said that she had wanted to be a nurse when she was about to leave school (at 16) but from her life story it is also clear she was a carer in childhood. The oldest of four children, she grew up in the inner city. Her parents split up when she was six. Her mother remarried, and when Kathleen was 11, her step-brother was born, and her step-sister a year after that. She described looking after her younger siblings when her mother became ill in her last pregnancy. In her opening life story she said she had wanted to train as a nurse when she was about to leave school after watching a promotional video at school about the armed forces, enticed as much by the glamour of travel as by nursing. Instead she went into nursery nurse training until she was old enough to join the army and did not in fact pursue nursing.

Two female family support workers reported wanting to go into teaching and nursing respectively during their last year at school. Clare Glover, aged 36 and the second girl in a family of four, was brought up in what she described as a happy family and was from a white working-class community in a rural part of Southern England. Clare began her narrative with an account of her family of origin and her childhood, going on to explain the influence of her female peers on her decision to work with children:

> "I got fed up with school. Like, you know, 16-year-olds do. So a friend of mine was ... [pause] going off to college to do nursery nursing, and I wanted to be a music teacher. But um [pause] but actually I couldn't be bothered to stay on to do the A Levels. So I thought 'Oh that sounds interesting, I'll go for that as well' ... which I absolutely loved. It was really my thing working with the, you know, under-fives.

Loved it. Um, when I finished that I actually wanted to work in a nursery 'cos one of my placements had been in a nursery."

Later in her interview Clare added that as a child she had always liked being with children and had done babysitting. However, it was also clear that earning her own money was an important reason for babysitting (and for other jobs) at that time, especially as her parents were not well off. She also referred to the way girls were sent along particular career routes in her comment "they didn't tell you about anything else".

"Just liked being with children. I used to babysit when I was like 13, 14 for different people on my dad's milk round. So I'd sort of [pause] and I used to do a paper round from the age of about 12, so I've always worked. Then I worked in the local supermarket at 16 when I was going through college. Always worked. But I always just wanted to [pause] I just always wanted to do teaching, 'cos I didn't know about anything else, didn't know about social workers, didn't know. And when you had a career interview then you went in and you said 'I want to be a teacher' and they didn't tell you about anything else."

However, as we will describe in Chapter Four, Clare's interest in working with vulnerable children while shaped in childhood was precipitated by circumstances not entirely of her own making. She 'fell' into family support work when the nursery in which she was working was turned into a family centre (Chapter Four).

Susanne Grant, a family support worker aged 39 from a black working-class family, worked with children with special needs. She said she had wanted to be a nurse when she was still at school: "I always wanted to do nursing, but never got the formal qualifications to go on to do that". Asked to elaborate, Susanne said that this may have had something to do with caring for her sick father when she was a teenager – "I suppose I've always kind of been in that caring role" – and also for her nephews and nieces (her siblings were much older than she was).

"But before [pause] I'm the youngest of six and my dad was [pause] had a stroke in his forties, so I used to do a lot of caring for him. *(Right)* Well because my mum had two jobs. So he'd go off to a day centre in the morning and come back for lunchtime. And she used to cook and leave his lunch in a flask and then I'd come home and she'd already have gone to her second afternoon job, cleaning job. So I used to do his dinners and get him ready for bed and whatever for when my mum came in. I used to go on little day centre trips with him.... He used to go to an Afro Caribbean class on Tuesday. So he used to do that. And that's how I suppose I've always kind of been in that caring role. And plus the age gap between me and my older brothers and sisters are quite large, so they had children when I was still at school sort of thing. *(Right)* So I had, you know, probably nephew, nieces to hang around with or look after."

Susanne's account was very matter of fact, conveying little about her feelings at the time concerning the impact of caring on her life: she did not get any qualifications at school. In fact Susanne described herself as a tomboy and more interested as a child in playing football "than sit and learn about silly babies". However, in her initial narrative, Susanne also emphasised her interest in people with special needs. When asked about this further, she reflected upon the impact of caring for her father as a teenager:

"As I said I think I've got an interest in medicine and *(Yeah)*, you know, people with broken bones and odd syndromes and whatever. I think I've always had that. But I don't know if that was triggered off from my dad being ill with a stroke and then he got Parkinson's disease. So maybe that [inaudible] was always there. Um, and then when I went to the nursery I ended up – not intentionally – but I ended up keyworking two children with Downs syndrome and two with autism."

However, as we will describe in Chapter Four, there were particular circumstantial reasons for going into childcare work at the time, namely to do with looking after her own children.

Two other female care workers also linked their motivation to go into caring work to being carers during childhood, but did not pursue it until later in the lifecourse. Marleen Bennett, a mixed-race residential social worker who grew up on a farm in Africa, recalled how she and her sister looked after their mother when she was sick. She also remembered *saying* as a child that she wanted to become a nurse, when she was about 10 years of age. Much later when she was caring for her terminally ill parents (at the age of 30) she reported deciding to do nursing (see Chapter Four) but did not pursue the idea until she had emigrated to the UK. Similarly, Sarah Butler, a 46-year-old white family support worker from a services background also reported that she wanted as a child to be a nurse. She did not take up this interest until much later when she became a single parent and was in need of paid work at the age of 42. She became a home carer for older people before moving into family support work.

Brian Stratford, a white 40-year-old male residential social worker, linked his desire to care and be a caring person to his upbringing. He described an untroubled childhood, referring only to his father and making no mention of his mother. In his initial narrative he recalled how his left-wing, politically active father took him to Speakers' Corner in London every Sunday where he would listen to his father's and other people's speeches. However, looking back to that time he suggested that this was not something he had valued then. However, now a residential social worker and a committed father, he saw things differently:

> "At that time I thought it [going to Speakers' Corner with his father] was pretty crazy. I thought 'What am I doing? I should be out playing football with my mates', but now when I look back on it, it was actually quite a good thing to do. Because it gives me a good rounded look on life, I think."

In fact Brian came to care work more by accident than design when his work as a chef took him to a residential home for young people (see Chapter Four).

Some suggested that they took a great deal of pride in having cared for siblings and other children. Sarah Butler, the family support worker mentioned earlier, grew up in a white, working-class armed forces family. Her father had married Sarah's mother when he was serving overseas and the family spent some while overseas. As the oldest (girl) in a family of five siblings, she was expected to help her mother look after the newest baby. In her opening statement she connected her love of children to this early experience of caring:

> "[F]rom a historical point, I'm the eldest daughter of a sibling group of five children. I parented from an early age myself within that family group. Which I suppose had a strong influence on my love of children and families and parents."

Wanting to be a good mother from a young age

For some (female) childcare workers, an ethic of care was attributed to wanting from a young age to become a mother and to be a 'good mother'. This is again an unsurprising finding given gender socialisation and the centrality of motherhood in female identities. In the UK context, moreover, until the late 1980s, being a good mother meant not being in paid work at least until children reached school age (Brannen et al, 2004a). Childcare workers with grown-up children would have become mothers in this period and so were particularly likely to have signed up to the ideal of full-time motherhood.

For some of this group an unhappy childhood infused their rationales for being good (full-time) mothers although how far this always related to explicit childhood aspirations is unclear. From a current perspective, a central story some care workers told was their determination to give their own children the care and affection that they had lacked in childhood. Carol Jones, a white 48-year-old residential social worker from a skilled working-class background, related at length how her father had dominated her childhood and adolescence, an experience that had made her determined to be a loving (full-time) mother to her own children. Similarly, Pat Foster, a 49-year-old white family support worker from a working-class background, linked her motivation to care to her mother's treatment of her as a child. She also suggested that her mother's lack of sensitivity to her needs and anxieties as a child had led her to "over-empathise" (her words) with other children. Like Carol, she had taken care of her own children on a full-time basis until they were in secondary school (a typical pattern at the time) before she entered the labour market and became a childcare worker. Moreover, judging her own mothering from the vantage point of her training as a childcare worker, she now considered that she may have been "overprotective" towards her own children and may have projected her own insecurities onto them. There is in Pat's use of the terms 'over-empathy' and 'overprotection' some suggestion therefore that her ideal of good motherhood may have been suffocating as well positive.

Understanding and identifying with the unloved child

The next narrative linking childhood with a later care ethic is about understanding and identifying with the unloved child through the experience of an unhappy childhood. The stories told by three childcare workers described traumatic childhoods and how through being vulnerable children themselves they had come to understand their own feelings and those of children they cared for who had been through similar experiences. A *lack of care* in childhood is hereby turned into a determination to help those in similarly deprived circumstances.

The first case, a female foster carer aged 44 from a black working-class background, might have been placed under the last theme of wanting to become a good mother. Debra Henry recounted a particularly difficult childhood. Debra's unhappy early experience had had a major effect not only on her understanding and desire to care for vulnerable children but had made her determined to instil in children and young people a sense of agency as she sought to do this for herself. Her unhappy childhood had made her identify with the *resistances* that such children engage in. Thus, just as she had sought to speak up for herself and develop self-care or self-esteem as a child and subsequently as an adult, she also sought to facilitate this for those in her care, including her own four children. In this sense Debra was unusual among foster carers whose model of a care ethic is typically protective considering their role to save or rescue vulnerable children (Nutt, 2006).

Born in the Caribbean, Debra was brought up by her grandmother and other relatives. She had no contact with her mother until aged 10 when she was reunited with her in Britain. In the meantime her mother had remarried and given birth to four more children. The reunion proved traumatic for Debra: her mother showed her no love and treated her 'like a slave', expecting her to look after her younger siblings. Debra ran away from home at 16. In her opening narrative Debra presented a story of maternal rejection:

> "Well my life story in a sense hasn't been really what you'd call a really good [laughs] [pause] a good life story. I was actually born in ... in the West Indies, so I lived there for the first 10 years of my life without actually knowing that I had a mum and that. *(Really?)* Yeah. So I sort of like was then whisked away from that and brought to England to meet the woman that was supposed to be my mum, who in fact sort of like treated me like her slave really. I was her slave I should say. So I didn't really get to do the things that children did, like to go out and be able to play with your friends and things like that. 'Cos my mum didn't like me like that, she just liked me as a slave and a servant. So started to look after my brothers and [pause] well my step-brothers and sisters. They didn't particularly like me either. So I eventually left home when I was 16 and a half. I in fact ran away. [laughs] But never went back, and up to this day."

In the lengthy and emotional argumentation that followed her initial story, Debra described how her childhood experience had shaped the care of her own four children and foster children: the importance of making children feel safe and loved, building their self-esteem, and giving them 'a voice', all the things she had lacked in her own childhood:

> "And I suppose a lot of that also comes from [pause] 'cos as a child nobody listened to me when I was a child growing up, and it was like you weren't an important person. So I [pause] in having my own children I've made them feel that, you know, although you're my children you're still important, and you've got to be important to yourself, first and foremost, you know."

Later in the interview Debra elaborated a theme of transmission. She reflected how her mother's treatment of her had made her 'hard' in making her determined that she and other vulnerable children exercise agency as 'persons' – "you're becoming the person that you want [to become]" and so break a negative cycle of transmission from mother to child:

> "So I suppose that's what being with my mum has taught me. I suppose it's made me hard like that I suppose. Not hard in the sense as in [pause] I think the love that I deem that I should have had I made sure they got instead. And I made sure when you're [pause] as they're growing that you're becoming the person that you want. I don't want you to become nobody, I want you to become who you choose to become."

Three other female workers also suggested that their survival of traumatic childhoods had helped them to identify with vulnerable children and also to become the strong persons they are today. Brenda Nelson and Eileen Wheeler were reticent about their traumatic childhoods while Mary Haywood, a 47-year-old white foster carer who had spent the first 12 years of her life in care and never knew her parents, gave little more than the bare, shocking facts. "If you ask me why I got into foster caring basically I think it was because I was in a children's home till I was 12 myself". Mary was taken into care when she was a few days old and because of her slightly dark skin said she was difficult to place (she had 47 placements). She described the children's home as 'horrendous' and recalled how she was made to feel 'different'. Aged 12, she was adopted and developed a good relationship with her adoptive parents. Mary's account suggested that her deep sense of moral responsibility towards vulnerable children emerged against the background of her own deprived childhood although there were particular factors precipitating her entry into childcare work (see Chapter Four).

> "I could never see any child out on the street or anything like that, or in trouble. I mean I just live for kids. I mean they bring me so much light and life. You know there is so much baggage that comes with kids through maybe their own parents' problems and things like that, which is pushed onto the child, you know. And childhood, because I never had a very happy childhood, I mean I was always watching my back, always fighting for my own things to be kept safe, you know I don't think any child should have that worry or problems and burdens on them."

Mary's story of an unhappy childhood has a redemptive quality, redemption achieved through the love of her adoptive father and her late husband and through becoming a mother herself (to her own child and her three step-children):

> "Never wanted children when I was young. 'Cos I never wanted to think that I couldn't love them the way that I [pause] you know I would never want to fail them and make them feel like I felt unloved. And, you know, just the problems of society if you like when I was younger. Because that's what I was. In my eyes. And I think that's [pause] But then you meet somebody don't you and you fall in love, and then you have a child."

Two other care workers reported abuse and neglect in childhood and had to take major responsibility for their younger siblings. Like Mary, Brenda Nelson became a childcare worker following motherhood. Again like Mary, her own childhood helped her to understand children from similar backgrounds. Brenda, who was aged 50 and a community childminder from a working-class background, was the eldest of five. As noted above, invited to tell her life story, Brenda hesitated and only hinted at the abuse and neglect that she had experienced as a child. In her initial narrative, she did not link being a vulnerable child herself to working with vulnerable children. Instead she dwelt on her circumstances when she became a mother and the need for an occupation that fitted in with bringing up her children (Chapter Four). However, later in the interview when prompted about her motivation to care for children, she gave a different insight, reflecting on the care she provided as a child and adult for her siblings. This emerged in response to a question about whether she thought of having children before the birth of her first daughter (aged 21):

> "Yeah. Always wanted them. Well not till I was about eight you know. [laughs] And even when I had mine people used to say to me 'Oh, you always....' and still now like if I had gone to the shop this morning they would be saying 'Oh, don't you look lost?' I brought our kids up, even, you know, like my mother's kids and that, and so I've always had them. So now when I don't have a pram or I don't have, people think I look strange. But I feel strange."

A similar story was recounted by Eileen Wheeler, a white community childminder aged 41 (also a foster carer). The second of eight siblings (she had an older sister), she came from a poor working-class background in the same city as the last informant. She and all her seven siblings were taken into care. Like Brenda, Eileen did not talk much about her early family life but was more forthcoming about the period after she left home, aged 11, to live with her aunt. She began her very concise account of childhood thus:

> "I think from 11 years old I lived in um, with a fam- [pause] my own family. Well it was a pretty deprived family. I came from a family of eight. We were all moved on to foster placements. At 11 I ran away to an auntie's, who wasn't a very nice carer. Then at 13 I moved [pause] I think it might have been 14 I moved with my gran, and then from 16 [pause] 15 and a half I got a job, and then lived independently on my own in a flat."

In follow-up questions in which Eileen was asked to give 'more story' based upon what she had said in her unprompted narrative, she remembered little of her early childhood beyond having a 'very unhappy time' living with her aunt (and then later with her grandmother) and having to care for her siblings. But Eileen was clear: "I think it's made me the person I am now, a stronger person". Later in the interview, she referred implicitly to her own childhood in describing the empathy she has for needy children:

> "I think I can meet their needs. Because I have a lot of empathy for the backgrounds they come from. All the different types of abuse I can see the children come in – their eyes, their face. It just reminds me of my past *(Yeah)* and how deprived I was. And I think I can give a lot to them emotionally. I hope. [laughs] And I understand where they're coming from. Although people say 'Oh they're awful', they're not – they're kids. So they're not to blame for that, what's happened to them. You know they're not to blame for how they turn out. If they're angry and aggressive. I have a lot of understanding why they're like that. I wasn't a very nice child.... I was quite a little thug. [laughs] [inaudible] But I suppose you know like you have to have an understanding why these children are like this. If they're bullying other children – they're bullying for a reason, you know. Or they're stealing or they're lying, you know. There's a reason for it all. And I have an understanding of it, did it myself."

Eileen related how she was able to see in the children for whom she now cares the frightened and angry little child that she once was. Through the process of dealing with her own childhood she developed an understanding not only of her own feelings at the time but also of children in similar circumstances. Moreover, as in the case of Debra discussed earlier, caring for vulnerable children also met *her* own needs for self-care and, importantly, constituted part of the process of dealing with the trauma of her own background and redeeming the past.

Eileen's continuing story hinged around care and a deep sense of moral responsibility for care. As a child she had responsibility for her young siblings and later, aged 22 and with two young children of her own, she became a foster carer to two of her siblings (a third one followed a year later). Contrasting her will to care with that of her older sister who had a marginally better childhood, Eileen said: "She didn't want to take on any responsibility for siblings and that. *[Yeah]* Where I did, I wanted to do that". Yet, while her identification with vulnerable children formed an important part of her *gestalt*, other lifecourse events played their part in Eileen's decision to become a carer (see Chapter Four). One was her need for extra income to top up her partner's low earnings and another was other people's encouragement for her to go into childcare work – the latter testimony to the low self-confidence so common among childcare workers who have had difficult childhoods.

Ethic of care attributed to later formative years

Finally, we turn to a case of a male care worker, Tom Jenkins, who did not refer to his childhood but who located his strong ethic as originating during his formative years as a young recruit to the army during which time he experienced some traumatic events upon which he did not elaborate. His account of his interest in vulnerable young people emerged in response to a narrative question that followed up key aspects of his initial life story. Asked what had sprung to mind about his time in the army, Tom reflected on his growing understanding of human beings and their fragility. However, as is clear from this next interview extract, Tom's reflections were not located in a narrative about the past but were reflections located in the present. Tom explained his reluctance to talk about his past army experience in terms of its traumatic nature making it "uncomfortable to talk about even now" and also his wish to protect the 'listener' (researcher).

> "[B]eing in the (army) taught me was that there's actually two planets ... two lives for everybody. Some people live in one life ... which is very harsh and crystal clear and hard hitting. And the other is this sort of life that they work at and make, and it's a lot more comfortable. And a lot of the real world in my view ... is actually shut out or blinkered."

Tom described his ethic of care in terms of feeling totally committed to his work throughout his time in residential social work. He drew parallels with the similar total commitment expected of him when he joined the army, commitment that meant sacrificing his family life to the demands of the job.

> "When I was an airborne soldier, right at the beginning of my service I was told by a regimental sergeant major 'Well in this mob, even if you're married, you're married to the army first ... I still in a similar sort of way, not quite so resolute, hold that type of mentality around my role ... I suppose at the end of the day when one sort of reflects on totally honesty, I can look back to my previous marriage and understand that the work did place me and in turn my

family under a great deal of pressure. And in that particular instance was a major contributing factor to the eventual breakdown of my marriage."

In his description of his ethic of care in practice, Tom evoked the army context and a male gendered perspective. For Tom 'caring about' others meant action: in terms of residential social work it meant being an advocate and a shield for young people:

> "I think people need to care and people need to [pause] it's best that we all try and care about one specific area, because we can't care about everything. But then to *actually do something about it*. And that's how it seemed to gel with me working with young people. Because I've always been a believer that young people more than anything need somebody as *an advocate and as a shield*, and that will speak up when nobody else is prepared to. And I think that all comes from that sort of experience."

Conclusion

In this chapter we have focused on care workers' childhoods and explored how far childcare workers made reference to their childhoods in their interviews. We have addressed the question: to which period of their lives did they attribute the *origins* of an ethic of care? In the next chapter, we ask what led care workers to start working with vulnerable children at a particular moment in time? In the subsequent chapters we turn to the ways in which interviewees created their identities over time as care workers. In separating out a commitment to care that is located *early in care workers' biographies* from what happens during the subsequent course of their lives and work histories, we have sought to demonstrate the need to understand care workers' lives and their commitment to this kind of work as *processual* and *multidimensional*. By this we mean that motivations to do care work with vulnerable children are shaped *over time* by early experience and by a complex of subsequent events, opportunities, meanings and motivations. Together these constitute pathways into and through care work and the identities that people forge for themselves.

In telling stories of their lives we found that most referred to their childhoods. Moreover the biographical 'facts' of some of these care workers' early lives suggest that their childhoods have some similarities with the children they now cared for. Their backgrounds in most cases were working class while some had suffered extreme deprivation. Some workers had been required as children to do a significant amount of caring work, for example caring for their siblings – some because there was no one else to step in. Some recounted childhoods characterised by loving parents, very different from those of the children they now looked after.

Telling stories of the past and about childhood involves theorisation and interpretation both for the narrator and researcher alike. Some care workers made clear connections between their experiences as children and a care ethic in adulthood while others did not. Yet we must ask what it means for both researched and researchers to make a connection between a person's past and their present life? For the research participant, accounts of the past are told from present perspectives and in the context of what has happened subsequently. Researchers are in a similar position but are at additional risk, namely of over-interpreting the evidence since they are reliant only upon what the interviewee has narrated. On the other hand, irrespective of the links made between childhood and an ethic of care in adulthood by researchers and research participants alike, a focus upon childhood can be said to have a particular importance not only because it shapes identities in adulthood – who we are and where we have come from – but also because childhood is likely to have a *continuing resonance* for those who care for children, especially children with troubled backgrounds.

For informants who reported happy childhoods or those who cared for siblings in childhood and were proud of doing this, we may hypothesise that their experiences provoked a desire to transmit these positive experiences and feelings to less fortunate children. We may therefore take Tronto's (1993) concept of care, discussed in Chapter One, a step further. A key aspect of her conceptualisation of care concerns the receipt of or responsiveness to care. What we wish to stress here is that the experience of receiving or giving care in childhood may encourage attentiveness in adulthood to the needs of others. Thus, a supportive or caring childhood may become a powerful personal resource, in this study translated into a concern to work with vulnerable children and one that care workers can capitalise upon in the provision of good care.

On the other hand, having a difficult childhood in which care was lacking is a handicap and may deter people from feeling or being able to care for vulnerable children. However, it is striking how some care workers seem to have been able to transform the experience of feeling unloved as a child into a resource enabling them to identify with similarly unloved children, and to empathise with those from emotionally deprived backgrounds. Some, like Debra Henry, described becoming strong persons through continuing personal struggle. For others with similarly little care in childhood, such a process was assisted when they had a partner who had had more positive childhood experiences of care and so was better resourced. Thus, Margaret Henderson, a white working-class foster carer, reported having come from a very close family that had made her feel she wanted to provide a similar experience to less fortunate children once her own family had grown up. By contrast, her husband noted that he had lacked such resources in his own childhood. Asked where the love he had given his own children had come from, he said: "That's got to come from [wife's] side and that. Because [wife's] very close to her mum and dad and that.... And I'm glad to say it rubbed off on me and that". This seemed to have helped him in fostering.

In sum, care workers' childhood experiences constitute a central resource for them, both in terms of motivating a desire to care for vulnerable children and also in helping them to understand and identify with the feelings and experiences of such children (see Chapter Seven on the importance of parenting for caring work). The resources that care workers bring with them from their own childhoods to this work need to be recognised and built upon in training. Given also, as we have found, there are likely to be a significant number of care workers who have experienced traumatic childhoods it is important that this is recognised in the training that they receive. In order for childcare work to provide the most vulnerable young people in society with the help they need, it is important that care workers themselves be given the support to deal with the vestiges of their own childhood-related problems. For issues may arise for care workers in their relationships with children and young people when the children's problems are similar to their own experiences, especially when these go unrecognised and hence are not dealt with. High-quality care requires not only training and support for care workers, but time for reflection.

FOUR

Entering care work with vulnerable children

Introduction

Making sense of people's lives and the stories they tell is a complex task. As described in Chapter Two, in the case studies we teased out the 'biographical facts' of care workers' lives and the contexts in which their lives were lived from the interpretations they provided as interview informants. Both the accounts of interviewees and the way we as researchers analyse them are multilayered. In this book we have disentangled accounts about the origins of their orientations to care (Chapter Three) from those events and circumstances that relate to their entry into care work (this chapter), and distinguished these from the orientations and identities that developed in the course of their careers in care work (Chapter Five).

The decision to work with vulnerable children by the four groups of workers in this study is an *occupational* decision to enter one type of work rather than another. We have identified the points in the lifecourse when they *first* entered care work with vulnerable children and young people, although, as many of these cases show, these workers also worked first in other types of care work. In the Postal Survey we were not able to explore care workers' work careers nor to discover the points in the lifecourse when they undertook training. It was not feasible to collect such detailed data while data on post-school qualifications related to care work are difficult to collect since there are so many post-school qualifications and we could only offer a limited number of options on the questionnaire.

In this chapter, drawing exclusively upon the case studies, we also address the question of *why* informants entered care work with vulnerable children when they did. We explore their reported decisions in relation to *past* events and circumstances while recognising and taking into account that these accounts are located in *present* time and current experience. Such precipitating events are sometimes momentous while often they are predictable or mundane such as the need to find another job or a person's suggestion to enter care work. Four broad themes are identified. These themes are not mutually exclusive, in some instances with several factors featuring in a given case. Table 4.1 gives an overview across the four groups. First, entry into childcare work is shaped in the context of a particular lifecourse phase, for example a mother at home caring for a young child sought employment that 'fitted in' around her family, as the literature on childminders suggests (Mooney et al, 2001). Second, entry into childcare work is shaped by other significant life events, for example where informants' own children experience major problems. Third, there is the impact of work–related events and changes, for example the need or desire to change occupations. Finally, there is the impact of other people who suggest a new work direction or provide validation for an individual's ability to do this kind of work.

Lifecourse phase

The survey evidence supports the contention of a link between lifecourse phase and entering a particular type of childcare work. We found in the Postal Survey that different groups of workers reported starting their occupation at different ages. In contrast to residential social workers and community childminders, foster carers were more likely to be age 40 or over when they started fostering with family support workers following behind them in age terms (see Table A11 in the Appendix). At the time of the Postal Survey, residential social workers were least likely to have children while community childminders were most likely to have young children.

Table 4.1: Distribution of factors implicated in entry into childcare work by type of care worker

	Residential social worker	Family support worker	Foster carer	Community childminder	All
Lifecourse phase	3	4	5	5	17
Significant life events	1	2	3	2	8
Work change/ voluntary work	5	3	1	0	9
Suggestions of others	1	3	1	4	9
Total	10	12	10	11	43

Note: There are 6 persons in each group of workers.

On the basis of the biographical interviews it seemed that the start of a career in childcare was prompted by a particular lifecourse phase (17/24 cases). A few female carers went into childcare training or childcare work straight from school, following gender-typical pathways that were influenced by peers and careers counsellors. For others, again women, the entry into care work was a strategy for managing work and family life during the transition to parenthood. Typically, women from working-class backgrounds, as most of the care workers were, had few qualifications. Becoming adult or becoming a mother with a young child constrained what they were able to do in terms of paid work. Those who had children young had accrued little labour market experience and could not afford to pay for childcare. Thus, some women opted to childmind or become foster carers, working in their homes while also wanting to bring up their young children full time. In other cases the entry of their own children into school or secondary school, or their older children leaving home, signalled women's decision to move into the labour market and into care work. This later entry into (childcare) work was common among women from older cohorts. Lifecourse was not such an influence among male carers.

Decisions to enter childcare work are sometimes compounded by other lifecourse transitions such as becoming a poor lone parent in the context of having few qualifications and little work experience (in the survey over a fifth of foster carers and community childminders; 12% overall). Becoming a lone parent for many working-class mothers meant having to find additional income. Getting a job outside the home involved finding childcare, an issue that was logistically and financially difficult. Thus, a number 'fell' into home-based childcare such as childminding principally because it provided a regular income while enabling women to look after their own children. Some lone mothers presented such strategies in a positive light even though the pay was low. Teresa Thomas said that childminding kept her mind off the unpleasantness of her divorce while Gillian Dunscombe said that it helped to restore her confidence in herself.

Clare Glover moved into care work with vulnerable children as part of the transition to adulthood. Of white UK parentage, Clare was the daughter of a milkman and a factory worker. She went into nursery nursing straight from school at the age of 16, having acquired some qualifications. Heavily influenced by her own family background, she developed a strong care ethic early in her lifecourse, as already described in Chapter Three. She was also influenced by her female peers one of whom had opted to do training to become a nursery nurse (NNEB). However, after qualifying, Clare was unable to find work as a nursery nurse and for a while worked as a nanny – "so I thought well if I can't work in a nursery, I have to work, I'll be a nanny". However, this was a stop–gap solution. When she eventually got an interview as a nursery nurse (in response to a letter she had written a year earlier), she dropped the A-level course she had just started and, aged 20, took a job in a local authority day nursery serving children of social services' clients. After three years, social services decided to close the nursery and replaced it with a family centre. The staff had to be redeployed and, with the encouragement of the matron, Clare applied for the post of senior family centre worker and to her surprise was appointed.

Looking back at her life, Clare now felt she had gained some confidence in her abilities, realising the amount of experience she had acquired working with the parents of the children in her care. She seemed to have welcomed the new opportunity. (It is, however, significant that during this time she turned down a further career opportunity to study for a social work diploma offered at the family centre since she now had a young child of her own.)

A family support worker, Susanne Grant, went into childcare work at a later lifecourse phase – the birth of her second child. Like Clare, she did post-school training in nursery nursing at the age of 18. However, unlike Clare, she was already a (young) mother and a single parent. Susanne was the youngest of six children. Of African Caribbean origin, her mother worked in low-skilled work and her father was disabled and unable to work. Aged 18, Susanne had her first child and was still living at home. Aged 22 and not working, she read a magazine article about a single parent who, like herself, was training to be a nursery nurse. Susanne went to college and met her partner while she was there. She had her second child three weeks after her final exams. She was both happy to have a second child but also proud of the achievement of qualifying as a nursery nurse. However, a year at home after the course ended was "enough of playing mummies". At 25 she took a part-time job working as a nursery nurse in a local authority day nursery.

With the exception of a further year's maternity leave, Susanne remained in work or education throughout the period of bringing up three children. Her motivation for working during motherhood was, she said, shaped by the strong work-oriented role model provided by her mother and siblings, as suggested by the research evidence concerning lone mothers of African Caribbean origin (Duncan and Edwards, 1999). Events overtook her work career as the local authority nursery she worked in was turned into a family centre following management changes, three years after she had joined it. Thus, Susanne became involved in family support work fortuitously and was given further training. Other subsequent events in her life reinforced her commitment to working with vulnerable families, namely that her second and third children were born with significant developmental problems (see under next section 'significant life events').

Foster carer Brenda Reeves also came into childcare work when she had small children. Unusual in our study being of (white) middle-class origin, Brenda trained as a dance teacher, eventually running her own dance school. Married at 32 and with a first child at 33, Brenda stayed at home with her first child, something she said she very much wanted to do, but worked in the afternoons and evenings teaching dance in her school. When she was pregnant the second time, the couple decided to sell the dance school. She felt she could not expect her husband to look after the children in the evenings – partly because he was getting busier (he was a builder), and partly because she considered that it was her job to look after the children. They decided to go into foster care and took on the placement of a young child with disabilities. Brenda was the main carer, but continued to do a little bit of teaching in another dance school on Saturdays. She explained her decision to enter foster care in terms of her new lifecourse phase of motherhood:

> "And children change your family life, don't they? They change the way you're going. You either stick with your career and the children sort of bumble along with you. I mean I know some people put them in nursery and things like this, don't they? Or they get nannies and things like that. But we decided that because my career was sort of children orientated and it was [pause] I was at home all day, 'cos my teaching was of an evening, I just, you know, looked after the children. But it was only when the second one was on its way and we decided that [pause] it became difficult with the building work to go and do the evening classes.... So it sort of like [pause] the family changed my outlook on my teaching as well. So it was sort of a joint decision – I'll sell the school, give up the teaching, then we'll do the fostering because then we can sort of be a family unit and work with children at home."

As we will show later, other factors contributed to this decision, although they did not prompt her initial move into fostering: an (unspecified) life event that helped her to empathise with vulnerable children, and the inspiration of a friend who had fostered and introduced Brenda to fostering.

An example of a carer who went into childcare at a slightly later lifecourse phase is Pat Foster, a family support worker, who did so after her children started school. This was a typical pattern for mothers of her cohort (Brannen et al, 2004a). Pat, of white UK origin, left school at 16 with few qualifications, had a child at 17, separated from her partner at 19 and repartnered in her early twenties. She and her new partner led an itinerant life, moving around the country, mainly living in rural areas. Having developed little self-confidence, and having little labour market experience, she was happy to be at home with her children. Only when her youngest started school did she feel drawn to think about paid work, even though there was considerable financial pressure upon her before this. First, she started doing voluntary work in her youngest child's school. There she met someone who suggested to her that she might come and work with them in a therapeutic centre for vulnerable young people (see under the last theme 'the suggestions of others').

Two mothers in the study started childcare work in the empty nest phase of motherhood. Carol Jones, a residential social worker of white UK origin, was a full-time mother for most of her sons' childhood even after becoming a single parent. Having left school at 17, she first worked in insurance, an occupation chosen for her by her father, much against her wishes. Carol resented her father's dominance over her life. While she had rebelled against him in adolescence, only later did she make her own occupational decisions. Their difficult relationship also shaped her life in other ways: Carol described how when she became a mother she was determined to be a loving parent to her children and so escape the pattern of her own unhappy childhood, a concern that reinforced her decision to stay at home with her children.

Carol's desire to be a full-time mother was further reinforced when she became a lone parent. However, her ex-husband was willing and able to contribute financially to their children's maintenance, unlike the case of other lone parents in the study. After a few years Carol took on some voluntary work with vulnerable young people when her children went to stay with their father overnight: she worked in a residential home for young people one night a week. It was only when her ex-husband was no longer obliged to support their children as they had left school that Carol sought full-time employment. She then had to sell the family house and divide the proceeds with her ex-husband. This empty nest lifecourse phase seems to have coincided with a new transition in her life – the decision to live with her partner of several years and to support him since he was unable to work because of ill-health. This confluence of lifecourse transitions led Carol to move to a cheaper part of the country. Prompted by her enjoyment of voluntary work with young people, she found a full-time job in residential social work (see further discussion of this case in Chapter Five).

Margaret Henderson, of white UK origin, also started fostering in the empty nest period of the lifecourse. By then, Margaret was a grandmother to several grandchildren whom she often looked after when her daughters were working (part time). Over the course of being a mother, Margaret had combined motherhood with a series of small part-time jobs but had always prioritised motherhood, as was the case with Carol earlier. She had done a variety of other kinds of work including care work in homes for the elderly since the shifts enabled her to fit the work around her family. In recent years she had mainly worked in community elder care, work that she then replaced with foster care, although she did not describe fostering in terms of paid employment. For Margaret and her husband the decision to become foster carers was prompted by feelings of emptiness after her daughters left home:

> "Well I think what it was, was we had three girls of our own, *(Yes)* and they all sort of grew up, got married and left home, kind of thing. And me and my husband thought that we had a three-bedroom house *(Yeah)* and we both always loved children and we just felt so empty. And we thought we could offer someone a home."

Significant life events

Life events, usually unforeseen and often traumatic, also constituted turning points leading to the decision to work with vulnerable children. Similar observations have been made in a study of care managers who described going into social work following caring for disabled children or those with a terminal illness (Carey, 2003). The story of Marleen Bennett, who became a residential social worker, involves a complex chain of twists and turns of fortune and is one of considerable determination and commitment. While Marleen located the origin of her ethic of care in childhood – a desire to be a nurse when she grew up and look after her ailing parents (see Chapter Three) – the move into childcare work came much later.

Of African origin and a British grandfather, Marleen grew up in the African countryside on a farm and moved into town to study at age 16. At 18 her twin sister had a terrible accident from which she died. This devastated Marleen and she gave up the course she was doing and got married at 18 "on the rebound", as she said, from the terrible event. She had her first child at 21 and did not work. Aged 29 with three children, Marleen's marriage was in trouble and around this time her parents became very ill. Marleen went to live with her parents in order to take care of them and never returned to her husband. She seems to have enjoyed caring for them. In the meantime her husband took her three children to Britain and refused to bring them back and slowly, Marleen recounted, turned her children against her. After her parents' died Marleen started working in a local nursery school as an unqualified assistant. She married again and had twins. She then vowed that she would find the money and come and live in England to be near her older children and help them (they were not happy living with their new stepmother). Marleen and her husband came to the UK; her husband had to give up his business. Aged 35 she started working in a home for the elderly, having abandoned her childhood wish to become a nurse, considering that the training was too long. She found the work 'hard' and soon moved into a private residential home for young people, first as an agency worker. After she was made permanent and working full time (shifts) she embarked on some vocational training courses (NVQ) and eventually got a place on a social work course while paying the fees herself plus a small grant.

For others, a traumatic life event had a more immediate impact upon the decision to work with vulnerable children. Mary, a foster carer of white UK origin, had the decision made for her. As described in Chapter Three, Mary's ethic of care was rooted in her childhood and her own terrible experience of being in a children's home for her first 12 years. The love given to her by her adoptive father (she was adopted in early adolescence) was redemptive, giving her a strong determination to care for others. Although she had trained in art after leaving school, she went into adult care work.

It was a major tragic life event in her life that propelled Mary into fostering. Aged 31, she got married to a man who had the custody of his three young children. And then a year after marriage and when she was several months pregnant her husband died suddenly. At 31 she became a widow with a ready-made family of four. Mary considered her deceased husband's children as her own. However, in legal terms this event bestowed on Mary the status of foster carer. With the help of social services, she fought for and eventually became their legal guardian (as the children's mother was alive, Mary had to apply for their custody). This tragic event set Mary on a course of long-term fostering during which time she said she had fostered 67 children. Asked if the tragic events had not happened whether she would have done this kind of work, she seemed to suggest that she would have done:

> "[B]ecause of the way it happened I suppose I didn't have to go through the processes and the [pause] I mean I have had all the assessments done and the interviews and what have you, but I came in through a side door rather than the front door if you know what I mean because of having taken the boys on and [inaudible] through court."

Justine Naisbitt, a family support worker of white UK origin, came to this work similarly through a complex chain of traumatic family events. She was working as an administrator in social services when she decided to move into family support work. Justine left school with no qualifications and worked in a variety of jobs from the age of 16. She got married at 20 and had three sons. Her husband was often violent and died some nine years before the interview in traumatic circumstances. All three sons had experienced mental health problems. Of the many terrible events in her life, Justine attributed one in particular to her decision to work with troubled young people. One of her sons was badly hurt in a motorcycle accident. He started to smoke cannabis to ease the pain, a habit that she thinks precipitated mental illness and self-harm. Justine found it difficult to get any help for her son even though by then she was working for social services in an administrative assistant capacity. Some help was only forthcoming after the son aged 18 committed a crime and was sent to prison. Justine decided to use the insight she gained from dealing with her son's problems to help other troubled young people and their parents and became a family support worker.

> "[I]t gave me an insight of what I wanted to do. I'd always been an admin worker, I really hadn't had any information to be, you know, good Samaritan type thing.... But I remember the despair I went through and how [pause] if you didn't know the system how hard it must be for normal mothers to figure out what to do or how to do it. So I thought well I would help these young people. That's how basically I ended up here in, you know, the Leaving Care team, helping young men of 18 plus."

Justine was one among several childcare workers whose children had serious health problems or disabilities – factors that contributed to their decisions to do childcare work. Brenda Nelson, a community childminder of white UK origin, mentioned several factors that were important in her decision to do this work. One was the discovery that one of her children was profoundly deaf. Diagnosed when her son was 18 months, Brenda expected to return to her factory job as she had done after her first child was born but was unable to do so because she could not find anyone who would look after him – the child was always crying. Becoming a community childminder was a strategy that enabled her to fit paid work around the care of her children.

A second life event was also important in her decision, namely the decision to look after her partner's son from an earlier relationship. Brenda had her first child aged 19 as a single parent and did not live with her partner until she was 26 when they had a second child. Her partner had a child of 10 by an earlier relationship. The boy had been in and out of care and was about to be put in care again. Brenda felt that she and her partner had a duty to take care of him:

> "[W]e sort of fought for him to come and live with us, but she [mother] didn't want him to come and live with us.... But anyway obviously we were quite upset about it and I had said, you know, there was no need for him to go into care when you know there's a perfectly good home here.... So after months and months of them meetings and seeing the mam, she had finally agreed that if he wanted to come and stay here then he could."

The stepson was very difficult and the social work support that they had been promised was not forthcoming. The 'placement' broke down when he pulled a knife on her. She contacted social services and asked for him to be removed immediately. This was very upsetting because she felt they had 'failed' him despite all their efforts. However, she did not attribute the decision to become a community childminder to this alone but also to a suggestion from social services (see 'The suggestions of others' at page 71). Which was the most decisive event is, of course, difficult to say.

Work-related events and contexts

The point at which care workers entered childcare was also influenced by work and the work context. This was noticeably the case for three male interviewees. On the other hand it is also the case that a number of female childcare workers came into paid childcare via voluntary work with troubled young people. Some did it as a route into paid work, especially among the older generation of mothers who stayed at home longer with their children: Carol Jones, a residential social worker who, following bringing up her children, started 'working' in a home for young people; Jenny Masters who started working in a youth club; and Pat Foster who started helping in her son's school.

Brian Stratford, a residential social worker of white UK origin, was born in 1965 and left school aged 16 or 17 with several GCSEs. He registered with an agency to work as a chef, because his "uncles were into chefing". After about four years he found a position as a chef in a children's home. He felt that he was able to connect well with the children, and spent a lot of time interacting with them rather than cooking for them.

> "And I thought, you know, there was quite a clear line of connection with them, good relationships. So the actual progression was to move out of cooking and into childcare. Which is a bit bizarre because I never really thought about it before to be honest with you. That's how basically I became [pause] working in childcare."

Still employed as a chef, Brian took some short courses to gain a basic understanding of child development and working with vulnerable children. With his colleagues' encouragement, he became a residential social worker. Shortly after he moved into childcare work his son was born, which further reinforced his commitment to working with children. However, while Brian's move into working with vulnerable young people was prompted by having close contact with these young people in his work as a chef, Brian attributed to himself an ethic of care that began to take shape during adolescence when his father, a political activist on the Left, took him along to political events and talked to him about issues of social injustice (see Chapter Three).

Similarly, the work context influenced Justine, who was working as an administrator in social services when she decided to become a family support worker, as described earlier. Her understanding of the problems of young people grew out of her job in which she was required to transcribe tape recordings of case conferences. However, this particular spur to move into childcare work was enhanced by events happening in her own family life making her feel that she might be able to help such young people.

Two male care workers described having to find new occupations. Tom, of white UK origin, was born in the North of England. He left school at 16 to join the army in preference to working in the local pit. He did a seven-year tour of duty during which time he was posted overseas, got married and became a father. After he left the army he became a bricklayer, mainly because of his love of the outdoors. The job caused him some health problems. His next job move was, it seems, suggested by one of the labourers he worked with (see later theme 'the suggestions of others'). As he put it "Fate took a turn" with his workmate suggesting that he try youth offending work, again because of his interest in the outdoors. Just as Tom had felt highly committed to the army, relishing in particular the challenge of the work, so he welcomed the challenge of working with vulnerable young people and he continued in the work for the next 20 years, becoming a manager and eventually qualifying as a social worker (see Chapter Five).

Obafemi Williams, of black African origin, grew up in Africa and after migrating to Britain studied part time for a professional qualification and eventually built up his own business. After his business failed in the early 1990s, he took up fostering, at a time when his children were moving into adulthood. However, unlike many female childcare workers in the study, he had not been a full-time carer of his children. Between foster placements, he worked in a residential home for adults with learning disabilities. Asked why he took up fostering at that time his response was framed in terms of altruism and his political commitment, in particular to black children. Significantly, in response to being asked why he became a foster carer, he made no reference to the collapse of his business and the need to find work:

> "[I took up fostering] … to keep my brain going. And also to help. Because I like doing jobs that help the society. *(Yes)* In fact I was politically involved too…. [We benefited a] lot from this society and we needed to put something back into the society. And we were motivated by the scarcity of black foster parents and we do see adverts all the time … you know, articulating the issues involved. You know, the tremendous amount of black children, you know, needing care, who are being forced to be fostered with white people."

Some informants' accounts underplay the contextual conditions under which they take on care work. This was particularly the case for those going into foster care since they saw fostering more in terms of a *commitment* to children than to paid work. Indeed, some were particularly concerned to present their commitment as having no pecuniary aspect.

The suggestions of others

As we have already seen, several interviewees were directed towards a caring occupation working with vulnerable young people by the suggestions of other people. (It is of course the case that those who took a care route on leaving school may have also been influenced by others' suggestions; this possibility has been referred to earlier in discussing the lifecourse phase.) Some described these suggestions as making care workers aware of their own potential for this kind of work while others described others' suggestions as one among several factors. An example of the latter is Kate Humphries who started childminding following her divorce. However, when private childminding placements dried up, her sister (who was already part of a community childminding scheme) suggested that she find placements from social services.

That informants felt equipped to follow up others' suggestions is of course an important point. According to some, these suggestions were 'a stroke of luck' without which the individuals concerned may not have gone into care work with vulnerable children. The influence of others is of course likely to have been particularly important in the early phase of the lifecourse in which young adults were finding their feet in the world of work and may have felt directionless especially where they lacked qualifications, work experience and had little knowledge about the labour market.

Eileen Wheeler, a childminder of white UK origin, was the second of eight children and had a very disturbed childhood. Fostering was something that she and her siblings had experienced firsthand. Aged 22, with a child of her own and some limited experience of low-paid work (her first job in a local laundry at 15 was found by her grandmother with whom she was living at the time), Eileen took on the care of two of her younger siblings when their foster care placement broke down. A few years on, aged 26 with three children of her own, having fostered yet another of her siblings for a time, she began to foster children who were not related to her. However, the spur to this was another's recognition of her "way with children" together with the fact that she badly needed the money:

> "I think how it started was just talking to my siblings' social worker and meeting up with other [pause] another foster carer who was looking after X, my younger sister.... And

they sort of said, you know, you should get into fostering, you're very good, and you've got the experience. And that's how it started really, and I think well it's a way of earning money …, to provide for my kids. 'Cos I wasn't working then. He was working in the laundry but it was a very poor income.... Just over £100 a week, so that's how I got into it really."

Eileen turned to community childminding when her marriage broke up and she needed some regular income and also felt a need to be at home for her own children and the siblings she was fostering. Again there is a complex of factors that propelled Eileen into this work.

In the case of Michelle O'Connor, of white UK origin, the effect of another's suggestion on her decision to enter family support work was also part of a chain of events although she started working with troubled young people earlier than this, a decision that was prompted by seeing an advertisement. Michelle left school with no qualifications at age 15. She took a series of unskilled jobs, including cleaning and factory work: "just anything that'd give me some money to go out and have a good time". She drifted into jobs, as she did not know what to do. Aged 21, she started working in a pub; she knew the owner, who asked her one day whether she wanted a job. She became the pub manageress for about three or four years. Aged 22, she married her current husband (whom she had met two years earlier), and together they rented a three-bedroom house in a small village "out in the sticks". Three years on she saw an advert for carers to provide supportive lodgings for teenagers referred by social services (a new scheme at the time). She and her husband agreed to apply to become carers. A few months later the couple decided to buy their current house in a medium-sized town, explaining that this location "made us even more desirable" as carers. They soon started to provide lodging for a teenage girl. The 'pay' was low and only covered their expenses, and Michelle kept on some cleaning work at the same time.

However, before providing supportive lodging via social services, she and her husband had been offering shelter to young people in their wider social network. These were mainly "friends, or friends of friends" who in some way needed help: "We'd get phone calls during the middle of the night from friends". Asked how it came about that people approached them, she explained: "I don't know, they just did. I suppose because I'd listen to them, talk to them, we were quite open …, non-judgemental.... Let them say their piece, you know".

Michelle found she was enjoying the experience, especially working with the various professionals concerned, and enquired whether she could become more involved. One of the professionals with whom she had contact suggested that she become a sessional worker for social services in family support work, working with teenagers. She went for an interview and was employed on an 'as and when' basis. Her account illustrates that the rewarding nature of her contact with young people and the realisation that she could make a difference to young people's lives were crucial in her decision to become more involved. However, Michelle had always seen herself as a caring person.

The attribution of decisions to the suggestions of others deserves some methodological reflection. It is a way of telling a story that diverts attention away from the agency of the self. In the context of this study of care workers, many of whom came from disadvantaged backgrounds and lacked educational qualifications, it demonstrates to the listener how in the public world others recognised their talents and potential. This enabled the informant to 're-present' the self in a good light especially when the individual concerned held a low opinion of their own talents. The lengthy life story told by Debra Henry, a foster carer, was peppered with attributions to the influence of other people upon the decisions she made. Her way of telling her story may be construed as a means of validating her sense of self through recounting the high esteem in which she was held by others in the context of her own low self-esteem.

Debra had a troubled childhood (see Chapter Three) and left school at 16. She had a series of low-skilled jobs and, like Michelle, was "trying to find a sense of direction I suppose". Following her daughter's birth at age 21, Debra was at home for a year living on benefits, her relationship with her daughter's father having broken up. She then worked nights in a mini-cab business. This enabled her to be at home during the day with her daughter. As a single parent a second time, after the birth of her second child (at age 24), Debra set up a mother and toddler group at home. After this period she embarked on an access course to gain some upper secondary qualifications, and next found a clerical job working for the local authority. However, she then gave birth to twins, again as a single parent. She thought: "Oh no, two babies. Look, there's no way I'm going back to work". At this point, aged 36, she recounted how her eldest child, now at secondary school, brought information about fostering home from school.

In her initial life story, Debra attributed her decision to become a foster carer to her children's persuasion – how they said she had the ability to do this work and referred to her own lack of confidence on several occasions in the interview. Her way of seeking others' validation was also reflected in the interrogative mode she adopted towards the interviewer, as can be observed in the following interview extract:

> "And it was those two kids that persuaded me to become a foster carer ... as far as they were concerned I sort of like had this way with children, especially if they happened to be naughty. I always got them to basically behave [pause] become good.... So they saw it as [pause] rather than, you know, always be doing it for your friends, why don't you become a foster carer and give some child what they felt that they were getting? ... It was, you know, they saw that I had something to offer rather than it was me that saw I had something to offer myself. Do you get me?"

The explanation Debra provided for becoming a foster carer at this time in her life unfolded over the course of the interview and had many facets. Asked towards the end of the interview if she would have become a foster carer if her children had not persuaded her, she asserted the importance of having foster carers from minority ethnic groups (referring to her African Caribbean origin). As a foster carer with a troubled childhood she felt that she could empathise with children from similar backgrounds. Still later she attributed becoming a foster carer to the need to find a companion for her son: "[H]e was the only boy in a household of women. And I didn't want him to feel, you know, out of place or whatever they feel, these boys".

Conclusion

In this chapter we have addressed one of the key questions of the study, namely when and why the childcare workers entered care work with vulnerable young people. We have focused here on the point of entry into this type of work and have found that this occupational decision was often part of a complex chain of events and explanations. We identified four broad themes that encompass the main routes into childcare work: lifecourse phase, significant life events usually in the family and of a highly problematic nature, the need to change occupation or the impact of the work context, and the suggestions of other people. We have tried to show how such 'explanations' for occupational choices are located in the contexts in which people live their lives and shape their own biographies.

Some of these explanations for entry into this work represent *gendered* practices or strategies concerning the entry into gender-typical work (for girls). They also refer to practices that mothers adopted in order to combine paid work with the care of their young children, or when an at-home mother decided to re-enter the labour market when her children were less dependent or grown up. In these cases, deciding to work with vulnerable young people was both propelled by lifecourse phase but also by the experience of being a mother and the resources developed in the course of bringing up one's own children. It was striking that the decisions of the three men in the case study sample were *not* made with reference to lifecourse phase nor their family lives and responsibilities. The significant turning points in their lives focused upon issues to do with finding employment and preferences for types of work. For some female care workers voluntary work constituted a route out of full-time motherhood and into childcare work.

Some explanations for this occupational choice point to *fortuitous* factors, such as when a job ended and other people directed informants to a different kind of occupation. Sometimes the precipitating factor was situational, such as when a person was working in the care sector in another occupation and thereby became exposed to childcare work. Thus, an informant was drawn towards working with vulnerable young people through direct contact with them and their families. Factors often came together in a series of events and actions in which private troubles became linked to public issues (Mills, 1959). An individual experienced personal troubles in their family lives and wanted to draw upon the resources, competences and insights developed through these experiences for the benefit of other children – notably children in the care of social services (see the theme in Chapter Seven concerning tacit knowledge).

These precipitating factors in the decision to move into childcare are part of childcare workers' explanations for caring but they do not constitute the whole of their explanations. For this we need to turn to the complex of motivations that generated and sustained an ethic of care *in practice*. Some motivations, as we saw in Chapter Three, often lay in childhood experiences. The motivations to care and the contextual explanations for why people entered care work with vulnerable children are not mutually exclusive but together form layers of explanation and understanding. Both are frames through which these different groups of childcare workers tell their stories. Thus, a community childminder typically chose to become a childminder when she was caring for her own small children and needed to earn an income, especially in the context of lone parenthood. However, this layer of explanation might be prefaced by a desire in childhood to care for others or to repair the damage done to her in her childhood so that others' children may be better cared for.

Such stories and accounts of motivations and explanations for doing care work with vulnerable young people are given in the present. They are thus framed in relation to the interests of the study and how the study was presented to informants – what they thought we as researchers were interested in. Stories and interview accounts are also framed through the lens of hindsight in the context of events that took place in the past and to which a range of meanings have subsequently been attached. Thus, present explanations are offered by individuals in the knowledge of the persons they have become and the experiences they have currently. They are framed too in the context of how they think about the future: their plans, hopes and dreams. To these issues we turn both in the next chapter in which we consider how care workers shape their own identities and in Chapter Eight.

FIVE

Care workers' careers and identities: change and continuity

Introduction

In this chapter we take up the story of care workers' careers from the point at which they first entered childcare, the focus of Chapter Four. We take the term 'career' to mean an individual's progression in paid work over the lifecourse and how it interacts with their other careers, for example the career of parenthood (Elder, 1978). Career as a term also has other connotations. As Rose (2004) has found, the popular notion grew dramatically in Britain between 1986 and 2002, in some cases replacing the word 'job' in employment opportunities advertisements. The popularity of this self-perception increased more among women (from 39% to 54%) than among men, including among part-time workers, with the steepest rise among those with no qualifications (23% to 36%) and those in the bottom of the occupational status hierarchy (where many care workers are located). As Rose suggests, the popularity of the term is surprising among those whose advancement is less likely.

Paradoxically, the growth in popularity of the term 'career' as applied to employment has occurred at a time of considerable change in the world of work. The 1990s have been described in terms of growing job insecurity and rapid change in the nature of work in which jobs for life are no longer guaranteed. As researchers have suggested (see, for example, the national survey findings of White et al, 2004) the disappearance of what has been called a male model of work needs to be seen in context, for example for some groups casual and self-employment have been longstanding features of the labour market while many jobs remain little changed. On the other hand, with the privatisation of public services, moving into the private sector may mean a significant diminution in the quality of employment conditions. Whatever the 'truth' about the changes in employment, the growth in popularity of the term 'career' needs exploring.

One important change that underpins the growth in popularity of the term is the growth of credentialism and paper qualifications.

This growth stands in contrast to the idea of career as a vocation or calling, the latter being premised on experience gained in the course of working in a particular occupation rather than on qualifications per se. Today's young people are expected to spend long periods in education. More and more occupations today require a degree or other higher-level qualifications, while many require workers to acquire further qualifications on the job. Care occupations require no upper secondary schooling on entry although those who lack such education – the majority in each of the four care worker groups in our study – are now required to gain an NVQ Level 3, which is equivalent to A level (see Chapter Two and Tables A14 and A15 in the Appendix for educational and training qualifications of the Postal Survey sample).

Despite the increased importance placed on qualifications, many care work occupations have relatively few 'career prospects'. Promotion in residential social work and family support work depends upon gaining a social work diploma while home-based care workers have few opportunities within their occupations for career development. For most care workers the opportunities for vertical mobility are limited; few routes exist into management and training opportunities are patchy. Horizontal movement is also problematic in terms of how local authorities organise care work. As we found in interviewing local authority and private sector managers there can be competition between different parts of the childcare sector to attract and retain childcare workers. Moreover, loss of workers from one occupation to another, for example from foster care to community childminding or vice versa, is treated administratively as a loss.

However, as both the survey data and the case studies suggest, many childcare workers do move across different fields of care work. Only around one fifth of the survey respondents (but rather more childminders) had *not* worked in another childcare occupation; nearly a third of those who *had* worked in another type of childcare had had three or more types of childcare experience.

In this study we are concerned not only with paid care work but also with informal care. Thus, our use of the term 'career' has other connotations, notably that first used by the Chicago School (Everett Hughes, 1958) in which career was conceptualised as referring to: (a) a number of role domains; (b) a future or prospective element; and (c) the agency of individuals who shape their own careers within a web of relationships with other people and in the context of wider historical, ideological and structural forces.

The lifecourse notion of career has particular relevance in this study. Here career refers to the linear progression of time but not in relation to a single pathway. Rather, according to Elder (1978), the lifecourse comprises a number of interconnected pathways or career lines relating to work, parenthood, friendship, sexuality and so on. As other research has found, many care workers make decisions about their work in the context of lifecourse phase and their family responsibilities. The spheres of paid work and caring are for some groups of women highly interdependent (Cancian and Oliker, 2000). Some organise their employment around their family responsibilities. Foster carers bring up their own children alongside those they look after. Childminders engage in this work at a point in the lifecourse when women want and expect to be home with their own small children (Mooney, 2003). When female residential care workers become mothers they tend to leave this type of work because of shift working, a practice that can make the organisation of family life difficult, as we discuss in Chapter Nine. Family support work is often chosen by mothers because of its standard working day, although as interview evidence suggests the pressure of caseloads is often so great that it is hard to resist the demands of the job. Working part time is not therefore seen as a viable option, added to which there are financial pressures since household incomes are low across the four groups (see Chapter Two).

The focus of the chapter

We draw here on the 24 case studies. First, we turn to the meaning of the term 'career' in its populist sense for the different care worker groups. Second, we examine the different structural factors that are likely to influence whether care workers saw themselves as 'having a career' in care work: (a) the attainment of educational qualifications over the lifecourse; (b) having experience of different types of childcare work; and (c) having a continuous employment career post parenthood. Third, taking up from the last chapter, we develop an analytic framework for examining the interpretive accounts given by care workers in their interviews: how care workers described their pathways in childcare from the point when they entered care work with vulnerable children. This latter focus involves exploring how care workers shaped their identities and the extent to which their identities appear to have undergone change. One particular feature of care workers' accounts that we draw attention to that is of methodological interest concerns the *form* that the interview took: how far they had a story to tell; how far the story was a narrative about the past or a continuing present; whether the story suggested a story about the self and the (re)construction of identity.

A career orientation or not

Ten of the 24 care workers saw themselves as having a career, reflecting Rose's (2004) finding for a national sample, as Table 4.1 indicates. But what did care workers understand by the term 'career'? The majority of interviewees, especially those working in organisational settings (residential social workers and family support workers), attested to the following features as intrinsic to the concept of career, including those who saw themselves as having careers and those who did not. A career was seen as such because, as one person put it – "it opens doors". Or, as another put it, it implies a "career path" or "stepping stones" defined in terms of the opportunity for vertical progression and personal ambition: "moving up", "moving across" (care occupations), the opportunity for self-development within an occupation or field of work. The counter to a career is a 'job' in which training opportunities are limited or do not lead anywhere. A few associated the term with money – "big bucks" and with "high-powered jobs".

Home-based care workers – foster carers and community childminders – had strikingly different views of childcare as a career compared to institution-based care workers. For foster carers their work was not seen as such, never mind as a career. Fostering was not equated with a job because it was seen as voluntary and as having a higher moral claim than employment. As one said, fostering is "a labour of love so that money cannot come into it" or as another put it, it is "just my life ... my giving ... my helping ... keeping kids off the streets", while a third said "a child can't be a job". However, perhaps reflecting changes in opinion that are taking place concerning the remuneration of foster carers (Fostering Network 2006) and the growth of Community Alternative Placement Schemes that offer foster care (Walker et al, 2002), two foster carers were clear that fostering *ought* to be a profession: attracting qualified people who had a calling to do this kind of work but who were compensated with a decent wage and given full employment protection.

By contrast with foster carers, community childminders, who were the least qualified of all the four groups, expressed a career orientation (in three of the six cases). However, the meaning they attached to the term 'career' lacked the sense of a career path denoted by an organisational context. The meaning of career to this group needs also to be understood in relation to the few work opportunities this group had encountered over their lifecourse. The three who thought of childminding as a career did so for the following reasons. One said that childminding was important to her in contrast to the dead-end jobs she had also done and had provided her with a sense of purpose and meaning to her life. Another two had been offered some training opportunities to do an NVQ, in one case making her feel different from 'ordinary childminders' and in another making her want to do more courses. By contrast, the other three childminders did not see their work as 'proper jobs': because of working from home, because it involved "looking after your own (children)", because the work is held in "low public esteem".

Structural factors that promote a career orientation

We turn now to structural explanations that may help to explain the presence of a career orientation among the minority of care workers (Table 5.1). The approach we have adopted is Qualitative Comparative Analysis (QCA) as devised by Charles Ragin (1989), a method of analysis seen appropriate to 'small N' situations. It involves dichotomising variables as present or absent, as high or low and so on. It is based on a process of logic rather than statistical probability. Through a logical inspection of a matrix of 'variables' it enables us to identify which are 'explanatory' factors for a dichotomously dependent variable, in this case the expression of a career orientation.

First, the attainment of qualifications (columns 1–3) may be expected to be influential. But only two workers left school with upper secondary qualifications. While these two saw care work as a career, so did seven others. By contrast, more gained post-school qualifications ($n=16$). However, 10 of the latter did *not* see care work as a career. Only a small minority of the Postal Survey respondents had a professional qualification at degree level such as social work, nursing and teaching (12%). Commonly, care workers gained a vocational qualification while working on the job – such as NVQ Level 3 (equivalent to A level) – 40% of Postal Survey respondents. Among the 24 cases, two did nursery nurse training (NNEB), three achieved qualifications in other professions (accountancy, teaching and dance); while the others attained NVQs carried out in the course of working as childcare workers. Four of the 24 (none of the community childminders) were offered the opportunity to do social work diplomas while working in childcare and three were currently doing the course or had completed it. Two further care workers had been offered places but had turned them down, while two others were thinking about doing the course in the future.

Having a continuous employment career with little time out of the labour market following childbirth (excluding maternity or parental

Table 5.1: QCA of factors contributing to 'having a career'

Cases	Completion of upper secondary qualifications	Attainment of post-school qualifications	Doing/done diploma in social work	Time out for parenthood (except maternity leave)	Other childcare experience	Sees work as a career
Family support workers						
Clare	0	1	1	0	1	1
Susanne	0	1	1	1	1	1
Justine	0	0	0	1	0	1
Sarah	0	1	0	1	0	0
Pat	0	1	0	1	0	0
Michelle	0	0	0	0	1	0
Residential social workers						
Tom	0	1	1	0	1	1
Marleen	1	1	1	1	1	1
Jenny	1	1	0	1	1	1
Carol	0	1	0	1	0	0
Brian	0	1	0	0	0	0
Natalie	0	0	0	0	1	0
Foster carers						
Obafemi	0	1	0	0	0	0
Brenda R	0	1	0	0	0	0
Mary	0	1	0	1	1	0
Debra	0	1	0	1	1	0
Margaret	0	0	0	1	1	0
Celia	0	1	0	1	1	0
Community childminders						
Gillian	0	1	0	1	1	1
Eileen	0	1	0	1	1	1
Brenda N	0	0	0	1	0	1
Kate	0	0	0	1	0	0
Teresa	0	1	0	1	1	0
Kathleen	0	0	0	0	1	0

Note: These are dichotomous categories (1 = present; 0 = absent); the one interval-level variable – time out for parenthood – is a crude representation.

leave) may also be expected to be important in developing a career orientation, especially among *mothers* working in female-dominated occupations. Again, as Table 5.1 suggests, this was a factor related to career orientation in only two of seven cases.

Finally, the last factor considered to shape a career orientation is having experience in one or more other childcare occupations. As we found in the Postal Survey, about half of all the care workers had worked in a care-related job (not just with children) before starting their current work, with family support workers most likely (63%) and community childminders least likely (31%) to have done so. More than three quarters had experience of childcare work, either paid or voluntary, at some point in their past. In the interviews, previous formal childcare experience across the four groups is not a condition for expressing a career orientation.

So what may we conclude from this analysis? First, the foster carers are unique in that none thinks in terms of a career reflecting the traditional character of our foster care sample. However, most had a post-school qualification, although not in childcare, and had worked in other types of childcare work. On the other hand, some of the least qualified, community childminders, had few training opportunities; yet some three of the six thought in terms of a career. But there are four cases in which two factors – post school training and studying for a social work diploma – are linked to a career orientation. On the other hand, there is one contradictory case: Jenny, a residential social worker aged 32 and a forces wife, who left school with upper secondary qualifications and did further training. However, her current plan was to develop a 'professional' career when her family situation enables this, suggesting that her case may not be so contradictory after all.

Frames for analysing care workers' careers

We turn now to the interpretive analysis of the cases: the ways in which care workers described their lives and work in childcare. We discuss first some theoretical ideas that offer a framework for understanding how the care workers and we ourselves as analysts made sense of care workers' lives.

Central to this study is the theoretical framework of the *lifecourse*. Individuals engage over chronological time in different fields of social interaction or careers as discussed above in its sociological sense (parenthood, paid work and so on) and they occupy different statuses related to these fields (Levy, 2005). These different fields and statuses make up an individual's lifecourse but how far the individual seeks to integrate them is another matter. Some fields and statuses are more dominant or become more dominant over time and have greater salience for the individual than others. Gender is a master status that shapes the dominance of some fields over others (Levy, 2005). For example, as we shall describe in the case of one male residential care worker, a career in childcare work while being lived alongside fatherhood was shaped by a hegemonic form of masculinity that precluded much integration between his career as a father and that of childcare worker. Moreover, as the form of his interview suggests, he engaged in a great deal of identity construction as he told a story of his developing commitment to care work in two senses: the gradual development of a professional ethic (through qualifications) and upward mobility – into management.

Identity is a second theoretical lens that assists us in understanding how people make sense of careers in care work. Here the focus shifts from the 'facts' of the life to the kinds of stories people tell about themselves. According to Antze (1996), stories are a means by which grand cultural discourses find their way into something resembling self-knowledge (p 6). *Memory* is employed in the telling of a life story; remembering the past plays an important part in the construction of identity. In this view, memory is not a simple recovery of a past reality. Rather, memories are interactive: 'Memories visit us unbidden, not simply as records of the past, but as responses to our ongoing needs, hopes and predicaments' (Antze 1996, p 10). The past is conceptualised in psychoanalytic terms as part of a 'timeless unconsciousness' in which the unconscious is made conscious and the past is turned into something that can be 'worked through'. As Antze argues, when an individual questions their identity or radically changes it then memories come to the fore in their account. Conversely, when an identity is taken for granted this is reflected in a lack of engagement in memory work.

One way in which an individual's quest for a new or reshaped identity may be gauged in our study is through the ways in which informants responded to the initial invitation to tell their life stories (issued at the start of the interview). For some informants, it may be that there was simply not much to tell. Narratives that were brief and unreflective related lives that were largely uneventful and unremarkable. In these cases, identities seemed not to have undergone any major transformation. By contrast, other informants responded to the invitation to narrative and talked without pauses or interruptions, often for an hour or more. Such narratives comprise detailed accounts of past events and experiences, often punctuated by argumentation and evaluation given by informants from the vantage point of the present.

These stories of journeys made over time suggest a process in which the self is constructed and reconstructed.

According to Ricoeur (1992) identity has a narrative structure by which he means that we come to know ourselves as persons who develop over time. The narrative structure of the self is revealed in life stories as a process of 'emplotment': the weaving and reweaving of past and present in which there is a perpetual tension between the self experienced as continuity and the self as representing discontinuity: 'demand for concordance and admission of discordances' (quoted in Antze, 1996, p 140).

Ricoeur's concept of identity links with ideas of lifecourse theory. On the one hand, the person sees themselves in terms of attributes that persist over time – race, gender, parenthood, birthplace and traits of personality and habit. This 'sameness' makes for similarity with others who share such characteristics. Thus, we may speak of 'identifying' with specific persons or groups. The other side of identity, according to Ricoeur, is about selfhood – the ability to see ourselves in time: as the persons we have been or will become. For our identities are composed of our ongoing sameness and uniqueness – the persons we recognise – but also the parts of ourselves that are open to change and dialogue. It is the tension between sameness and change – who we are and who we are becoming – that sustains a life story, as we shall observe in some of the cases discussed in this chapter.

Four cases: career development and identity (re)construction

Our choice of cases to be discussed in this chapter is not made on the basis of typicality. Rather, the intention is to demonstrate *theoretically* some possible pathways in childcare work identified in the interview material. Other pathways may be teased out. However, the following were selected as they represent those care workers whose pathways are already developed while others have only just started out. This case analysis will seek therefore only to offer explanations at the individual level but will suggest how such explanations may apply to other similar cases. On the one hand, we pay attention to the conditions that facilitate and inhibit the development of a career in childcare, in terms of a career route in the progressive sense of the term. On the other, we explore the extent to which the individuals concerned provide narratives of the self in terms of identity change or stability over time as they engage in care work, whether this be in terms of having a career, having a job, or being committed to caring for a child.

We have selected four cases – two residential social workers and two foster carers – from which we abduct in each case different processes of identity construction.

Developing a professional career and identity

Tom, a residential social worker, was unusual in our study, the single case representing achievement (a professional qualification in social work) *and* promotion into management (in residential social work). This is very much a man's story. Yet in his biography, Tom is both typical of other care workers (male and female) and different. Like other care workers, he left school with no qualifications. He was resistant to gaining qualifications until he was in his forties, preferring to draw upon an ethic of care developed through his own life experiences. At this time Tom became a manager of a residential home run by the local authority and his antipathy to qualifications weakened and he started studying for a professional qualification in social work. Like many of the female interviewees in the study he got divorced but unlike them this did not influence his work decisions.

Tom moved from one work career to another. He joined the army for seven years after leaving school at 16 and was highly committed to army life. Clearly his attitude changed after some unpleasant experiences about which he did not speak and which seem to have changed his views on life as well as making him decide not to sign up for another tour of duty. Indeed, in emphasising his strong commitment to paid work, in contrast to his family life, he described care work as replacing his 'marriage' to the army. Such an exclusive career orientation dominated his family life and represents a hegemonic form of masculinity unique in this study (but unlikely to be so in the workforce). Thus, as the strongest exemplar of vertical career development, Tom represents a benchmark of male success.

Tom's story consisted of 11 pages of single-spaced A4 text in which he spoke without interruption. It is a narrative about the self both as shaped by and shaping the events of his life. The story is marked by its strong framing in terms of its primary location in the public domain. Family life barely features in this account. While Tom's story is about a journey of the self and towards the end of his career about an upwardly mobile career, it also suggests reference points of sameness as well as identity change.

Born in 1953 in a mining area in the North of England he joined the army at the age of 16. After several periods of duty abroad he came out of the army. The army had introduced him to 'a wide array of backgrounds' and to many aspects of 'everyday life'. But he found it a "hard act to follow" and missed the excitement of jumping out of planes and living in the wild. After a succession of jobs he trained as a bricklayer and, by then married with a young child, he moved to the South. He had to give up bricklaying for health reasons and at "a mate's suggestion" took a job working with young people in the outdoors. After 18 months he was employed as an intermediate treatment officer, working with troubled young people. After five years he felt he had met 'all the challenges' and thought it "time to move on" again. His presentation of self contains a sameness of self described as a strong wish for 'challenge' and a love of the outdoors, desires that he noted drove his original decision to join the armed forces and his later decision to work with vulnerable young people. There is a struggle going on between his sense of sameness in terms of never having been 'judgemental' about others and his desire for challenges – "I've always been like that" – and his self as changing and developing. The story is one of tension between his desire to be understood as the person he 'is' rather than as the person he is 'becoming' and the qualifications he has attained:

> "It seemed my nature not to be judgmental about anything, so if I hear something I don't accept it as fact. I've always been like that, and I remember at the time thinking 'Well what am I going to do?' Clearly I'd developed a real sort of enjoyment and a lot of satisfaction from working with what were described as extremely challenging young people. I didn't actually find them to be like that [pause] um, very much the opposite in reality [pause] um, and I enjoyed the work thoroughly. So I thought, right, I want to stay in the care profession."

One of the key stories Tom tells is about a shift from an almost disdain for qualifications – the self that follows his own judgement feels pride in not being qualified – to a high respect for knowledge. Thus Tom presents himself in his early narrative as following his own 'natural' curiosity, questioning lay orthodoxies about residential care from his own still under-informed position:

> "And I suppose really I'd always prided myself on the fact that I'd gone as far as I had *without* [his emphasis] a qualification, and I was reluctant to sort of go down that route. But at the time – and it's not in my view changed that much today

> – at the time [pause] travelling around various London
> boroughs and in discussion with colleagues, it seemed to
> me that everybody was saying that the residential childcare
> sector, children's homes in particular, and the resource and
> assessment centres that we used to have in London, were
> appalling places, and that the calibre of staff that worked in
> the homes and assessment centres was very low."

After a brief experience in the private sector, an experience that
"reinforced [his] fears" about it, he returned to the public sector. For
11 years he has successfully managed a home that had been in crisis
when he joined it. Tom had only planned to stay for two years but
became 'hooked on residential childcare'. He liked the challenge and
opportunity. And then, as he put it, he reversed his "tradition" and went
off to get qualified – completing a social work diploma and courses
in management. In short, his narrative suggests a questioning of his
former identity:

> "I remember thinking at the outset what I'm doing this
> for is I'm jumping through the hoops so that I can actually
> progress to a higher level so that I can actually have more
> of a say in policy making."

Gradually he came to see the benefits of further education in being
taken seriously by managers above him, and having a say in policy
making. Slowly he came to feel benefits for himself.

Tom's story is marked by a number of turning points related to his
developing identity and career. These turning points are sometimes
marked in his narrative by graphic turns of phrase (noted in the post–
interview commentary made by the interviewer following the end of
the interview). For example, Tom referred to his entry into care work
following a career in the army and a spell as a bricklayer as taking an
'alien route', signalling his strong will in withstanding peer pressure to
follow the crowd. He referred to his entry into management – the point
when he became "hooked" on residential care work – as "fate taking a
hand". These latter words suggest a departure from his earlier narrative
form in which he attributed most of the steps in his career to his own
agency – his strong desire to embrace different kinds of challenge. In
the post–interview commentary it was also noted that Tom swallowed
hard when describing his move into management and the "scope"
the job provided "to bring about change", signalling the emotion still
surrounding this step away from his natural inclination to follow his

own instincts and bent (his sense of sameness), that is not to become a manager. His choice of words is also significant in his description of deciding to get a qualification as "breaking with tradition". Thus, through the language he uses we may see the interaction between 'events' and human agency.

These linguistic framings capture the shift in his presentation of self thus far in the interview: as a person who throughout his life (he left school at 16 with no qualifications) had placed higher value on action (rather than managing others' actions) and on being judged as the person he started out as compared to the person he has become (with qualifications and managerial status).

A professional identity thwarted

Carol, a residential care worker, was born in the South of England in 1952. An only child, she left school with some qualifications (unlike Tom) and went into office work aged 17 at her father's insistence. For 10 years and following divorce she was more or less a full-time mother, fitting small part-time jobs around the children (when they stayed with their father). Her desire to care for others (as paid work) came rather late in her lifecourse; she did not start care work until she was in her forties (first working as a voluntary worker). The critical resources needed for gaining the necessary qualifications were lacking at the time:

> "I'm thinking 'Maybe there's something else I could do' ... But I couldn't financially afford to sort of stop working and go off to university for two or three years and do that. So I thought I've got to try and get in the door, whichever way I can.... And that's the way I did it. And I used to work a night when my boys went to their dad anyway, so they didn't even know."

Carol was 48 when she started working full time as a residential care worker in a private residential home where there were no opportunities for training (workers were expected to do training in their own time). In contrast to Tom, whose army experiences were pivotal in developing an ethic of care, Carol developed her ethic of care early in her life as a response to a lack of care from her father (see Chapter Three). However, for Carol this meant that she expressed her desire to care through mothering, a desire reinforced by being a lone parent.

Like Tom, Carol's story was long, consisting of many pages. Like Tom she had a story to tell. She began with her divorce, seeking to justify being a more or less full-time mother for 10 years ("they were my first priority") and her late start in care work. Next she focused upon her lack of qualifications when, aged 47, she took a full-time job as a residential care worker, so justifying her failure to develop a career, something she now clearly regretted.

> "Care work's something I wanted to do when I was younger. It was difficult with small children and also that I was divorced, so I was the carer. So funny hours don't fit in when you have small children. So it wasn't until they got older that I thought maybe I could give this a go. Found it very hard to get into it because I hadn't got the right piece of paper to say I was qualified as an X,Y,Z or whatever they were looking for, but started doing voluntary work. And that was my sort of foot – and they were very good because they said 'Well okay, even though you're not qualified X,Y, Z, but you've got experience of life, you've had children'. And to them that counted for an awful lot, which I appreciate. 'Cos I think it's important."

The next focus of her narrative was about her sons leaving school and the need to sell the house following divorce in order to divide the proceeds with her ex-husband. This provoked further decisions, namely to move to an area with cheaper housing in the context of her long-term relationship with her current partner. Carol moved and set up house with her partner. As her partner was on long-term sick she had to find a full-time job. However, she was not able to get a permanent contract in the private residential home where she found work and her contract was not renewed after it expired. She applied to a new home and worked there for four years.

Several long narratives followed later in the interview concerning a complex of events that precipitated a major crisis and questioning of her identity. It is of course the case that Carol was looking back with hindsight, recalling what it had been like to be both a 'senior' and 'the new girl' in a private residential home and the unsupportiveness of the staff: how the "old hands" had wanted to "catch her out". Carol expressed considerable dissatisfaction with the home: the way it was run, not being paid when on call, the lack of management support, lack of specialist training for very difficult young people who were in considerable mental distress. This account culminated in a story about her recent serious illness just as she was about to move to a new job which had been handled very badly by management while the staff appear to have been singularly unsupportive. The manager had said that she was "skiving" – despite evidence of her hospitalisation and had not paid her for the last two shifts that she had been unable to complete.

Her sudden illness and the dispute with the home clearly provoked some considerable identity questioning. The fact that her new employer, this time in the public sector, was likely to be so much better than the private agency – offering her further training opportunities (for which she will be paid), higher pay, a pension, and sick pay even before the start of her job – seems to have reinforced Carol's sense of having missed out on opportunities and making her *more* conscious of her potential in care work, a potential she now realised she might never attain. Moreover, it emerged that Carol's new job was a demotion albeit with better pay. At the end of the interview, when asked why she had not moved into local authority work earlier, it became clear that she had applied before but had been turned down, the reason she thought having to do with her low-level qualifications.

The sense of unfulfilled or thwarted potential in terms of attaining qualifications and promotion was most evident in Carol's response to the question about 'having a career' posed towards the end of the interview:

Interviewer:	"Do you think of it as a career?"
Carol:	"To an extent. I tell you what is the slight thing, is probably my age. I really wish I'd just said to my dad 'Pfff ...' and I'd done it when I was 20."
Interviewer:	"How would that have made your career different?"
Carol:	"I would have got more qualifications, I may be a manager somewhere. I may be doing something like that. I started probably later than I should have done ... I think considering that I started later I've done reasonably well so far.... But you know I'm 53. Now I'm thinking [pause] I'm getting a bit tired to do too much. And really I just want to do the best I can and jog along. And if, great, they say 'Would you like to do this?' or do that – fine. But career to me, I should have started at twenties or thirties.... Do you know what I mean? ... But it doesn't mean I'm less dedicated."

Carol justified her lack of a career in lifecourse terms – 'starting too late' in the context of a poor employer and lack of training. Also relevant is her story about a strong ethic of care. This ethic of care was inspired by a difficult childhood in the form of a domineering father who had pushed Carol into a particular line of work and stopped her from pursuing her own caring inclinations (see Chapter Three).

An array of identities

Celia, a white foster carer, was aged 57 at interview. She had four children of her own with a son aged 20 still at home. She was also a grandmother. Born in London, Celia came from an unconventional background: parents who were politically active and who devoted themselves to working with young people in deprived areas; her father a political organiser and her mother a teacher. The family moved around a lot, which affected Celia's schooling. She left school at 17 having got several O levels and did not finish her A levels. When she left school she had no clear idea of what she wanted to do and went to work in an office: "I had various God-awful jobs. Were totally wrong for me as being an office something or other, you know". She left paid employment at 20 to live with her husband – who was of African Caribbean origin and a widower – and to care for his two young children. By the age of 23 she was caring for four young children – her two stepchildren, and her own twins. She described this time as 'awful' because she and her husband were not getting on. They divorced when the twins were about two and she took a full-time job in a local authority family centre, a job that enabled her to bring her children with her to work.

> "And they had this wonderful idea of it employing mothers to give them some training to [pause] whilst having their children in the nursery.... Which they did, they had the twins there. And I worked there for two years, which I didn't receive much training. In fact which is why I decided to go to teacher's training after that, because I wasn't really [pause] they didn't give us any piece of paper at the end of it, you know."

Next she qualified as a teacher; both her parents were teachers, her mother training while bringing up Celia, just as Celia has done. She worked as a supply teacher part time as a single parent with three young children and found it tiring. During this period she met her second partner. After the birth of another child Celia took maternity leave, returning to teaching when her son was four months old. However, following the return to work she said she "got the chance to become involved in catering, because I'd always been interested in that, then I took it" and eventually ran her own business over the 1990s. Then in 1996 she began short-term fostering, returning once again to catering. Her rationale was: "Well I just like doing different things, you know. I really like doing that". Celia also hinted at doing other types of work that she said she did not want to go into. When in 2002 Celia and her partner separated she gave up the catering business, but continued fostering.

Celia's story was long, indicative in itself of having a story to tell. It suggests the creation of a number of identities across both her public and her private life. Asked to recount her story, Celia did not know where to start, hinting that there was not enough time to cover the whole of her life. Once she got going her initial story covered six pages with the odd comment from the interviewer. It traced the path of her life (marriage, divorce, motherhood, a return to education and engagement in different lines of paid work) and an account of the events that led her to foster a boy, via the friend of one of her children whose mother did not care for him. This latter event happened when she was 50, after she had already had two work careers, brought up four children and had gone through a divorce.

Significantly, Celia devoted a lot of time to arguing in favour of foster care being a paid profession. She did so from her position of having developed an array of identities. While Celia saw teaching as a career, this did not preclude her from trying other possibilities. When she got the chance to become involved in catering: "because I'd always been interested in that, then I took it".

Also significant is the fact that Celia was a member of an older cohort of women born in the 1940s. Such women commonly gave up work for a number of years to look after their children. Yet Celia was atypical for the time and did not do so: "No, I think I assumed that I'd work actually. Yeah I would work. I didn't think that I was going to stay at home, no".

Thus, Celia developed an unusual career for a mother of her generation in having a number of work careers. Celia had therefore accrued a number of resources that would be helpful in fostering. Her expectations of fostering reflect not surprisingly the expectations she had developed in these other professions, namely for proper pay and good conditions of employment. Celia was also adamant about the need for professionals to be accountable if they did anything wrong. Accountability, Celia believed, should be accompanied by the 'protection of being employed'. She also insisted that foster carers should not be subsidised either by their working partners or by the state, and was highly critical of people who claimed benefits while fostering as a way of enhancing their income. In Celia's view, fostering should be rewarded properly.

Thus, Celia considered that training is crucial to making fostering a proper profession while she also adhered to a strong belief that foster carers ought to provide children with a normal family life (see Chapter Six). If foster carers are to be treated and remunerated as 'proper professionals', Celia argued that fostering would be more successful in attracting professionals from other fields, notably teaching (like Celia had been) and social work. Such professions, she considered, would have a lot to offer to foster care. As she said, fostering "has to become a professional job" if "a better class of people" is to do it.

> "Because if you were paid you would probably get a lot more teachers and social workers, because they'd be thinking: well you know like maybe my partner's working and so therefore I could work a little bit of part time and then I could be at home for the children and I'd be earning an income.... Because you'd already had a training. You know they're not going to get professionals, people who have [inaudible] professions who would have something to give more. I mean we're not treated like professionals.... It's outrageous because they do have something to contribute."

Celia's storying of her life consists in 'an array of identities'. In her account she made no clear links between the succession of one identity to the next: from teaching to foster care for example. Indeed in some cases these different lines of work were combined at the same time. On the other hand, fostering seemed to represent to Celia a profession that was not easy to combine with other work although she had done this at times in her life.

It may also be that Celia saw fostering now as a single occupation because she had come to it at a later point in the lifecourse after several work careers and after her children had grown up. Fostering was a way for Celia to step down from full-time work. But she also noted that she had thought about giving up fostering because of the impact on her family and family relationships, and also since becoming a lone parent she found she needed more time to herself: "you want to have a break or you want to go away". But she also said that she did not *want* to give up. The previous year she had done a refresher course for teachers because she wanted to get into mentoring (having done some youth work in the past) but felt she was 'too old' to return to teaching. This coupled with illness resulted in her not finishing the course. Celia planned to continue with the current foster placement until the boy was 18. After that, in accordance with her life thus far, and all the different things she had done and experienced, she hinted that another career and identity beckons in the future, namely to travel.

Core identity as informal carer

Margaret was of white UK parentage. She became a foster carer, like Celia, later in the lifecourse, once her children had left home and set up their own families. Like most of the care workforce Margaret left school at 16 and, by contrast with Tom and also with Celia and Carol, she had not attained any qualifications since leaving school. She had been on few training courses since becoming a foster carer, apart from a very short course on drug awareness.

In her life story and the form of her narrative, Margaret's presentation of self and the structure of her career were bounded by core identities, namely those associated with being a mother and an informal kin carer, with care pervading her life. Margaret did not question these core identities. Her career both in paid care work and in informal care does not imply a sense of personal journey or self-discovery.

Born in 1953 in an industrial town in the South of England near to where her family and her wider kinship network still live, Margaret left school at 16, as mentioned above, and did a number of low-skilled jobs – working in a shoe shop and a factory. Married at 19 to her current husband, a lorry driver, she had a child at 21, gave up paid work and had two subsequent children, returning to a variety of short-term, part-time jobs in order to earn some money in between staying at home to look after her three children. When her youngest was at school she began to work in care homes for the elderly and then moved into community care. However, it was when her youngest daughter married and left home that she decided to do fostering, mainly because she and her husband found the house so "empty" – with no children in the house, even despite the fact that she regularly helped look after her many grandchildren.

> "Well I think what it was, was we had three girls of our own, *(Yes)* and they all sort of grew up, got married and left home, kind of thing. And me and my husband thought that

we had a three-bedroom house *(Yeah)* and we both always
loved children and we just felt so empty. And we thought
we could offer someone a home."

Margaret's core identity or identities are bound up with being a
mother and an informal carer. Her initial life story is framed in term
of positional identities rather than personal identities, in Bernstein's
(2000) sense of these terms. In her first narrative Margaret positioned
herself firmly within her family of origin (in relation to her brothers),
in relation to paid work ("done all sorts of kinds of things"), her
marital status, motherhood and grandmotherhood. By definition this
is a static rather than a dynamic account of the self as a set of roles
accompanied by an ongoing but unchanging commitment to care.
It is less of a 'personal' story – of a newfound identity or an identity
questioned or thwarted, as in the cases already described. Rather, it
conveys a sense of identity continuity in the context of a close-knit
network of family ties.

Margaret's initial life story is given in very brief bursts, presented
in report form; it ends with a presentation of self as defined by and
embedded within the lives of her wider family, which is where she
began.

Interviewer: "Tell me about you and your life."
Margaret: "Um, I've got two brothers.... Lived in X until I
                  sort of grew up and then my mum and dad and
                  all the rest moved down to C. Um, I've worked
                  doing all sorts of kinds of things and then I've
                  gone into um care assistant, and I now work
                  looking after people. But I'm self-employed now,
                  so I work with myself. And got married when I
                  was 19. Had T when I was 21. And we ended up
                  having three girls.... Really we would have loved
                  a boy and I think I would have had another one
                  but I became ill and I couldn't have any more
                  children. So um, um, my oldest daughter is 30.
                  She's got L and Y.... And then my next daughter
                  is 28, just coming up 28. She's got T and T....
                  And then I've got my other daughter, she's 25.
                  And she's got B, M and S."

Asked for more narrative, Margaret continued in a similar vein:

> Interviewer: "So can you just tell me a little bit about when you were born and a bit about growing up with your two brothers?"
>
> Margaret: "And then from there, after having the children, I used to do a couple of nights in a nursing home.... And then from there I worked for actually social services. I left there and I went to [private agency] and work for myself. I had a real happy childhood. My family's very very close.... We all live sort of very near each other. I see my brothers all the time as well. I see my mum and dad every day, I go up and see them. They live just up the road."

The rest of her account was related in the present tense as conveying a life that did not change to any great extent, her core identities being a mother, daughter, wife, grandmother and carer. In addition to foster care and her grandparenting duties Margaret looked after her disabled parents who lived nearby. Her motivation for fostering was expressed in terms of an ethic of care based upon a commitment to children – "they are part of your life" – seeking to provide what her parents were unable to provide rather than to help the children change (see Chapter Six). Indeed, the very idea of anticipating problems that may be encountered in caring for foster children was anathema to Margaret; she wanted to give the children "a normal life". Being too attuned to possible problems might work against this. She hinted: "I don't like to keep throwing that back at him".

> Interviewer: "So what would you say um your main motivation for going into [fostering] is?"
>
> Margaret: "I think being able to give something to a child, that the child can't have at home. It's like I've always said, 'I'm not X's mum and [husband] isn't his dad'. We're just here looking after him and we're giving him something that his mum unfortunately can't do at the moment."

The opportunities for training as a carer, while limited in terms of availability, were not welcomed by Margaret. Training was not important. Rather it is "better to be hands on", "you learn by what you do" (see Chapter Six):

> Interviewer: "And do you think training and qualifications are important for this kind of work, or not really?"
>
> Margaret: "Not really. I always think that you learn by what you do and [pause] you're better off hands on and learn as you go along. And anything you don't know, having the support there that you could pick a phone up and say 'I've got this problem, you know, I need help' rather than keep sending you off on courses. I mean it's like at the moment they keep on they want us to do a course. But it's in the evening, and to tell you the truth, by the time you've worked all day and you come home and see to the children, I don't want to have to go and sit somewhere for three, four hours."
>
> Interviewer: "So you haven't been on any?"
>
> Margaret: "Yeah we've been on a couple. But at the end of the day I don't get anything for doing it and I'm not [pause] unless I'm in that situation it most probably wouldn't affect me anyway if you see what I mean."

Margaret did not see foster care as a career. Looking after children she considered akin to parenting: being patient, giving them guidelines, providing them with a sense of continuity and security – "you can't ever switch them on and off". While her successes with her charges made her feel successful, Margaret was adamant that being a good carer was like being a mother: mothering was about giving, and receipt of money would tarnish it. Indeed her strong preference for working for the local authority rather than a private fostering agency reflected this attitude: "But the private sector, the money they get, I really [pause] to me it's as if it's a job and it's money first, then the child".

Conclusion

This chapter has sought to pick up the story after the point of entry into working with vulnerable children. It has focused upon the ways in which care workers forged pathways within childcare and how these pathways shaped the meaning of their work: in particular whether they thought of childcare as a career or not. It explored the impact of structural factors upon subjective assessments implied by 'having a career': completing upper secondary-level schooling, post-school qualifications, movement between different childcare occupations, having significant amounts of time out the labour market during the childrearing years, taking a professional qualification. None was found to be a necessary or sufficient explanation. In practice 'having a career' had many meanings.

In the four cases analysed in detail a more complex picture of care work over the lifecourse was revealed in the stories told by care workers in their interviews. In addition to the 'facts' of their lives, the interpretations and the form of their stories – the nature of their narratives – were significant, suggesting the creation and in some cases the questioning and recreation of existing identities. Thus the first story considered (Tom) was a story of personal change and 'sameness' of the self in which a struggle was manifest in the tension between the person he still remained (committed to action and the challenge of the work) and the person he had become (an educated person with a high respect for knowledge). By contrast, Carol's story was about opportunities missed and glimpses of the person that she might have become as she realised that the moment and opportunities for developing a career in childcare had passed. Her story was about thwarted ambition, ambition only realised after considerable disappointment and dissatisfaction while working in a private residential home. At the centre of her narrative was a set of critical events relating to a life-threatening illness and wrongful treatment by her employer. In this narrative context, Carol was questioning the person she had become and thereby suggested the person that might have been.

Celia related a disconnected story of her life as a partner, mother, student, lone parent and a succession of work identities – teacher, caterer and foster carer. Her identity as a foster carer was shaped in the context of these other identities. Both the narrative and argument that she developed in her interview suggested that these identities constituted resources that she brought to fostering: particularly in the claims that she made for the proper recognition and remuneration of fostering as professional work. The story told by Margaret, another foster carer, suggested an identity that was more fixed or less subject to change, and less about a journey of the self. It focused little upon the past, with limited narration of events and developments (there was little memory work). It was an account told in the present tense that focused largely upon ascribed identities in which motherhood sat at the centre and flowed into the other spheres of her life. For Margaret fostering was not a profession; it did not require training and education.

In addition to being about the development of identities, the chapter was also about the lifecourse and how the lifecourse shapes the opportunities available to people and of which people avail themselves at different points in their lives. Thus, what is possible for one person at one moment in time, for another may be ruled out. In Tom's story, we witness the development of a work career through professional qualifications attained and management experience gained. Tom's career in childcare takes off in his thirties; for him, divorce and parenthood were no obstacles in his quest for challenging paid work. His life story and identity construction, however, is about an unplanned project of the self – a journey of self-development as well as a pathway of commitment to vulnerable children.

In the three other cases, the women embarked on childcare work when they were a little older than Tom. They did so when their children were less or no longer dependent. The pattern of their lifecourse was very differently structured. Carol's lifecourse exhibits limited progression in childcare even though she described her childhood as having provided her with an early impetus to rebel (against an unloving and domineering father who pushed her into work she did not want to do). Conversely, this early experience injected in Carol a strong desire to be a good mother to her own children (to give them the love she lacked as a child), especially when her marriage broke up. Thus, Carol put her employment pathway on hold until her children were less dependent, while as a lone parent living in a particular place she could not access the resources to retrain. Finally, when she branched out into a full-time job in residential care in her early fifties she realised that she had missed the boat and that it was probably too late to make up the lost time and take a professional qualification.

Celia also came into childcare work later in the lifecourse. However, in contrast to Carol she did so in the context of having gone back to education and retrained as a teacher. She did this as a mother of several young children. Celia's resources to do this were greater than those available to Carol or Margaret: in terms of her location in the inner city and also the role model provided by her own mother who had done the same. Also, when Celia became a foster carer, she did so with two professions behind her. This array of achieved identities that she brought with her to foster care shaped her expectations of fostering as an occupation: her view being that fostering should be treated as an occupation and profession and remunerated properly. For Celia care work could be seen by an outsider as a 'step down' in her career but it represented for Celia a new identity in which resources gleaned in two other types of service work were brought to foster care.

Margaret likewise entered childcare work towards the end of parenthood. However, unlike Celia she did so with far fewer material and cultural resources and no desire to re-enter education, do training courses or be financially independent (beyond being a secondary earner in the household). Moreover, in this context she placed value on her identity as a mother and viewed foster care as being akin to parenting. Unlike Carol, Margaret did not tell a story of self-development, for example as expressed through training and qualifications.

The issues raised in this chapter and the cases we have discussed have focused on the notion of care work as a pathway of the self as well as an occupation. Such understandings may pose challenges for policy – in terms of the different groups that it seeks to attract to childcare work and recruitment and retention strategies. For people forge identities for themselves as well as being shaped by the opportunities available to them.

The case of Carol represents an opportunity for policy to target training and support to those who lack the necessary grounding early in the lifecourse and may think it too late to do further training, even though they are disposed to make the effort.

The case of Celia is more of a challenge, highlighting the fact that some come to fostering with greater cultural capital and resources and hence have high expectations in terms of monetary rewards and employment conditions compared to those who lack such resources – the case of Margaret. Yet policy needs to consider how best to support workers like Celia (a foster carer) if it wants to attract and keep the valuable resources they bring; professional foster care schemes are an example of new opportunities. Issues arise as to whether and what kinds of experience and expertise should attract greater remuneration and the consequences of such differential treatment for recruitment and retention among different groups.

The cases also raise issues of *gender* and the different routes that men and women take in care work including the rewards they seek and competences they bring. However, interestingly, in Tom's case, progression into professional training and management were by no means smooth as he sought to remain true to the person he was and the reasons why he came into the work in the first place – to be hands on and respond to difficult challenges raised in working with very troubled young people in residential homes. The increasing demands on social care managers (in terms of paperwork, liaison with other services and so on) may leave little time for the direct work with children and young people that has often attracted them to and kept them in the work. Such issues have implications for the design of management roles in the sector.

SIX

What do vulnerable children need? Understandings of care

Introduction

Having looked at how and why people entered childcare work and the identities they forged, in this chapter we turn to how care workers currently understand their work and what it means to care for vulnerable children and young people. Drawing largely upon the case studies, we consider the goals they aim to achieve with their work and the types of knowledge they draw upon including worker's own experiences of and attitudes to parenting, their experiences of training and the attainment of credentials and professional qualifications. How care work is understood affects not only the way in which the work is experienced, the focus of the next chapter, but reflects the types of knowledge available for this work and perceived as important.

In discussing what care means we turn first to how care is conceptualised. Ideas about what care of children might mean are affected by changing policies and practices (Brannen and Moss, 2003). Even the word 'care' has come to have several different meanings over time from burden and concern to protection, responsibility and having a liking for someone (Petrie, 2003). As discussed in Chapter One, Tronto (1993) has described an ethic of care in which care involves caring *for* and caring *about*, and a practice that 'should inform all aspects of moral life' (p 127). Care is understood as both relational and task orientated, but as well as caring about and taking care of children, it is about being competent to ensure adequacy of care and responding to children by taking their perspective while not expecting them to be 'exactly like the self' (p 135).

It is important to note that understandings of children and childhood are both socially and historically constructed, transcending as well as changing over time and across different cultures and countries (Prout and James, 1997; Brannen et al, 2004a; Moss et al, 2006).

Rousseau's construction of the child as an empty vessel, or tabula rasa, who needs to be 'filled' with knowledge, skills and cultural values through a process of transmission both resonates today and belongs to a different era. Many post-war ideas about childhood, which continue to be influential, view children as following a biologically determined course of developmental stages and phases associated with age (Mayall, 1996). As many sociologists of childhood have stressed, both constructions place emphasis upon the child in the future as a person who is 'becoming' rather than the child in the present who is 'being'. Hence, children are seen as 'incomplete' until they have reached adulthood, while understandings of when adulthood is achieved have also undergone considerable change (Brannen and Nilsen, 2003). A third understanding of children builds upon deficit notions of care and resonates with 19th-century ideas about poor families and children as 'in want and in need' (Petrie, 2003). None of these lenses sees children as active and competent, able to engage with other children and adults in relationships where together they co-construct knowledge, culture and identity (Moss and Petrie, 2002).

Social policy too affects the way in which children and care are understood. In an analysis of childcare policy, Cameron (2003) notes the emphasis that has been placed on children's *protection* as a means of controlling children's behaviour and the child's environment. Given the problems in residential care services in the past it is understandable that current policy has a strong prescriptive and procedural approach as evidenced in the *National Minimum Standards for Children's Homes* (DH, 2002). However, the need to ensure security and safety, and the prominence they are given, risks turning the carer into 'a warden or a minder' rather than emphasising their 'developmental role [and] less concerned with the 'upbringing' of children in a pedagogic sense' (Boddy et al, 2006, p 106). The social pedagogic model found in countries such as Germany and Denmark emphasises *practice*, particularly physical contact between carer and child (to comfort and reassure), and pedagogic relationships in which carers nurture relationships with children through practical activities, although this is not to suggest that residential childcare work in the UK precludes consideration of the whole child or relationships (for a fuller discussion of social pedagogy see Petrie, 2003 and Boddy et al, 2006).

The level of training and qualifications care workers have influence how they view and understand the children they care for and the work they do. Care may be seen as the same activity across settings and carers, so that apparent similarities 'lead to viewing services and workers as replicating, consciously or unconsciously, the home and informal carers, such as mothers' (Johansson and Cameron, 2002, p 18). Traditionally, care work has been seen as the domain of women for which little training or qualification is required, the assumption being that looking after someone else's child is the same as looking after one's own. Although this attitude has changed and, as we saw in Chapter One, there are a number of initiatives underway to establish a better-qualified and more flexible workforce, the question remains as to what education and training are appropriate for childcare workers.

Over recent years education and employment policy in the UK has stressed the acquisition of *skills* reflected in the development of NVQs that are awarded at different levels and which parallel different tiers of the formal educational system (for example, NVQ Level 2 is equivalent to a school-leaving qualification and Level 5 to a university degree). These work-based competency awards are based on National Occupational Standards, which are statements of skills, knowledge and understanding. An alternative model of childcare work is that of pedagogy, some of the key principles of which are an holistic approach focusing on the child as a whole person; reflective practice, which involves theoretical understandings and self-knowledge; and an emphasis on team work (Petrie et al, 2007). Pedagogue training combines academic studies, professional skills and practical training. It integrates theory, practice and personal qualities, and stresses the importance of combining 'head, heart and hands' in work with children and young people (Cameron and Boddy, 2006).

How carers see their work

One of the main reasons care workers in the Postal Survey gave for entering care work was because they believed they could make a difference to the lives of vulnerable children. As we see in the next chapter, it is this aspect of the work that often brings the greatest satisfaction. Many of our interviewees understood their role to be about changing young people's behaviour, improving their self-esteem and, for family support workers and community childminders, working with families to improve parenting skills. Other interviewees saw their role more in terms of compensating children for what they were perceived to be lacking such as love, a 'normal' family life and activities that were not provided at home.

These goals were not mutually exclusive so that some workers talked about both change and compensation. Furthermore, giving children what they had missed was seen as the means by which to bring about change. There were, however, notable differences between the four groups of workers in the emphasis they placed on change and compensation. The discourse of compensation was more prominent among home-based workers (community childminders and foster carers) than among institutionally based workers (residential social workers and family support workers), while the change model featured more among family support workers and those caring for looked-after children (foster carers and residential social workers) than among community childminders.

These differences are likely to be attributable to the different contexts within which care work takes place. These contexts include not only whether care is home or institutionally based but also the age of the children and reasons for their being cared for. Thus, family support workers referred to modelling and transference of good parenting skills as integral to their work with parents. Their work with teenagers was very much about improving their self-esteem, providing support and letting them talk through their problems. In this role, workers often saw themselves as the young person's confidant, helping them to work through the difficulties they were experiencing in their lives. For example, Michelle O'Connor, describing how she had helped a young girl who was self-harming, says: "just asking her why she felt the need to do it ... and however she felt about whatever, it didn't matter, she could tell me".

But whether subscribing to a model of change or compensation, workers used different practices in seeking to achieve their goals. These included the provision of boundaries and offering children a 'normal' family life, practices that relate to the condition of children's current lives. Another is relational, namely about forming attachments with children and making good relationships. A practice that was located from the perspective of the future was about encouraging children in their education in the hope that they would achieve good outcomes, while advocating on children's behalf that they received the help they needed in the present. These practices – managing boundaries, creating a 'normal' family life, developing close relationships and promoting education – can also be seen as comprising key elements of care. Although here we discuss each separately, they were not mutually exclusive.

Managing boundaries

Within families and between children and their parents, boundaries are negotiated and put in place. However, they are not static but evolve and change over time (Hill, 2005). Setting boundaries is an aspect of parenting (Pugh et al, 1994) and it is therefore unsurprising that childcare workers, who often understand their role to be similar to being a parent, considered setting and maintaining clear boundaries important in their work with vulnerable children. This is underscored in the legislation for children's homes where Standard 21 of the National Minimum Standards for Children's Homes (England) requires that 'staff employed at the home are able to set and maintain safe, consistent and understandable boundaries for the children in relation to acceptable behaviour' (DH, 2002, p 31). Care workers in our study reasoned that children's challenging behaviour was in part attributable to the fact that they had lacked such boundaries in their families.

Foster carers and residential social workers tended to emphasise the need for boundaries more than did family support workers and community childminders. Not only are looked-after children likely to present more challenging behaviour and to have experienced several different carers, which may exacerbate their difficult behaviour, they are also in full-time care. The need for boundaries is therefore seen in terms of the context of their past and present situations.

Brian Stratford, a residential social worker, saw his role as giving the young people in his care 'a future' by providing boundaries, alongside several other goals including building their self-esteem. When asked about his practice, he responded:

> "Myself personally I try and make sense of their past and try and give them a future, you know. A lot of parents, a lot of these kids we see in care, I mean their parents are not bad people, they just don't know how to look after kids. Not born with parenting skills.... So for the kids it's just making them feel [pause] I think it's making them safe as well, and giving them some boundaries that they haven't had before and saying 'actually no, you're not going to walk out the front door, or no you're not going to do that'. And 'actually no you actually are quite good at this'. 'Cos a lot of them never get told they're good at something."

Protecting children is an integral part of caring work and many, like Brian, were of the opinion that clear boundaries helped children feel safe and know where they stood. Susanne Grant, for example, a family support worker, said: "I think children need boundaries to be safe and to feel safe". Tom Jenkins, a residential social worker and a manager with many years' experience, took this further, explaining everyone's need for consistency:

> "Children need consistency. They need to know when, why, what and how. And they need fixed goalposts. The way to

freak any kid out is to keep switching and chopping and changing. I apply the same principle to myself in my work. I apply the same principle to my staff team.... Because I'm a great believer that if you're objective about things and you're clear then people are more settled and stable and gel together better and respond better as a result of that. And children are no different. I was in a discussion earlier [supervising a colleague] ... I said: 'What's the worst thing at the moment?' She said: 'Well it's the way his mum keeps saying she's going to do something and then changes her mind'. And that encapsulates where I'm coming from. Kids don't need that. We don't like it as adults. We like to know why, what, where and how."

However, foster carers and residential social workers often encountered difficulties in enforcing boundaries, with some speaking at length about a sense of powerlessness. For example, Jenny Masters referred to being unable to stop teenagers absconding from the home:

"[T]he rules and regulations [are] that we can advise the child not to go off and obviously make them aware of the risks and, you know, dangers and all of going out late at night and so on. But we can't physically stand there and go 'No you're not going out that door'. Nor can we lock the door."

A number of residential social workers expressed concern about the welfare of young people leaving the home late at night. In their inability to prevent them leaving, they felt unable to 'protect' the young people in their care and keep them safe, which many saw as crucial to their work.

The sanctions available to residential social workers and foster carers for managing unacceptable behaviour were sometimes viewed as insufficient or inappropriate for the seriousness of the 'offence'. This led some residential social workers and foster carers to believe that their powerlessness in such situations left young people with the impression that their actions were of little consequence: "they can get away with what they like" (residential social worker); "[the message to the child is] 'Oh, I could do that and get away with it. Why? – nothing ain't going to happen to me'" (foster carer). This perceived leniency was viewed as exacerbating the young person's problems and undermining the carer's position.

Powerlessness was further reinforced by the way that some of those working with looked-after children felt that their own rights were given less prominence than those of the young person. This is not to say that these workers believed that children's rights were unimportant; they did much advocacy on their behalf for their rights. This feeling of powerlessness was expressed when workers described having a complaint made against them by a young person. Obafemi Williams, a foster carer, in talking about accountability, said with respect to allegations made by foster children: "You are guilty before you are proven guilty as far as they [authorities] are concerned". Debra Henry, another foster carer, felt that an allegation made against her had not been handled well by the local authority who, she felt, had not listened to her nor taken into account the child's history of making allegations: "And that made me feel really terrible".

These feelings of disempowerment could lead to constructions of vulnerable children as 'powerful'. They could also lead carers to develop strategies to counter the perceived imbalance of power. Celia Anderson recognised the limited sanctions she could use with foster children and managed the situation by 'keeping them guessing': "You don't want them to know what you would do. Because you're not going to – what are you going to do? You're not going to do anything". By contrast, Debra was able to withstand feelings of disempowerment in her determination not to treat foster children as special or different from her own and thus swayed them from developing a 'false' sense of their own power:

> "And sometimes it is the things that gets said to them, you know. Like they're made to feel special. 'Well what's special about you? You're just a child, just like mine' ... when you give them [those] kind of ideas. That's when the trouble and the problems come into it, really in truth."

Family life: striving for normality for children

> "A bit of childhood. Do the normal things. Being a real child.... All the things that [pause] they know what normal is even though they haven't had it.... Kids want a family life, they want a family." (foster carer)

The desire to create a 'home-like' environment and give vulnerable children experience of 'normal' family life was evident in the accounts of most foster carers and community childminders and some residential social workers. Carers often achieved this by assuming a parental role although recognising they were 'substitute mothers' or 'second-hand parents' in that they did not have full parental rights. As some pointed out, most children still had a family of their own, and for some carers such as Obafemi Williams and Mary Haywood their ultimate goal was reuniting children with their birth families.

Brenda Reeves, a foster carer, wanted to feel more like a parent than a carer and was pleased that the foster child, whose parents were deceased, was calling her mummy and her husband daddy: "she obviously feels so secure with us ... and I actually feel like I'm a proper parent to her". Eileen Wheeler, a community childminder, was "trying to be a little mother" and focused on meeting children's emotional needs: "Nurturing, love, time spent on them, understanding ... I mean they are frightened children". Eileen, as with some of the other care workers who had experienced an unloving childhood (see Chapter Three), referred to her own unfulfilled needs as a child. Wanting to provide children with a 'normal' or 'good' family life was about reparation both for their own unhappy childhood and what the children in their care had experienced.

Debra Henry, a foster carer, drew little distinction between her role as a mother and that of foster carer: "being a foster carer is just like being a mum, there's no difference. The only difference is you actually didn't give birth to that child". This meant that Debra saw the children, whether her own or those in her care, "in the same light ... I'm not going to treat them differently". Two community childminders, who also understood their role in terms of integrating children into their family, referred to how the children they cared for were just like their own (see also Chapter Nine).

Yet others were unable to equate the care of vulnerable children with the care of their own children in this way. The involvement of social workers, the different backgrounds and challenging behaviour of the children, the carer's inability to enforce boundaries and apply sanctions, the rules that workers themselves had to abide by, and the need for respite care (for themselves and the children) all contributed to an understanding that caring for vulnerable children was different from caring for one's own child. Tom Jenkins drew a distinction between his own children and children in the residential unit, not least because of their different backgrounds and behaviour, but explained how he applied similar values:

"[A]ny practitioner needs, ethically needs a baseline and a set of values that you can apply. And so in a way I don't apply any different values to these kids than I would my own.... But I'm not one of these people that has this twee idea that you can ever say that they're the same."

Although residential homes should be 'home-like' as far as possible (DH, 2002) and workers such as Natalie James and Jenny Masters spoke about trying to achieve this, others questioned the practicality of such an approach. Tom Jenkins pointed to the "stark difference" between the two environments: "Children in a normal family environment, they're not subjected to that [behaviour of distressed and damaged children]" and both he and another residential social worker, Marleen Bennett, believed that residential children's homes as they were currently conceived were inappropriate "because they [the young people] simply don't gel together. You know they all sort of challenge each other and add to each other's problems and distress".

Physical contact was another area that illustrated the difference between carers' own children and those they cared for. Carers talked about 'safe caring' and how they could not behave towards children in their 'care' as they did with their own children, further underlining the 'otherness' of such children and making for constraints in integrating them into family life:

"Because you are not their parents, okay, and you can never be. All right [pause] otherwise you would be depriving them of their natural rights. Okay. So but treat them as best as you can, knowing the limitations. You must look after them, you know, safely. You know, keeping some boundaries. Yes. Otherwise you can get into trouble. You have regulations for safe caring and things. Where my children would jump into my bed. If they're your own children. You can't do the same with [pause] you know. So those limitations, those boundaries, must always be observed. Otherwise you know you'd be in trouble." (Obafemi Williams, a foster carer)

Yet despite the constraints upon creating a 'normal' family life, home-based carers in the main emphasised the benefits of family life for children in their care. Margaret Henderson's comments encapsulated what a 'normal' family life can provide in terms of long-term outcomes for her foster child: "And hopefully when he grows up and he marries or whatever and he's got his own children, he'll remember where like the family was all very close together, the security, rather than the threats and being frightened". Margaret was not alone in believing that her input now would have benefits in the future and, like others, saw her work as having the potential to 'break the cycle' of abuse, neglect, poor parenting and poor outcomes.

Forming attachments and making relationships

All the residential social workers and many of the family support workers referred to the importance of establishing good relationships between children and carers as a chief means by which they could meet their needs. Home-based workers also talked about forming close attachments with children and the loss they often felt when children moved on:

> "I just got too close probably. And when he left I asked his mum to keep in touch . let me know how he was getting on. And she never did ..., and that night in bed I just cried my eyes out for ages, thinking I'm never probably going to see him again. It was awful." (Kate Humphries, a community childminder)

Community childminders appeared to receive little preparation for dealing with the loss of children and learned to cope as best they could:

> "As I went on I had to make sure that you've just got to try not to feel that way again. Not feel close to them, just realise they're going to be leaving one day and it's up to the parents and you might not hear from them again."

Being able to listen and communicate with children and gain their trust were seen as key skills in developing good relationships. Justine Naisbitt, a family support worker, explained that she could relate to the care leavers she worked with, mostly young men, because she lived in the same area as they did and had young adult sons herself: "And I can speak their language as well.... I can understand what they're saying and talk back to them in the same way. And that also gives, you know, they'll say 'Oh well she knows what I'm talking about'". Michelle O'Connor, another family support worker and again working mainly with older teenagers, emphasised the need to: "Give them space, let them talk. That is the main thing that you can do – talk to them. But not at them, with them".

A relationship based on trust enabled childcare workers to be a confidant to the young person or parent who found they could talk to the family support worker, foster carer or residential social worker in a way they were unable to with their social worker or others involved in their care. A critical element of this relationship was a non-judgemental attitude often coupled with the ability to 'talk their language'. Susanne Grant, a family support worker, illustrates this attitude with the following comments:

> "Everybody needs support at some point and not all of us have the parenting we need to cope with life to begin with.... You know, I don't think 'Right we're going to remove your child, you're useless parents, so I don't have to treat you like a human being'. I think I still show my families respect and still talk to them. And I've had a lot of feedback from families where they said, you know, 'I prefer to talk to you than a social worker'. But then maybe I'm non-threatening because I don't have the power to remove their child. But, you know, they prefer to tell me something than the social worker. And I suppose probably the role I'm in I'm able to give them more time than a social worker's able to do."

However, some found developing good relationships while maintaining a professional boundary initially difficult. Reflecting on when she had started working with vulnerable children, Carol Jones, like several other care workers, had high expectations, but came to realise that she was being unrealistic: "But I thought 'Oh, you know, they'll all like me, and we'll all be best of friends', and I've since found out they don't all like you" [laughs]. She went on to explain how friendships could be problematic when it came to asserting her authority: "At the end of the day you're the one that's going to say 'No you can't do that'. And if you're trying to be their friend they're going to hate you even more". Others expressed disappointment that they could not disclose personal information about themselves to young people because this could be used against them when the young person became angry or distressed: "You can't disclose any of your own personal information to any of these young people. And I think that's incredibly sad, incredibly sad".

Good relationships were facilitated by continuity and stability, features of care that were seen as important and what vulnerable children needed. Yet, high staff turnover and short-term placements at times compromised continuity and stability. Commenting upon turnover among social workers, Pat Foster, a family support worker, said: "I actually really believe it gives a poor quality of service to service users to change all the time. You know. I think it must be awful for children and young people who have, you know, 10 social workers going through their lives". Short-term placements, sometimes for assessment purposes, placed constraints on the "ability [of staff] to try and engage and build up effective longstanding relationships", a point made by Tom Jenkins, a residential social worker. Obafemi Williams, who had been a short-term foster carer, was considering a permanent placement: "So that there will be stability … short-term placements don't give us the opportunity to have as much impact on the children. Because it takes such a long time to change a child".

Creating change through education

Supporting and encouraging children in their school education was seen as a means to help children both in the present and future although it was not explicitly expressed by many workers working with school-aged children. Jenny Masters, a residential social worker, recounted an incident of talking to a young boy who was excluded from school about his aspirations to be an architect. The conversation she recalls shows how Jenny supported his ideas and encouraged him to 'study hard'. Whereas Jenny's motivation for supporting children's education comes largely from the requirement of staff to work to each child's care plan, including a personal education plan, other carers were influenced by their own experiences.

For example, two foster carers, both from minority ethnic groups, emphasised the importance of education for their foster children while reflecting on the importance that education had played in their own lives. Obafemi Williams had come to Britain from Africa to further his own education (see Chapter Four). In describing a typical day and how he helped children with their homework, Obafemi said: "I'm particularly interested in helping them with their education. Because I believe that it's very important, that's the key, you know. And you work with the teachers too".

Debra Henry, of Black Caribbean origin, had been actively discouraged from staying on at school by her mother and had left at 15. Aged 44, she was still seeking 'to improve herself' and was in her final year of a psychology degree when interviewed for the study. Referring to the way foster children were no different from her own, she said she did not accept anything less from them in terms of educational achievement and thereby challenged what she saw as the low expectations of social workers and others towards children in care:

> "One [social worker] once told [foster child] 'It'll be all right if you come out of school with one GCSE', you know, 'cos statistically [pause] And I went mental. I just simply asked her 'Would you tell your own child that? Would you be satisfied of your own child coming out with one GCSE?' So she goes to me 'No'. So I says 'Why are you telling her that?'"

Understandings and types of knowledge

We turn now to the resources that workers drew upon to help them achieve their aims and inform their practice. As we saw in Chapter Two (Table 2.17), around a half of the Postal Survey sample had a qualification relevant to care work although rather fewer foster carers (37%) compared to community childminders (47%), residential social workers (55%) and family support workers (55%). Unsurprisingly maybe, formal training and qualifications were considered essential by only around two in five (44%) of the Postal Survey sample, although a quarter were undecided (Table 6.1). There were significant group differences with foster carers less likely to agree that training and qualifications were essential for their work compared to the other three groups.

Table 6.1: Agreement with the statement 'Formal training/ qualifications are essential'

	Type of worker				
	Residential social worker (n=82)	Family support worker (n=84)	Foster carer (n=72)	Community childminder (n=64)	All (n=302)
	%	%	%	%	%
Agree	52	48	25	52	44
Neither agree nor disagree	18	32	25	28	26
Disagree	29	20	50	20	30

Notes: 3 missing cases.
Percentages do not always total 100 due to rounding.

The fact that many workers were recruited to the job without a relevant childcare qualification may well have led them to conclude that qualifications were not essential. Support for this hypothesis is suggested by the Postal Survey data: two thirds without a childcare qualification (67%) compared to a third with a childcare qualification (33%) agreed that qualifications were not essential. Interestingly, those who were undecided were just as likely to have a childcare qualification (45%) than those without (55%). This perhaps suggests some ambivalence as to how helpful a childcare qualification was perceived to be in their work, and this was supported, as we shall see, in some of the biographical case studies.

In the context of work-based competency awards such as the NVQ alongside the fact that many lacked formal qualifications, childcare workers drew upon different types of knowledge: tacit knowledge, functional knowledge and professional knowledge (Cameron and Boddy, 2006). Tacit knowledge is attained through personal qualities and experiences, including parenting and informal care. Thus, for example, carers said they can empathise with the young person because they have been through similar experiences themselves (see Chapter Three). Functional knowledge, on the other hand, implies a set of work-based skills or competences by which carers can demonstrate that they can perform a set of tasks to agreed standards, as in the NVQ. The third type of knowledge is professional knowledge, providing workers both with credentials, but also with a theoretical base that they can apply to their practice. Such knowledge is usually acquired at academic institutions through higher-level qualifications, such as a diploma in social work.

Three groups emerged when workers were asked about their attitudes to training and qualifications and the skills needed for their work (Table 6.2). While all considered tacit forms of knowledge to be important and all drew on their personal experiences in their caring work, the relevance of tacit, functional and professional knowledge

Table 6.2: Distribution of cases with respect to the primary importance of different types of knowledge

Type of worker	Type of knowledge		
	Tacit	Functional	Professional
Residential social worker	2	1	3
Family support worker	1	2	3
Foster carer	3	3	0
Community childminder	4	2	0
Total	10	8	6

varied depending upon how care work was understood and the level of training and qualification that workers had achieved.

Tacit knowledge: the importance of being a parent

Ten childcare workers, the majority of whom were home based, saw tacit knowledge, particularly the experience of parenting, as the most essential form of knowledge. Many saw little point in the need for further training or qualifications because they understood their work in terms of being a parent, as communicated by Brenda Nelson, a community childminder:

> "And isn't that not what's wrong now, everybody wants you to have NVQ or whatever they're called in whatever job you do now, you know, isn't being a mother enough? You know, you've brought your own up, you've brought other people's up. You know, I don't need qualifications to make me a good mother."

Few in this group had a childcare qualification and therefore had little else to draw upon, but having such a qualification did not necessarily lead to a change in attitude towards training and qualifications. Debra Henry, as we have already seen, made no distinction between fostering and parenting. Although she had gained an NVQ Level 3, she was dismissive of what this qualification provided beyond enabling her to recognise child abuse. Although she saw the professional knowledge provided by the psychology degree she was pursuing as useful – helping her to understand children's behaviour and to apply different strategies – she saw the value of tacit knowledge as paramount:

> "There's no point in you becoming a foster carer if you didn't have no children yourself.... [And] You can't train me to be a parent. It's either I've got it in me to be a parent or I don't have it in me to be a parent. What you can train me to do is to cater for particular needs of children."

In the following case we show how tacit knowledge permeates the way that a community childminder viewed her work. Kate Humphries, of white UK origin, was 37 years old at interview and had an 18-year-old son and a five-year-old daughter. Kate had been a single parent from the age of 18 until meeting her husband, a builder, at the age of 28, and having her daughter some three years later. She had been community childminding ever since she started childminding some four years earlier when her own daughter was a year old. When considering what vulnerable children need, Kate projected her own needs and those of her daughter:

> "I think 'Oh this could be my little girl in someone else's house and she's upset looking for me', you know. And I've seen [childminders] in the past and they're like 'Oh that's enough of that moaning there', and I think 'How can you do that?' They're only like one and two years old and they're probably missing mummy, you know. So that kind of thing is so important for you to give them lots of attention. Even more love than you probably would normally."

As a single parent, Kate had intermittently worked part time when her son was young, leaving him with her mother while she was at work. Although she sympathised with mothers who worked for financial reasons she was less accepting of mothers who worked through choice. For Kate, good care equated to mothers 'being there' for their children. She confessed that she could never have left her daughter with anyone else. "[I] wouldn't give my child to a childminder. And it's not because you don't think they're any good, because you know you're good and you know all the other childminders you know are good, it's just that [pause], just couldn't actually do it. I mean not just a childminder, anybody really."

Caring for other children was seen as both similar to and different from caring for your own. "You know I give them just as much love and attention as I would my own children. I treat them as my own when they're here definitely.... But it's different in the way I think you just worry that bit more because they're not yours, more than anything." Unlike other community childminders, Kate did not go so far as to say she was a substitute mother, but clearly adopted a mothering role.

Care was also seen as about providing children with opportunities that they might not get *at home*, such as messy play, and ensuring that "they feel really safe, really happy and really secure". She achieved this, she said, by staying calm and avoided shouting or raising her voice, and cuddled children so that they felt comfortable and were not upset. A calm manner and putting children first were the key criteria of 'good childminding' "they [children] come first. You know, not you, not your life, they do". In her emphasis on these aspects of care – love, attention and stability – lacking in her own childhood (see Chapter Three), Kate revealed how her understanding of care has been influenced by her own upbringing.

Although Kate valued training in some aspects of the work, she saw childcare qualifications as unessential since her experience as a parent had taught her what she needed to know. She also attributed childcare skills to a natural ability, "you're either good at it or not", leading her to the conclusion that not all parents would make good childminders and those without children could be good carers.

Functional knowledge: skills for the task

The eight cases placed in the functional knowledge group were drawn from across the four groups of workers. For them, tacit knowledge was important but on its own insufficient to equip them with the skills for the job. They spoke about training and qualifications in terms of their value in providing knowledge and understanding about the regulations, for example, to do with safety and child protection. The cases in this group was less likely to describe themselves as substitute parents and more likely to stress that it was not appropriate to take on this role. One or two referred to 'corporate parenting' (a formal term used to describe the collective responsibility of local authorities and those caring for looked-after children for achieving good outcomes for children).

Teresa Thomas, a community childminder, was proud of the NVQ Level 3 qualification she had attained and her attendance on numerous courses. When asked if training and qualifications were important in her work, her response reflected the way in which she divided childcare skills into those that can be learnt through being a parent and which she saw as coming naturally such as playing with children, and those such as first aid and child protection for which training is necessary. For Teresa, a qualification brought public recognition of the knowledge she brought to the job and evidence that she was a good childminder: "I didn't have any piece of paper saying the knowledge that I thought I had. I didn't have anything on paper saying, you know, that I'm a good childminder".

The following case of Jenny Masters, a residential social worker of White British origin, illustrates how functional knowledge is applied. Jenny was 33 years old when interviewed. Her husband was in the army and they had two children aged 10 and 7. She had worked for two years in a local authority residential unit providing long-term care and was working there 18 hours a week.

Jenny's understanding of care focused on meeting children's needs, which she sought to achieve by following each child's care plan. Jenny explained what a care plan involved and in so doing illustrated how she saw children's needs and the *tasks* required to achieve desired outcomes:

> "And basically the care plans are the likes of the emotional side, how the emotions are. The work plan – if there could be low self-esteem well how you can work to build their self-esteem, do your plan, what you would do, you can discuss it with the child, even have it down on the care plan what the child is willing to agree to do and so on. You would have health needs, education needs, which you've got a plan on every one of these. So basically everything more or less going on in that child's life you've got more or less a plan for. How you're going to work with that, how you're going to aim and achieve, and [meet] these goals."

Jenny saw 'achieving' change in young people as the heart of her work and emphasised the role relationships played: "[getting] that relationship going with the kids and work[ing] with them and start[ing], you know, to get a turn around, where they are starting to achieve things and so on, it's good to see". However, she was disappointed and frustrated when children did not respond despite her efforts and assigned responsibility for the 'failure' to the child's unwillingness to cooperate:

> "I'm just not getting any of that [turn around] at all, because I've got such a difficult child to work with.... And we're trying and trying and trying, but at the end of the day if the child's not willing to work to it there's not a lot we can do. 'Cos like I said you can't force or make that child do something that they don't want to do."

Jenny described her role in terms of corporate parenting and stressed the difference between this role and her experience as a parent, not least because her own children were expected to abide by her rules. Her frequent comparisons with her experiences as a parent, however, pinpoint the difficulty she was having in coming to terms with the role of corporate parent given its limitations on authority and responsibility:

> "[Y]ou can't physically stop children leaving the unit at night. Where if my son turned round and said to me at

10 o'clock at night 'I'm going out' I'm like 'No you're not, you're at home'. But that's where it comes [pause] when I say you're a corporate parent, remember, you're a corporate parent, not the parent.... But um, our child [in the residential unit] she basically does what she wants a lot of the time when she wants. And there's not a lot we can actually do."

Asked what skills were needed for the job, Jenny spoke about needing to be a caring person and considered that she had a predisposition to care: "I'm always helping everybody else before I'd help myself". She thought that listening skills and the ability to follow through on tasks were also important as was knowledge gained through her training. Jenny had an NVQ Level 2. In discussing the courses she has been on, she focused on the requirements to follow policies and procedures, suggesting few opportunities for reflection:

"At the end of the day, you know, you're covering your own back, you're doing everything right. When you're in that job, you're writing down everything, recording everything, so should anything happen, God forbid, that nothing can ever come back on you. You've proven, I'm qualified in the job, I know I'm not allowed to do this, however I can do that."

Professional knowledge: a deeper understanding

Six cases, all residential social workers and family support workers, differed from the former groups in that they saw professional training and qualifications as more important than tacit knowledge and were less likely to elevate the importance of parental experience. The cases within this group regarded training as providing a theoretical base for understanding and reflecting upon their practice. This might enable a carer to challenge received wisdom and to become a more reflective practitioner, as in the case of Tom Jenkins who initially in his career had been resistant to formal qualifications. Most within this group had already gained, or were in the process of gaining, a diploma or degree in social work and many took a therapeutic approach in their work.

The case of Clare Glover exemplifies how this group drew on all three types of knowledge. Clare was 41 years old at interview, of white UK origin, with two children aged 11 and 14. Her husband was a psychiatric nurse. She had been working as a family support worker for eight years and previously had worked as a nanny and nursery nurse, having studied for a nursery nurse qualification (NNEB) (see Chapter Four). After her first child was born and six months maternity leave she returned to her job as a nursery nurse in a family centre, leaving her daughter with a childminder. She stopped work after her second daughter was born, but found full-time motherhood not entirely satisfying. There followed a return to family support work with a three-year break for childminding. Clare was attached to a family support team and involved in intervention work and supervision of contact visits. She was undertaking a degree in social work sponsored by her employer.

For Clare, family support work was about keeping children out of the care system although she acknowledged that in some cases it might be in their best interests:"But actually seeing families being able to stay together with the input that's needed and the support is very rewarding". Clare herself came from a close, supportive family, which was an important resource for her when her daughters were young. She believed many young parents lacked such support, which through her work she was trying to provide:"And that's why I think sometimes when I'm working with families and they've got nobody nearby and they're not talking to their mum or they haven't got any siblings, they haven't got that support network. And I think it's really important".

In seeking to understand parents' behaviour, Clare also sought to empower parents to make changes in their lives. Rather than lecturing parents on 'good parenting' she tried to teach them in a practical way that did not alienate or undermine them, while also referring to what had worked for herself as a mother:

> "'Oh have you ever thought of doing this?' or 'Have you thought of doing that?' and giving them different choices.... But I always say to parents, you know, you could do planned ignoring, time out, loss of privilege, all these different things and uh [pause] and 'What would work for you?' 'That worked for me', which was time out, 'but I couldn't do planned ignoring'. 'But you might be able to', you know."

Clare was also reflective about intergenerational patterns of parenting both in her own family and those of the families she worked with, understanding that what one generation considered to be 'good parenting' was not necessarily the same in the next generation. For example, she had rejected her mother's rather strict parenting style for a more laissez-faire approach. The knowledge she drew upon involved being reflective about and making connections between her own background, her work and her current social work training:

> "And I think doing this type of work you get more of an insight. Especially now I'm doing the training I look at all the different theories, you know, and psychology as well. You think 'Oh', you know, 'my mother'. And my grandmother who had like 13 nervous breakdowns through her life and that. And I think 'Oh I can see patterns of behaviour here'."

Clare gave a number of illustrations in her interview of how she had applied theoretical ideas to her professional practice. When Clare discussed her work with a looked-after 15-year-old girl with learning difficulties whom she had helped come to terms with the death of her parents some years previously, she illustrated how she had been sensitive and responsive to the young person's needs:

> "We didn't do any more about feelings, we didn't do any more about loss, because I think she'd got to that point where I just picked up that she didn't want to do that any more, and if we come back to another time that's fine. But it wasn't an area she wanted to go to. And because of her understanding levels it was difficult to get her back on track, I had to work at her pace. And you know I didn't want to push anything. We weren't on time-limited sessions. It was when we felt we were ready to finish sessions.... It's about using the words and communicating effectively but not threatening. And making sure you're at their level."

Clare's case therefore combines different forms of knowledge: tacit knowledge ('experience'), functional knowledge ('tasks') and professional knowledge ('theory'). The last two forms of knowledge are evident in the way she compared herself to many social workers whom she felt had theoretical knowledge, but not always the 'people skills', whereas she felt she had the skills and was learning the theory. She saw theoretical work as providing frameworks to understand children's behaviour better and as giving her the confidence to try different approaches.

> "So it's all about what I've learnt over the years. And some of it is just from experience as well. Which I do give to

parents, 'cos it worked for me, you know, and it might work for them.... I can say well the reason why I'm working with this family is because of, you know, the neglect and the parenting ability and that and it's [pause] and I'm doing task-centred bit. We're going to work on this task and we're looking at this solution. So we're looking at solution focused. I never had all this task-centred, solution-focused stuff before. I knew I was working on a specific problem with the family, but I wouldn't know why I was. But I now realise with the theory and why these theories evolved and who by, I now know the way they approach it."

Although not a topic explored in the interviews, Clare was unusual among the interviewees in explicitly highlighting the value of multi-agency training, although others spoke about the benefits of sharing information with their peers. She saw such training as enabling a coordinated approach to the care of children and providing opportunities for new ideas about how to work with children as well as exchanging crucial information about children and the services they were receiving (or not):

"[What] I really find interesting when I'm on the course is the talking through and thinking about and sharing practice with other childcare workers and teachers. Because you just get a load of ideas from others and ways of working. You think 'God, that is such a good idea'. And they'll say 'Oh have you seen that book by so and so? It's really good, I've used that'. And you think 'Yeah that's great'. So, but even in your workplace, talking with other co-workers and colleagues, you pick up so much stuff that you just think 'Why didn't I do that before? I wish I'd known about that before'.... And that's why I'm quite into multi-agency working now where you've got other agencies like from Health and Education, where we haven't worked before together, we don't communicate well, and, you know, the things like Victoria Climbié happened because we didn't do that. And I think more training, multi-agency training is very important, so people know where you're at."

Conclusion

How childcare workers understand their work depends upon the context in which they work, their preparation for the work in terms of personal qualities and life experiences, skills and training and professional qualifications, and the needs of the children they care for. Context is not just about the settings in which care is provided, whether institution or home, it is about the history and current provisions available within a particular service, local authority and country. In this chapter we have focused upon the perspectives of the carers in terms of how they made sense of their roles, the aims they sought to achieve, and the knowledge resources they saw as important and which they drew upon.

We saw from the Postal Survey that childcare workers wanted to make a difference to the lives of young people and the families they worked with. As the case study evidence suggests, making a difference was interpreted in a number of ways, which can be encapsulated within two views: compensation and change. In the first approach care workers considered that their role was to compensate for the deficits in the situations and histories of the children and young people. In particular, they sought to remedy the lack of love from parents, and to provide them with a 'normal' family life, thus making good the deficits. Alongside but also often in conjunction with this view is the second view, namely to bring about change in the young people themselves. Such a model therefore extends the compensation model of providing the necessary conditions for change to bringing about change itself. Care workers who sought to change young people spoke in terms of changing their 'behaviour' so that it became 'less challenging', raising their self-esteem, and giving them confidence to articulate their problems and feelings, and to make progress in their education (in the case of older children). Workers across all four groups referred to the importance of boundaries and good relationships in achieving their goals.

Providing children with a 'normal' family life in the case of foster carers and a 'home-like' environment in the case of community childminders and some residential social workers translated into care workers positioning themselves as 'substitute parents' and wanting to treat children in much the same way as they did their own. This could be particularly problematic for foster carers and residential social workers. In the case of foster carers they were expected by social services to care for foster children as members of their own families but, unlike with their own children, they lacked parental rights and authority. This ambiguity in their role could lead to feelings of disempowerment, which were further reinforced by the way in which allegations made against them were investigated. Not only is a complaint or allegation distressing for all concerned, it also brings into question the carer's ability to provide good-quality care (Nutt, 2006). Foster carers' ambiguous status is particularly emphasised when allegations are made because carers suddenly find themselves no longer trusted by the authorities (Walker et al, 2002).

In order to both protect and control the children in their care, carers set considerable store by 'boundary setting', considering that the children's families had failed to provide them with sufficient guidelines. However, childcare workers could feel helpless and undermined in their inability to enforce boundaries. Again, in the case of foster carers, this underlined the ambiguity of their relationship to foster children – as a parent but not a parent. Foster carers felt that children needed to learn that their actions had consequences and were upset when they felt that children were learning that they could do what they wanted.

The relational aspect of care came out forcefully in the case studies. Carers saw the creation of good relationships with children and young people as key, while stability and continuity of care were important to facilitate the development of such relationships. Relational goals were sometimes expressed in terms of 'friendship' although there were contradictions here, often unarticulated at the time. For one thing, friendship implies equity, which was not achievable in contexts in which care workers were governed by clear understandings that they should not become 'too attached' and that they were in *adult* positions of responsibility. Moreover the physical expression of affection could not be proffered without due consideration of the formal limits to their role. This was especially difficult for foster carers whose aim was to give children in their care 'normal' family lives.

The aim of enabling children's school progress was not commonly expressed, which may be due to the different contexts within which each type of worker worked. Day-to-day responsibility for looked-after children's education rests with foster carers and residential social workers, unlike community childminders and family support workers. Furthermore, community childminders were usually working with pre-school children. Family support workers worked with older children and families with young children and tended to be undertaking time-limited and focused pieces of work.

The chapter drew upon a typology of different kinds of knowledge – tacit, functional and professional – that has been found relevant to understanding childcare workers' cultural capital. Workers were asked to identify their priorities for childcare work in terms of the necessary qualities, skills, training and qualifications for the work. According to their responses and how they described their own practice, workers were placed into three 'knowledge groups', with some suggesting that all three types were important and relevant to their work. Tacit knowledge was typically emphasised by foster carers and community childminders. This might consist in personal qualities defined in terms of 'natural instincts' such as being patient, confident, sensitive, calm or having a sense of humour; or it might arise from life experiences such as dealing with problems with one's own children. Such tacit knowledge was bestowed typically through ascribed statuses of being a mother or grandparent rather than through attained statuses of being a student on a training course or diploma in social work.

Functional knowledge was associated with skills and competences to perform tasks that were often acquired through courses and workplace training such as NVQ qualifications. Workers who placed priority on this type of knowledge belonged to all four types of care workers in the study. Those who considered professional knowledge important also mentioned examples of tacit and functional forms of knowledge. All six were residential social workers and family support workers.

Professional knowledge was typically acquired through a social work diploma or degree and was seen as providing a theoretical base to enable the worker to understand better children's behaviour and apply different approaches. It is important, however, to stress that those who had a training or qualification in childcare did not necessarily shift their view about the paramouncy of tacit knowledge although this depended upon level of training and qualification.

Given that social services (particularly residential care) has had a number of high-profile cases of child abuse and been found wanting in terms of failing to protect children in their care, it is unsurprising that many childcare workers saw children in their care principally in terms of needing help and protection and requiring good-quality care. Such views of cared-for children as 'needy' were rarely tempered by *cultural* understandings of children's services (Dahlberg et al, 1999). Ideas that reflect the wider debate about what childhoods *can be* like for vulnerable children were unsurprisingly not articulated by care workers. While care workers' goals need to be achievable in the shorter term and embedded in everyday life, different visions of childhood can be important influences on practice, in particular ideas that accord children active citizenship and the ambition to become responsible members of society. Such visions are very different from offering a 'service' to children (Moss, 1999). Rather they are about creating with children and young people a 'place for them to be' (Moss and Petrie, 2002). Such silences in the data (Brannen and Nilsen, 2005) emanate from the still relative lack of opportunities for professional and pedagogical training for those who work in children's services and from the history of British childcare. Nonetheless, the different types of knowledge – tacit, functional and professional – are open to these different visions of childhood.

SEVEN

Experiences of care work

"They should be a lot more honest [about the nature of the work].... Because I think people tend to be put off because of the bad press that they get. And that tends to highlight like the bad things rather than the positive things." (Debra Henry, a foster carer)

This chapter sets out to document the everyday reality of working with vulnerable children in both home and institutional settings. There is a fairly substantial literature on the attractions of care work with vulnerable children and their families, whether this be foster care (Triseliotis et al, 2000; Sinclair et al, 2004), residential care (DH, 1998; Mainey, 2003), childminding (Statham et al, 2000; Mooney et al, 2001) or family support work (Carpenter and Dutton, 2003). Common motivations across these groups include wanting to make a positive difference to people's lives, enjoying working with children and young people, and gaining satisfaction from helping them to overcome challenges and difficulties.

But how do these expectations match up to the reality of the everyday work? Previous research involving residential social workers, foster carers and childminders has reported a high level of job satisfaction (for example, Penna et al, 1995; Aldgate and Bradley, 1999; McLean, 1999; Mooney et al, 2001; Mainey, 2003; Milligan et al, 2005; Sinclair, 2005). Much less has been written about the *lived experience* of providing care for children who need support from social services. Yet there are good reasons for looking in depth at the nature of care work with vulnerable children. There is little public understanding of what such work entails, or the range of ways in which it can be carried out. Research commissioned by the Department of Health found 'a lack of basic knowledge about both social work and social care' among the general public, and generally negative perceptions that are thought to contribute to recruitment and retention difficulties in this field (Central Office of Information Communications, 2001, p 61).

Some types of work with children, for example family support work and community childminding, have received relatively little attention in the literature, perhaps reflecting the lower priority often attached to preventive work compared to the services needed by children who live away from home. This sense of invisibility, even within their own organisation, was reflected in the comment of a family support worker in the current study who referred to herself and her team as 'the silent workforce'.

Both childcare workers and managers in our study thought that there was a need to prepare people better for what the work entailed, balancing honest information about the difficulties with a positive portrayal. They talked about how difficult it was for people to imagine what the work was like, and several recounted tales of people who had begun the job with false expectations and then left. This was particularly the case in residential social work. As Carol Jones (a residential social worker) noted, "You can't breeze in and be this fairy godmother and make them all better" An overview of key messages from fostering research has similarly concluded that it is important to convey positive but realistic messages about fostering to the general public (Sinclair, 2005).

The experience of providing care for vulnerable children will be influenced by the amount of support – practical and financial – that carers are offered and their conditions of employment. A recurrent theme in the UK literature on care work with children, and indeed care work in general, is dissatisfaction with the typically low pay and status (Johansson and Cameron, 2002). One survey of 2,000 foster carers in England found that less than 4 in 10 of those with children placed by the local authority expressed satisfaction with their remuneration, although those working for independent fostering agencies tended to be more satisfied (Kirton et al, 2003). The level of allowances paid to foster carers has varied considerably across the UK, although a national minimum allowance was introduced for foster carers in England for the first time in April 2007.

Whereas foster carers working for independent agencies are usually paid higher fees and allowances than those working for local authorities, the reverse is true for residential childcare workers. Care workers in the public and voluntary sector earn on average 22% more than those in the private sector (Eborall, 2003). A survey of staff working in residential childcare has shown a high level of job satisfaction, with around three quarters either satisfied or very satisfied with their jobs (Mainey, 2003). Factors considered to produce high morale were good teamwork (the most important single factor, mentioned by 72% of respondents), clear guidance, supportive management style, support from colleagues, access to training and recognition of good-quality work. However, staff and managers alike felt that their work was undervalued and that field social workers in particular did not appreciate the work they did. A more in-depth study of children's homes (Whitaker et al, 1998) reported similar sources of satisfaction and stress. Rewards included feeling supported by a strong staff team, seeing that the young people in one's care actually benefited, feeling that difficult situations could be handled competently and feeling valued by colleagues and managers. Sources of stress included a pile-up of tasks, being at the receiving end of abuse, and knowing that the unexpected and unmanageable could occur at any time.

Insufficient information about the children they are required to care for is another issue for some childcare workers, in particular home-based workers such as community childminders (Statham et al, 2000) and foster carers (Morgan, 2005). For all types of childcare worker, the extent to which they *feel* supported in their work is an important consideration. Foster carers in particular appear to value support equally or more highly than financial rewards: one survey showed that only a minority would favour higher payment if it meant less support (Kirton et al, 2003). Informal sources of support such as partners and children can also be very important (Sinclair, 2005). One study of carers who fostered difficult adolescents found that the two often went together: carers who felt they had good formal support also reported good informal support (Farmer et al, 2004).

Much of the literature we have reviewed examines the experience of care work for just one type of childcare worker. A particular feature of our study was the inclusion of four different groups providing care for vulnerable children, which enabled us to explore similarities and differences between their experiences and the factors that might help to account for this. All four groups worked with children or young people who were in contact with social services, and who would be defined as 'in need' within the terms of the 1989 Children Act. Their care work varied along a number of dimensions, as described in Chapter One, but despite the differences between the four groups of workers, there was a remarkable consensus in the overall picture that emerged from analysis of the satisfactions and frustrations they currently experienced in their work. The overriding message was of people who were strongly committed to working with vulnerable children and to helping to improve their lives, who obtained enjoyment and satisfaction from the nature of the work, but who more often than not were dissatisfied with at least some of the conditions under which the work was carried out. Other research has likewise made a distinction between the intrinsic rewards of care work, which tend to be high (at least for those who remain in the work); and the extrinsic rewards such as pay and status, which tend to be low (see, for example, Balloch et al, 1998; Statham et al, 2000; Cameron et al, 2002; Mainey, 2003; Greenfields and Statham, 2004; Sinclair, 2005).

The rest of this chapter begins with an overview of responses to the Postal Survey questionnaire, drawing out similarities and differences between the four groups of worker and seeking explanations for these from the case study material. This is followed by a thematic analysis of satisfaction with different aspects of care work with vulnerable children, both intrinsic and extrinsic, using the case studies to illuminate the subjective experience of care work and to examine the factors that influenced reported levels of satisfaction. Finally, two cases are presented in more detail to illuminate the interplay of different factors in determining how care work is experienced overall. These cases cover different types of care work, and workers who are situated at opposite ends of a continuum of enjoyment and satisfaction with their work.

Satisfaction and dissatisfaction: Postal Survey findings

The focus of this study was care work with vulnerable children in contact with social services, so all four types of worker supported children or young people who would be defined as 'in need' within the terms of the 1989 Children Act. Table 7.1 shows the ratings given by respondents in the Postal Survey to indicate their satisfaction with different aspects of the work. Overall there was a high level of satisfaction, particularly among childminders. More than half the sample, regardless of type of childcare work, reported satisfaction with the place where they worked, the children and families they worked with, the way in which they worked within a team, their hours, the control they had over the work, and the support and training they received. Ratings were made on a five-point scale and were then combined for analysis purposes into a three-point scale, so it is important to note that those who were not counted as satisfied were not necessarily dissatisfied. Often it was the case that they opted for the midway point on the rating scale, indicating neither satisfaction nor dissatisfaction.

The least satisfactory aspects of the work for all groups were extrinsic factors – pay and other working conditions (such as access to a pension and sick pay), and the pressure and low status of the work. Managers of the respective services confirmed that pay levels were generally poor. One of the private companies providing residential childcare was paying unqualified workers just 20 pence an hour above the minimum wage. Childminders working in community childminding schemes received an hourly rate for sponsored children that was little higher, and in some

Table 7.1: Proportion of childcare workers satisfied with different aspects of the work

	Type of worker					
	Residential social worker	Family support worker	Foster carer	Community childminder	All	
	%	%	%	%	n	%
Place where I work	74	63	84	97	298	78
Children and families I work with	74	71	68	92	298	76
The way in which I work within a team	70	74	60	63	295	68
The hours	60	69	58	81	293	67
The control I have over my work	54	61	55	86	295	63
The support I get in my work	63	63	56	64	296	62
The training I receive	59	51	55	68	294	58
Feeling secure in this kind of work	45	52	34	41	295	44
Pressure of work	39	26	40	61	298	40
The status of the work	39	38	39	39	295	39
Pay	28	37	37	38	295	34
Other working conditions	39	56	6	16	292	32

Note: Respondents could give more than one response therefore percentages do not total 100.

cases actually lower, than the normal fee they could charge to parents looking for childcare so that they could work. One childminding scheme did cover five days sick/dependency leave and four weeks paid holiday a year, but neither authority offered community childminders a retainer to keep places open for social workers to access at short notice, so most childminders needed to care for children placed privately as well. In fact, half of the community childminders were not caring for a child placed by social services at the time of the survey, and 4 in 10 had not done so for over a year.

Foster carers received a range of fees and allowances, but the independent fostering agencies in our study paid significantly better than did the local authorities. They also provided better support and training opportunities, as other studies have found (Kirton et al, 2003; Sellick and Howell, 2004; CSCI, 2006). The foster carers in our survey who worked for independent agencies (sample size of 33) were more satisfied than those working for local authorities (sample size of 35) with most aspects of their work including pay, status, support and training, although the numbers are too small to draw definite conclusions.

The survey findings suggested some other differences between types of childcare worker. For example, home-based workers were more satisfied with the place where they worked than those who were institutionally based. The influence of the setting in which care work is carried out on the experience of care, for both care provider and recipient, has been discussed elsewhere (Statham and Mooney, 2006). Childminders and foster carers tend to be highly satisfied with care work that can be undertaken in their own homes (and indeed this is often a significant factor attracting them into the work) because it allows them to combine paid work with the care of their own children. However, our interviews suggested that this co-location could also be a negative experience, for example when the children cared for had an unwanted impact on the carer's family or caused damage and disruption to the family home.

The highest levels of satisfaction were found among community childminders with many aspects of their work, including the children and families they worked with, their hours and the control they had over their work. The interviews suggested a number of possible explanations. The hours children attended when in a community placement were often shorter, since they were typically collected by their non-working parents at the end of the school day, rather than at 6pm or even later when parents finished work. The children cared for by community childminders often had less challenging behaviour than those looked after by the other three groups. This was partly a function of age, since childminders mostly cared for young children and babies, but also reflected the fact that daycare places were often provided to meet parents' needs rather than because the children themselves were exhibiting difficult behaviour. Working from home gave childminders greater control over how they organised their day, and the interviews showed that 'being my own boss' was a particular source of satisfaction for this group. They enjoyed the autonomy and control they had over their work: "I'm my own person ... if I want to leave here at half past nine and on a summer day not come back till four, I can do that".

Although foster carers also cared for children within their own homes, they scored lower than childminders on satisfaction with the control they had over their work. This could be because they were less likely to see foster care as 'work', but also because they felt more constrained than childminders by rules and regulations about what they could and could not do with the children in their care (see later in the chapter).

Family support workers in the survey were the group most concerned about the pressure involved in their work. Little more than a quarter (26%) rated themselves as satisfied with this aspect of their work compared to 40% of the childcare workers as a whole. This is likely to reflect the changes being made to the family support worker role in all three local authorities from which this group of workers was recruited for our study. They were seen by managers as a key group in relation to increased integration of children's services. In two of the authorities, the post had been renamed (to social services assistants in one, social work assistants – family support in the other). Although this rebranding and incorporation within social work teams was presented as developing a career route, the interviews with managers and family support workers raised a number of issues. For example, not all family support workers wanted to take on more responsibilities or develop a career, and one manager was concerned that the move to base family support workers within social work teams as 'para-professionals' was creating additional stress and problems with burnout for this group.

There was a lower level of satisfaction with working hours among residential social workers responding to the Postal Survey compared to the other types of childcare worker. Unsocial working hours were particularly common among this group: most worked shifts (83%), evenings (71%), overnight (61%) or at weekends (78%). Managers in our study reported that full-time residential social workers generally averaged 37 or 38 hours a week, but that this could alternate between 'long' weeks of 45 hours and 'short' weeks of 30 hours. Most units employed day staff doing either early or late shifts plus regular sleepovers (once a week or once a fortnight), and separate 'waking night' staff who provided overnight care. However, one of the private companies did not employ separate waking night staff and workers were expected to sleep in as part of their shift. The manager explained that "a shift is 15 hours ... well, it's 24 and a half hours really. It's 8 o'clock in the morning until 11 o'clock at night. Then a sleep, and then go home at half past eight the next morning after the handover".

However, over half (60%) of the residential social workers in the survey nevertheless rated themselves as satisfied with the hours they worked. The interviews suggested that part-time or evening shift work, particularly when managers were flexible over rotas and were sensitive to family commitments, could be welcomed by some workers as it helped them to combine paid work with family responsibilities.

Care workers' experiences

The case studies provided an opportunity to explore sources of satisfaction and frustration in more detail and to locate these in the context of the workers' everyday lives. The 24 childcare workers who were interviewed in depth were asked to think of a recent 'typical day' when they were looking after a child in need, and to describe that day in detail including how they felt at various times during the day and what they liked and disliked about their work. Many also provided vivid examples elsewhere in the interview of situations and events that had occurred in their care work with children.

The children and young people they cared for covered a broad continuum of need, with residential social workers tending to deal with the most disturbed and difficult children at one end and community childminders the least challenging children at the other end. However, almost all workers had experience of difficult behaviour and dangerous or stressful situations. For foster carers and residential social workers this was usually related to the children and young people themselves, whereas for family support workers and community childminders potentially violent situations were as likely to be caused by their work with parents, including situations where they felt their work put them at risk of repercussions from within the community.

Intrinsic rewards

Making a difference

Despite these difficulties, the high level of satisfaction with the children and families they worked with was very evident in the case studies as well as the survey. It was important to these workers that they were providing care for children who had experienced difficulties and disadvantage in their lives (two thirds rated this as 'very important' in the survey). Being able to make a difference to the lives of vulnerable children was a strong motivating force for all groups of childcare worker. In their stories of care work, recurring themes were their pleasure in being with children and young people and establishing relationships with them, and the satisfaction they obtained from seeing the children they cared for develop and make progress.

Community childminders talked about the rewards of being able to give children experiences they would not receive at home, and seeing them "with a full tummy and a smile on their face". Brenda Nelson, who had herself had a difficult and traumatic childhood, said the satisfaction lay in "just seeing the difference. The difference from somebody taking notice and taking care of them and seeing how they react to that and how they grow with it". Workers in children's homes likewise spoke of the huge satisfaction of getting traumatised children finally to smile or to respond to their approaches, of helping young people to "get on and achieve things", and of feeling that their work was important.

Residential social worker Brian Stratford described how he was "kept going" by the occasions, even if they occurred rarely, where young people went on to make a success of their lives and credited this to his input. "There's not many people in this world could say they've done a job where it helped somebody." Family support workers also spoke of the fulfilment of helping families to stay together, and hearing later that they were doing well. Foster carers stressed their pleasure in building relationships with the children and young people they cared for, and seeing their lives improve. "Them moving on and getting married and having their children, their grandchildren ... it's worked and you're the one that's put them on that road. I mean what more could you want?" (Mary Haywood). Not all carers were able to stay in touch with the children and young people they cared for – in fact one residential social worker described how the company she worked for forbade ongoing contact between workers and children after they had left – but the satisfaction of knowing that they had been able to make a difference was a powerful motivating force. "You can't beat it, it gives you a buzz." (Natalie James)

Being able to give children something they had missed out on, and creating a homely atmosphere where children felt safe, was an additional source of satisfaction to many carers (see also Chapter Six). This was particularly clear in the accounts of the home-based workers (childminders and foster carers), who stressed the 'normality' of their everyday lives – going shopping, going to the library, visiting relatives – and who enjoyed being able to share this with children who might not have had such experiences.

The satisfactions of sharing everyday life were also evident in the descriptions that residential social workers gave of their work, even though this took place in a setting that was home to the children but not home to the workers. They talked about going to the park, 'chilling out', planning meals, helping with homework, making cakes and watching television with young people. For Jenny Masters, working less than two years in a local authority long-term unit that housed five young people aged between 14 and 16, the best part of the day was when the children came back from school. She enjoyed "that feeling of everybody being there together", sitting down asking how their day had gone, "just that quality time with the kids where you're getting to talk with them and that". Brian Stratford, a team leader in a voluntary sector home providing short-term assessment places for 12- to 15-year-olds, described a typical day when most of the young people were at school, and the activities that occurred once they returned around 4pm:

> "We've got this really nice big house, we've got a big massive dining room, kitchen area, lounge. We've got another area which has got computers for them and a pool table and stuff. So we've got the separate areas. So wherever they are, we are. And if they want to sit in the lounge and watch, we'll sit in there and just chill out in there, have hot chocolate and stuff. Or when they want to play pool we go and play pool with them. Or if they want some free time in their bedroom [inaudible] go upstairs, their own spaces."

However, having asserted that "we try and keep it quite normal like a family", Brian in his typical day went on to describe how a project worker from a charity had come into the home to run a group session for girls about sexual abuse, and the impact this had on the young people's behaviour afterwards. In children's homes, even relatively small ones catering for only a handful of children, everyday activities co-existed alongside less 'normal' events. Accounts by residential social workers also included handover meetings at the beginning of each shift, significant amounts of paperwork and record-keeping, breaking up fights and patrolling the landing at night to ensure that young people did not enter each other's rooms. The tension between providing a normal family life and meeting the specific needs of disturbed and damaged children is a part of the care work experience that was discussed in greater depth in the previous chapter.

Challenge and competence

The difficult and challenging nature of some children's behaviour could itself be a source of satisfaction, provided that workers were well supported and felt able to deal with such situations well. Such support was not always forthcoming, and in the next chapter we show how children's behaviour was one reason why some Postal Survey respondents had gone on to leave their jobs, especially those who had been working in children's homes. However, when workers were well supported and felt competent in their ability to handle challenging behaviour, this could be a motivation to remain in the work.

Residential social workers were the closest to the 'front line', dealing with a number of children all of whom typically had a high level of need. A constant theme in the residential social workers' accounts was children's often difficult and challenging behaviour. They described incidents of attempted self-harm, violence towards other children and staff, verbal abuse and children generally 'kicking off' and pushing boundaries. But they also stressed the importance of understanding such behaviour and not taking it personally. Brian, for example, gave an example of a child biting him and then crying and finally starting to talk. "You just knew he wasn't biting me, he was biting his dad or someone else in his head." Having good support made such behaviour manageable. Natalie James described a dangerous situation where a teenage girl was lashing out and attempting to wrap a cord round her neck, but presented this as a challenge she felt able to deal with because there were other staff ready to help. She described her manager and colleagues as "very supportive" and told how they would sit together chatting after the young people had gone to bed.

Foster carers also experienced a high level of challenging behaviour, although this depended partly on the type of placement. Short-term and emergency placements appeared to be particularly difficult and demanding. Mary Haywood, an experienced foster carer, remarked ironically that fostering was fine "if you like swearing, you like kids that are sexually activated at seven, you've got a kid of nine on the pill....". Like others, she thought it important to be able to accept such behaviour: "I've seen four-year-olds effing and blinding and kicking doors down, and you know if you haven't got the temperament for it that isn't going to change overnight".

Justine Naisbitt, a family support worker in a leaving care team, obtained satisfaction and pride from her ability to work well with difficult young men and to obtain their trust: "I've had bad 'uns, really bad ones [laughs]". Being able to deal with the stressful nature of her work was a source of self-esteem: "You have to be strong to take the abuse and sadness of it all". Community childminders tended to downplay any challenging behaviour by the children they cared for, and to focus instead on how the children fitted into their daily routine. They were more likely to describe problems with the parents of sponsored children rather than with the children themselves. But even for community childminders, the fact that sponsored children came with what one childminder referred to as 'issues' led them to feel that their work was particularly worthwhile. Kate Humphries thought that caring for sponsored children was "probably the most important job you can do", and Gillian Dunscombe said that she liked "the challenging side of social services, you know. That it's not a normal nine-to-five job, you've got something a bit more challenging than just being a childminder". Again, feeling well supported and able to contact someone in an emergency, such as a parent turning up drunk or when the carer was concerned about a child's welfare, was important in enabling community childminders to deal with difficult situations.

External conditions

Constraints on the ability to provide quality care

The downside of the pleasure and satisfaction that all carers took in children's progress and development was the frustration experienced when they were unable to make a difference or felt constrained by external factors that hampered their ability to meet children's needs. These factors included a lack of autonomy to interact with children in the way they judged best; decision making that was led by budgets rather than the child's needs; inadequate staffing levels leading to too much pressure; and being given insufficient information about the children they were asked to care for.

A concern expressed particularly by residential social workers and foster carers was being constrained by external rules and regulations that impacted on the care they were able to provide. Both groups looked after children who needed full-time care, and their work thus entailed involvement in all aspects of children's lives – their education, health, relationships and so on. Residential social workers and foster carers were expected to act as 'corporate parents', yet often felt that they were constrained in their ability to act as a parent would. They disliked having to check with social workers or parents before taking fairly routine decisions about children's lives, such as whether they could sleep over at a friend's house or have their navel pierced. One residential social worker explained how it was difficult "not being able to sometimes say to a young person 'yes that's fine, you can do that' or 'no it's not'". A common complaint was being unable to prevent young people leaving the residential unit or foster home late in the evening, and fearing that this placed young people – especially teenage girls – at risk of harm.

Another factor that reduced both residential social workers' and foster carers' experience of being in control of their work was the risk of false allegations being made against them by the children and young people they cared for, and the sense of powerlessness that this engendered. This led them to behave differently with the young people they cared for than they would with their own children, for example in terms of intimacy and showing physical affection (see Chapter Six). As other researchers have found (Sinclair et al, 2004), the way in which allegations against carers are handled has a significant impact on how they felt about the work and their intentions to continue. Debra Henry described how she thought of giving up fostering after a child (an emergency placement over a weekend) made an allegation against her, which she was not aware of until she enquired why no further children had been placed with her and was told she was under investigation. Debra 'felt terrible' that social services appeared to believe a child with a history of making false allegations and felt she had not been listened to. Although persuaded to continue fostering by the link worker, she continued to feel distrustful and resentful of social workers.

Frustration at lack of resources took different forms depending on the type of care work, but was evident across all four groups of worker. Brian disliked the way that recommendations made in their assessments could be ignored by social services due to cost, and children sent back to their parents instead. "It happens all the time. And then it gets frustrating and you think, what is the point of doing this job?" Family support workers had experienced resources being "sucked away", such as losing access to rooms where they had been able to do one-to-one work with young people or having contact time with them reduced, making many activities impracticable. This left them feeling their work was not valued, as well as making it harder to do the job well. Foster carers found it difficult when they could not access resources that children needed, such as counselling. "You get frustrated that there's not enough put in place for them" (Celia Anderson). But when they were able to help the children improve and achieve, the work was a source of considerable satisfaction.

Staffing difficulties sometimes created situations where workers felt too stretched to do their work properly, especially when high turnover or sickness rates were combined with unsupportive managers. Family support worker Pat Foster's typical day left her with "no time to breathe", feeling stressed and under pressure as two young people's care arrangements broke down and she was unable to get hold of social workers to set up alternative placements. Carol Jones, who at the time of her interview had actually handed in her notice at a private residential home (see Chapter Five), gave a lengthy account of unsupportive managers who left her to find her own cover when staff called in sick, expected workers to do sleep-ins without the support of waking night staff, and regularly allocated insufficient staff to a shift to be able to cope with the high level of children's needs. She felt that "they don't give a damn about their staff ... it's all about money, they don't look after you".

Low pay and status

There was widespread dissatisfaction with poor pay, although foster carers held differing views about the importance of financial rewards for the work (see Chapter Five). For the other three groups of worker, it was clear that the issue of pay was closely linked to dissatisfaction, with a perception of the low status and value attached to their work. They felt that poor remuneration gave a message that their work was not important. This was especially strong among the family support workers interviewed, who had been relocated into social work teams and saw themselves as doing the same kind of work as social workers, but for lower pay and without perks like golden handshakes and travel allowances. They also resented the title of 'social work assistant'. Justine Naisbitt, attached to a leaving care team, believed that family support workers were treated "like a second-class citizen":

> "We're not social workers, we don't profess to be social workers, but we'd like some recognition. You know we do a damned good job. And we actually fill the gaps that the social workers don't do, and can't do. And that's what I find is really upsetting, you know. That I could do a social worker's job tomorrow, and that's not being big headed or boasting or anything, but I would say that 50% of the social workers could not do my job. Because they just don't have the skills or the experience or the knowledge. And we never get that kind of acknowledgement. Specially pay-wise. I'm still on [pause] I am on the same scale as an admin worker, and yet I deal with death, murder, you know, debauchery. You name it, I've dealt with it. And I go out into the field and could be hurt at any moment. And that's not taken on board, I'm still paid the same as an admin worker."

Like Carol Jones who complained that the company running her private home "didn't look after you", those caring for vulnerable children wanted themselves to feel cared for and valued in their workplace. Some appeared to be looking for elements of a 'family' in their work environment – people to socialise with, who cared about them and looked out for them. When this was not the case, due to high staff turnover, unsupportive managers, feeling "put upon" or unappreciated, the experience of care work was far less satisfactory. One family support worker who was considering leaving explained that this was largely because of a new manager, who lacked social skills and didn't make workers "feel loved".

For childminders, who in general were highly satisfied with their work, the most frequently mentioned dislike was the isolation and lack of adult company. This was the flipside of the autonomy and control that was a source of satisfaction. They enjoyed having "no one telling you what to do", but also found that "it's quite lonely work on your own".

A continuum of satisfaction

So far in this chapter we have taken a thematic approach and separated out the rewards, constraints and difficulties of the work, such as making a difference to young people's lives, dealing with challenging behaviour, autonomy and control, pay and status. But both negative and positive themes typically co-existed in individual workers' accounts, and the overall experience of care work depended on the balance and interaction between different factors. For example, difficult and challenging behaviour was experienced differently by carers who felt well supported by managers and colleagues, and who thought that their views were respected and had the resources to do their work well.

It was possible to distinguish three broad levels of satisfaction among the 24 case study workers, although individuals were situated along a continuum rather than falling into discrete groups (Table 7.2).

First, there were those carers whose overall experience was generally positive (categorised as 'high satisfaction'). They were very engaged in and focused on their care work with vulnerable children, felt well

Table 7.2: Overall satisfaction with experience of care work (number of cases)

	Residential social worker	Family support worker	Foster carer	Community childminder
High satisfaction	3	0	3	4
Medium satisfaction	1	2	2	2
Low satisfaction	2	4	1	0

supported and enjoyed the challenge of the work even though there might be some things they would like to be different. The difficult situations they dealt with were presented as challenges and they stressed the rewards of the work and its importance. This group included staff in voluntary and local authority children's homes, foster carers working for local authority and independent fostering agencies, and childminders working for different placement schemes. None of the six family support workers fell in this first group. Foster carers and residential social workers were more evenly distributed.

Midway along the continuum were the 'medium satisfaction' carers who gave roughly equal weight to both positive and negative features of their work. They enjoyed some aspects but expressed strong dissatisfaction with other aspects of the work such as the pressure, lack of status or the low pay. At the other end of the continuum were those we have characterised as 'low satisfaction'. They still often enjoyed the contact with children and young people, the sense of being able to make a difference to their lives, and the variety and challenge of the work. However, this enjoyment was compromised by organisational factors such as poor support from managers or colleagues, lack of appreciation of their work, too much stress and pressure or insufficient resources to do the work properly. The overall tone of their accounts was more negative than positive, and some had seriously considered leaving. None of the community childminders fell into this group, but four of the six family support workers did.

The two cases presented below have been selected from each end of the continuum, and provide a more holistic picture of how positive and negative aspects are interwoven to produce different experiences of care work. Both Brenda Nelson, a community childminder, and Susanne Grant, a family support worker, are strongly committed to improving the lives of disadvantaged children and face difficulties and challenges in their work. But Brenda feels well supported by the local authority and enjoys the autonomy of working from home, while Susanne is unhappy with the pressure of work, lack of support from her manager and with her employment conditions.

High satisfaction: community childminder

Brenda Nelson is aged 50 and lives on a council estate with her husband (a builder) and the younger of her two adult children, who is disabled. She has cared for children placed by social services for approximately 20 years. In the early days, before regulations changed, children were initially placed for a short period but occasionally ended up living with her for up to two years, despite the fact that she was not a foster carer. At the time of the interview Brenda is providing respite weekend care for a seven-year-old boy with Attention Deficit Hyperactivity Disorder, whom she describes as a "lovely boy", easy and fun to be with, "just a bit hyper". She is also caring for another child in a private arrangement during the week. Her care work thus involves long hours, starting at 7.30 in the morning during the week and providing overnight care from Friday to Sunday for the child placed by social services. The pay is poor, but there is little mention of financial considerations in her account, apart from a joking reference to the fact that "I'll never be rich me. It costs me more to look after these kids than I get paid".

Brenda's commitment to helping vulnerable children stems from her own difficult and unloved childhood (see Chapter Three), and she obtains great satisfaction from being able to improve children's lives. "It makes the job more rewarding when you see how much a little love and understanding makes to these children." She identifies with their distress, and the work fulfils her need to care: "It meets my needs … I think I can give a lot to them emotionally". She loves being with the children, seeing them grow and develop —"I just love it". She also likes the control that she has over her day, with no timetable and no one telling her what to do.

Brenda's husband is very supportive of her childminding work, which is essential since Brenda's home and work lives are so intertwined and there are children in the house "all day, all weekend, night-times". Her husband gets involved in the children's care but avoids bathtimes and bedtimes due to his concerns about false allegations. Brenda has been impressed by his sensitivity in this area, recounting an episode where a boy who had been emotionally neglected kept asking for kisses and cuddles. Although both responded, they realised there might be a problem when the child began asking for physical affection from the taxi driver who took him home. "So [husband] said to him 'You're too big for kisses, I'll shake your hand. I'll give you a cuddle and then I'll show you how to shake hands'. You know, like nice."

Brenda has considered fostering, but prefers community childminding as it allows her to help a greater number of vulnerable children. She enjoys working from home and part of the satisfaction is creating a warm, caring home environment for children who have not experienced this. Although she has at times thought about moving on to other work with children, such as a teaching assistant in a school, this would not provide the same satisfaction: "It just wouldn't be the same as having them at home, would it? Just writing and reading with kids that go home at the end of the day – and then nothing". Brenda has experienced some very difficult situations with abusive parents and damaged children, and at one point had to have a panic button installed because of threats from a child's parents. This has just made her more determined, rather than leading her to think of giving up. The fact that she can access support from social services or the community childminding scheme coordinator makes a lot of difference: "You've always constantly got back-up, there's always someone there. Weekends, they're always on call at the civic centre, so there's never a time when you're not [supported]". Training is widely available and can be tailored to particular needs, although Brenda herself has not taken this up to any extent.

One of the few things that Brenda dislikes about the job is the paperwork, which has increased hugely in recent years. She was indignant when inspectors rated her care 'satisfactory' rather than 'good' because she didn't have a filing system. "And I thought how dare she sit there and tell me, you know, she wasn't going to pass me as a good childminder because my paperwork's not right. I don't do the job for the paperwork."

Some of the children she has cared for have been severely neglected by their parents. This makes her angry, but she has learnt to manage these feelings so that parents "wouldn't know I didn't like them". The work does take an emotional toll, however, especially worrying about children's safety when they are returned to unsatisfactory situations. After a placement that has been particularly emotionally draining Brenda does sometimes think of giving up, but can't bring herself to do so because of her strong commitment to the work.

> "I wish you knew how many times I'd gave this job up, but I can't ... it just takes it out of you, and then I think 'I'm not doing it any more. I'm not doing it. You'll just get too upset about it'. And then you just do it again [laughs] ... I think 'If I didn't, who does it?'"

Brenda says that one of the most rewarding aspects of the work is being able to see the difference she has made to children's lives, especially when they are removed from damaging home situations and placed in foster or adoptive care. "I get to see where they're going to live and what's going to happen to them. So it's nice ... I still see all the kids that I've had and I haven't seen one of them that's gone back into a bad situation."

Low satisfaction: family support worker

Susanne Grant is a full-time family support worker with training and experience in a variety of childcare settings who is attached to a duty and assessment team. She has two children at home aged 8 and 15, and an older son away at university. Her job involves direct work with families, duty work that necessitates dealing with emergencies and is totally unpredictable, report writing and administration. Susanne's typical day reveals the stresses caused by the heavy workload, variety of duties and unpredictability of demands. Although her hours are nine to five, in reality it very much depends on what is going on:

> "If we have to place children or do some emergency on duty then it could be really late. I mean like one Friday night the school rang at five past five to say they had a child not collected. *(Right)* So he had to be accommodated, so by the time I got home it was half seven, 8 o'clock. 'Cos we couldn't find his carer."

Her account of her experiences includes many examples of dealing with difficult behaviour and risky situations, such as supervising a potentially violent father's contact visit to his partner and newborn baby in the hospital (with a security guard in the background), helping a family where the mother had died and the father had an alcohol problem, and helping a young mother with four children and a chaotic lifestyle. She describes children kicking, spitting or swearing at her, and at times has to take charge of a situation that is growing out of control because the parent is unable effectively to do so:

> "So in the end I had to get him and put him in the chair next to me and told him not to move, 'cos I'm not happy with him, and that's not how we behave. He did listen to me, screamed for a while, but then after a while he sat down and read a book and whatever."

Susanne obtains satisfaction from being able to deal with such situations. She also likes the variety of the work: "I think that's what I like about the job. No day's the same and you're always learning new skills. You can never know everything about families". But she is not at all happy with her manager, whom she feels does not understand the family support worker's role and who has discouraged staff from socialising during work hours, thus altering the atmosphere at work. She just wants to see people working all the time, "that social side of it is gone". In common with other care workers attached to organisations, Susanne values the camaraderie of colleagues, and losing this is a source of dissatisfaction.

Susanne is also unhappy with the pressure of her work, feels put upon and that there are not enough hours in the day. For example, describing her typical day, she reported getting into work at 7.45am and did not break for lunch until four. The high turnover of staff in her department exacerbates the situation: "There's a lot of agency staff and a lot of staff from abroad ... talk about clients experiencing loss, you do it every week 'cos every Friday there's a leaving do".

The removal of children is a particularly difficult, upsetting and stressful aspect of her work even in the knowledge that it is being done for the child's safety. Susanne describes how a mother reacts at being told her three children are to be removed:

> "She was really screaming 'I want my children, I want my children', she ran outside and tried to throw herself in front of a bus and was rolling around in the road screaming. And that was difficult because even though children are removed for their own safety it's quite a hard thing to say to parents, you know, 'No you can't see your child, no I'm taking them to foster care'. Yeah I think that's really difficult."

On another occasion she recalls having to accompany a social worker and the police to remove a baby and thinking that the baby had died when the social worker came out crying, but without the baby. Recriminations from relatives of children who have been removed are also a concern. In recounting the above removal Susanne says: "I said to them 'I'm not willing to go into the house, I'm sorry. I don't think I could put myself in that position' 'cos I still have to walk around [the community in which she lives]. I'm not going to do that". Dealing with the emotional reaction of such events is likened by Susanne to dealing with a loss: "It's almost like losing something". The local authority does offer up to six sessions of counselling in these circumstances.

Susanne has considered leaving her current job (although not childcare work altogether), despite enjoying much of what she does and the variety and challenge of the work. She is currently undertaking social work training, sponsored by the council, and once this is completed she hopes to move on, ideally to a post where she could provide longer-term support to vulnerable children and their families rather than crisis interventions.

Conclusion

Overall, our study found a high level of commitment to working with vulnerable children and enjoyment of the intrinsic satisfactions it provides. The experience of care work involved a combination of positive and negative factors, with workers situated at different points along a continuum of satisfaction. Most were making the best of poor working conditions, but for some the frustrations and difficulties were beginning to outweigh the rewards.

The positive and negative aspects of the work were often two sides of the same coin (Table 7.3). For example, the variety and challenge was one of the attractions, but could also be a source of stress and danger. Intrinsic rewards such as having a strong commitment to the work and gaining satisfaction from an ethic of care were balanced by frustration at external conditions such as the low status the work was accorded and lack of resources to provide good-quality care. While it was a source of great satisfaction to workers to see children improve and achieve, the downside of the workers' emotional engagement was a sense of failure and disillusionment if children did not improve or a placement broke down, and sometimes not knowing what happened to children after they left. The pleasure that many workers took in the affection shown to them by the children they cared for also had to be set against the sense of loss that could arise when children they had become close to moved on, and against the risk of false allegations.

Table 7.3: Two sides of the coin: positive and negative aspects of care work with vulnerable children

Rewards	Difficulties
Variety and challenge	Stress and danger
Ethic of care	Constraints on ability to provide good care, low status
Children's achievements	Placement breakdowns, lack of further contact
Affection of children	Separation issues, fear of allegations from children
Creating a home-like environment	Can't act as a parent
Autonomy and control	Isolation
Convenience of home location	Negative impact on own family
Opportunities for career development	Current work not valued

Creating a home-like environment was a rewarding aspect of the work, but could create tensions when carers were unable to act as a parent in terms of enforcing rules, showing explicit affection or keeping children in (this was a particular issue for those who lived with children). The autonomy and control that childminders in particular enjoyed over their working environment was balanced by the isolation of their work and lack of adult company, which featured in four of the six childminder accounts. For home-based workers, the convenience of caring within their own home meant that it was harder to separate work and family lives, and their work was more likely to have a negative impact on their own children or partner (see Chapter Nine). Finally, increased opportunities for career development and encouragement by employers to obtain social work qualifications, as in the case of the family support workers in our study, could create tensions for workers who did not want to progress in this way and who felt that this gave the message that their work was only valued as a 'stepping stone' to other work.

The above analysis suggests that some of the difficulties are inherent in the nature of the work, such as the tension between needing to engage emotionally with children and wanting to improve their lives, while also being able to let them go, and to accept that not all children can be helped. But other difficulties could be more easily addressed, and we return to this in Chapter Ten. The study points to the crucial importance of a supportive working environment. Institutional workers placed a high value on there being a good atmosphere at work and having colleagues and managers who would provide back-up, especially when dealing with challenging and stressful situations. However, it is also important for home-based workers (foster carers and childminders) to feel part of a team and to be well supported, particularly given the more isolated nature of their work.

It was also very important to childcare workers to be able to provide good-quality care. They saw themselves as on the child's side, and wanted to be able to do their best for them. This meant that external constraints perceived by workers as restricting their ability to do this were strongly disliked – whether this meant being unable to obtain the resources they thought children needed, having insufficient time to work with a child on a one-to-one basis, or having insufficient authority to prevent young people going out late at night. This reinforces the need for managers and commissioners of childcare services to share with workers an understanding of what constitutes good care (see Chapter Six), and to create, as far as possible, the conditions that allow workers to provide this.

Despite the difficulties and frustrations of care work with vulnerable children, these workers bring to and develop a strong commitment to their work. For most, the rewards appear to outweigh the negatives. Looking back to Table 7.1, the majority of survey respondents reported satisfaction with most aspects of their work, apart from pay and status. Yet the case studies revealed a more complex picture, with positive (usually intrinsic) and negative (usually extrinsic) factors interwoven in the experience of caring for children in need. What would it take to make them stop providing this kind of care? And if they did leave, would they be lost to care work altogether, or would they move on to a different kind of childcare work? In the next chapter, we look further at workers' intentions to stay or leave, and at findings from a one-year follow-up of those responding to the Postal Survey.

EIGHT

Leavers, movers and stayers

Introduction

In this chapter, we consider questions concerning who stays and who leaves childcare work and why. We also examine movement between different types of work with vulnerable children, since this has particular relevance for government policies to encourage greater flexibility and transferability across the childcare workforce (see Chapter One).

A number of studies have examined reasons for the recruitment and retention difficulties affecting the social care workforce, many of them based on cross-sectional quantitative data. For example, an investigation by the Audit Commission (2002) identified six key factors in people's decisions to leave public sector work: a sense of being overwhelmed by bureaucracy and paperwork; insufficient resources leading to unmanageable workloads; a lack of autonomy; feeling undervalued by managers, government and the public; pay that was felt 'unfair' compared to that of people doing similar work; and a climate of change that felt imposed and irrelevant. A survey of over 2,000 readers conducted by *Community Care* magazine on the reasons why people stay in or leave social care jobs found that the main reasons for staying were job satisfaction and good relationships with colleagues and managers, while the main reasons for leaving were poor relationships with managers, poor pay and working conditions, and workloads that were too high (Winchester, 2003).

Turning specifically to studies of retention among childcare workers, most findings are again based on survey data. Research with foster carers has identified four main reasons for ceasing to provide such care: seeing fostering as no longer fitting into their lives (for example because of getting older, their family situation changing or wanting to take up work outside the home); lack of support for the fostering work; the impact of caring on their families; and distressing events such as placement breakdowns, allegations being made against them by the children or difficulties experienced with birth families (Sinclair et al, 2004). Among staff in children's homes, reasons given for thinking about leaving include wanting to make more use of qualifications, children's difficult behaviour, feeling discouraged by children's lack of progress, and feeling it is time to make a career change (Mainey, 2003). Childminders often take up the work in order to remain at home while their own children are young, and may stop once their children start school (Mooney et al, 2001), although those who care for children placed by social services tend to be more experienced and remain in the job for longer (Statham et al, 2000).

The UK government's response to these recruitment and retention problems in the children's workforce has been to set up a Children's Workforce Development Council and to develop a Children's Workforce Strategy (HM Government, 2005a). A key aspect of this strategy is to promote greater flexibility within the children's workforce through the introduction of a 'common core' of skills and knowledge for all those working with children, young people and their families (HM Government, 2005b), and through developing an integrated qualifications framework (Johnson et al, 2005).

In our study, the prospective element of the research design enabled us to consider how care workers' trajectories developed over the course of a year or so and to relate what they did to what they *thought* they would do at an earlier point in time. As we shall show, it is important to be attentive to the importance of time in shaping what people say and what they do. It is also important to note the different types of methods we have used and the evidence drawn upon in terms of the kinds of claims that can be made about the study findings. For example, the attrition of the original Postal Survey sample followed up at Time 2 may have skewed the likelihood of finding more people who have left childcare work. Definitions of what counts as 'leaving' also need to be kept in mind, particularly when comparing findings from different studies. Retention rates are often calculated on the basis of numbers leaving their current employer, regardless of whether or not the worker moves to another job of the same type and thus remains within the care workforce. In our study, 'leavers' were defined as those who moved out of a particular type of childcare work (in a children's home, or as a foster carer, for example), but not those who moved between sectors or employers while remaining in the same type of work.

In the rest of this chapter we draw on four data sources: the Postal Survey with four groups of childcare workers, the Telephone Survey conducted one year later with the respondents to the Postal Survey who had agreed to take part, interviews with managers and the selected case study interviews.[1] These data span the range of structured, semi-structured and unstructured interview types.

To leave or not to leave: workers' intentions

The four groups of workers in our study responded in a Postal Survey at Time 1 to a number of pre-coded questions that were designed to assess their future employment intentions. They were asked whether they saw their future in their current type of work as short or long term (five years or more), how long they thought they would stay, how often they thought about giving up, and whether they would continue in care work with children if they left their job. They were also asked to indicate, from a list of potential reasons, those that might cause them to give up the work.

The results indicated a high level of commitment to work with vulnerable children, and some uncertainty about future plans. Almost two thirds described their future in the work as long term and more than 4 in 10 thought they would still be doing this work in five years, while around a third did not know. Only 11% of childcare workers ticked that they had 'often' thought of giving up and almost a third that they had done so 'hardly ever or not at all'. Community childminders were least likely to think of giving up and residential social workers most likely to do so, but even so, only 13% of the latter group had thought of giving up 'often'.

However, it is important to be aware that present time horizons reflect current experiences and that the concept of plans for the future may not necessarily refer to ideas for future action that are concrete and specific (Brannen and Nilsen, 2007). Indeed, the reasons given by respondents at Time 1 for thinking about leaving closely mirror the aspects of the work that they agreed caused them the most dissatisfaction, such as the low pay, workload pressure and low status of the work (see Chapter Seven). Their reasons for thinking about leaving may thus reflect current experiences in the job, rather than actual intentions to leave.

The reasons given by those who said they were thinking of leaving nevertheless suggested some interesting differences between home-based and institutional workers. Work–family issues were more commonly mentioned by foster carers and community childminders, whose care work was undertaken in their own homes, than by those working in an institutional setting (see Chapter Nine). Averaged across all four groups, the three most common reasons for thinking about leaving were the pay/fee, the effect on the carer's family, and better opportunities elsewhere (see Table 8.1).

Table 8.1: Potential reasons for giving up the work (Postal Survey)

	Type of worker				All (n=213)
	Residential social worker (n=62)	Family support worker (n=57)	Foster carer (n=52)	Community childminder (n=42)	
	%	%	%	%	%
The pay/fee	57	46	42	62	51
Effect on my family	34	23	67	43	41
Better opportunities elsewhere	37	42	21	41	35
The hours	55	21	23	17	31
Workload/pressure	29	40	33	7	29
Low status	18	32	27	41	28
Funding/resources	26	33	27	17	26
Feeling insecure	29	21	25	24	25
Unsupportive management	31	30	23	7	24
Cost of living/ housing	23	18	15	31	21
Other working conditions	16	0	35	33	20
Not part of a team	18	14	12	2	12
Having a baby	27	12	10	10	16
Client group	13	11	25	14	16
Little control	15	16	21	5	15
Isolation of work	11	16	12	21	15
Atmosphere at work	19	19	8	2	13
Lack of training	16	21	8	2.	13
Unsupportive colleagues	18	14	12	2	12
Service closing down	18	5	2	5	8
Part-time study	16	11	2	5	9
Other	7	12	15	5	10

Notes: The figures highlighted in bold show the more important differences.
Respondents could give more than one response; therefore, percentages do not total 100.

One year later: Telephone Survey at Time 2

Approximately a year after completing the Postal Survey, follow-up telephone interviews were carried out with those respondents who had agreed to further contact, which was just under two thirds of the total. Excluding those who provided no contact details and those who were selected for case-study interviews, 87% of potential follow-up interviews were achieved, with 34 residential social workers, 36 family support workers, 35 sponsored childminders and 24 foster carers (129 interviews in total). The aim was to find out how many were still doing the same type of work, how many had left, their reasons for moving on and what they had gone on to do. Those who were still in the same type of work were also asked if they had thought about leaving and, if so, what had made them stay.

Movement among the childcare workforce: myth or reality?

The great majority (82%) of childcare workers were still in the same type of work some 12 months after the original survey. The figure rises to 84% if the case studies (who were also still in the same type of work) are included. Residential social workers were the most likely to have moved on. Nearly a third (10 out of 34) were no longer working in a children's home a year later, and another six had remained in the same type of work but moved to a different home or agency, all within the private sector. Losses had been particularly high at one chain of private residential homes. When interviewed at Time 1, the human resources manager for this company said that exit interviews suggested this was due to "hours, long shifts, pay – and head office I'm afraid".

By Time 2, eight of the 35 childminders were no longer accepting placements from the local authority, although three of them continued to care for children placed privately by their parents. Given that managers of the placement schemes had earlier reported few problems with recruitment and retention, this suggests that some childminders may have considered they were no longer part of the scheme even though the local authority regarded them as still available for this work.

There had been very little loss among the foster carers and family support workers during the intervening year, with only 2/24 and 3/36 respectively no longer doing the same type of work. These figures reflect retention within a particular workforce, not necessarily remaining with the same employer. Five foster carers had changed their employer in the past year, with two changing to a different independent agency and two moving from the local authority to an independent agency because they felt they would receive better support. One foster carer had moved in the opposite direction, however, from a private agency to the local authority, because she had not been offered sufficient placements.

This apparent stability among the childcare workforce masked the fact that a surprisingly high proportion of the home-based carers did not have a child placed with them at the time of the follow-up (a third of the childminders and one in six of the foster carers), although they remained available for this work. Among these, some had not been carers for some time: two thirds of those without a current placement had last had a child placed with them over six months previously, suggesting some under-use of a potential resource although providing greater opportunities for matching and placement choice.

Who had left?

The number of leavers was therefore small – 23, including three where it was only possible to obtain minimal information (that the person was no longer doing the same type of work) from a relative or colleague. However, it is possible that a higher proportion of leavers would have been found among those who did not offer to take part in the follow-up Telephone Survey. The small number who had left is an important finding in itself, but it means that the sample size is too small to allow generalisations about the characteristics of leavers, and the following analysis is indicative only.

A higher proportion of those in their twenties and fifties had left than those in their middle years. Nearly a third of those in their twenties at the time of the Postal Survey had left a year later, compared to less than 1 in 5 of those in their thirties and less than 1 in 10 of those in their forties. The proportion rose again among those in their fifties, to nearly a quarter, possibly reflecting general trends towards early retirement especially in the context of the end of the mothering phase of women's lifecourse (Table 8.2). On the other hand, leaving rates were higher among those who had been doing the work for less than two years at the time of the Postal Survey, who were from a minority ethnic group and who did not have children. Most of these differences probably reflect the fact that the largest group of leavers (10 of the 23) were residential social workers.

Table 8.2: Leavers by age band

	Age band at time of postal survey					
	20-29	30-39	40-49	50-59	60+	All
	n	n	n	n	n	n
Stayed	13	23	42	24	1	103
Left	6	5	4	7	1	23
Total	19	28	46	31	2	126

Note: 3 missing cases.

What did the leavers go on to do?

Of the 21 leavers for whom information was available about what they had gone on to do, two thirds were still working with children or families. Three childminders were no longer offering sponsored placements but were still providing childcare for working parents, and two family support workers had left to do a social work degree or diploma but were doing their placements in children's services. Two of the leavers had retired, four (who had all been working in children's homes) were still doing care work but with adults, and only one of those who had left had moved into a completely different area of work, in the music business.

A similar picture of continuing engagement with care work was evident when childcare workers who were still in the same type of work at the time of the follow-up survey, but who had considered leaving during the previous year, were asked what they had considered doing instead. Over half (18/32) said they would still be working with children or young people, and most of the rest did not have particular plans or ideas. Residential social workers mentioned jobs such as care work in a children's hospice or with disabled children, social work with children (but not residential), and work in a respite children's home. Family support workers expressed a preference for jobs involving some kind of therapeutic or counselling work, such as play therapy, counselling abused children or psychotherapy. A quarter (8/32) of childcare workers who had considered leaving had thought about moving into care work with adults instead, such as working with adults with learning disabilities or mental health needs. Only four were considering moving out of care work altogether, and three of these were residential social workers.

Why did they leave?

Childcare workers who had left at Time 2 said they had done so for a variety of reasons. These included issues relating to dissatisfaction with the work such as the hours or pay (six leavers) or other aspects of the job such as the children's behaviour or lack of support from management (cited by six leavers). Other reasons related to professional career development, also discussed in Chapter Five (eight leavers) while others were lifecourse related such as approaching retirement, ill-health or wanting to spend more time with their family (seven leavers).[2] In four cases, the decision to leave was effectively made for them, for example no placements being offered or a contract coming to an end.

Among the residential social workers, there appeared to be three types of response to why they were no longer in the same work. One response was given by those in their fifties – they were approaching retirement or felt they were getting too old to do this kind of work. A second response from a group of young people in their twenties suggested stressfulness of the work (see Chapter Nine) and disillusionment with the kind of care the children were receiving, especially in privately run homes (see Chapter Six). Finally, for two mid-career women in their late thirties, other work opportunities had arisen that were more attractive. Across residential social workers as a whole, concern at the quality of care was the reason most frequently cited for leaving this kind of work, followed by the increasingly challenging nature of children's behaviour (often involving physical violence), which they did not feel empowered to deal with, and the (related) pressures of the work.

The following two examples taken from the Telephone Survey represent perspectives at different points in the lifecourse, and reflect themes that also arose in the case study interviews among the stayers. One of the telephone interviewees was a woman in her late fifties who had been in the job for four years, and the other was a younger woman in her mid-twenties who had left within a year. Both had worked in the private sector. The older woman had been finding it difficult to do sleepovers and felt she was getting 'too old' to keep in touch with the 11- to 16-year-olds she was caring for. She found the young people hard to control, said that staff were subject to false allegations 'with no comeback' and that morale in the home was very low. She had moved to a new job as a project worker with homeless people. The younger woman described the work as "emotionally, mentally and physically stressful" and thought that she had been too young in her mid-twenties to cope. She had left to take up a nursery nurse post, which she saw as a stepping stone to work in a school setting, perhaps as a classroom assistant. Her main reason for leaving had been dissatisfaction with the profit-oriented ethic of the private company and the poor quality of care she felt the children consequently received due to frequent moves, high staff turnover and not enough staff on each shift. Little training was provided and she had been left in charge after only three months in the job, with no deputy around.

Of the two foster carers who had left, one had done so because no suitable placements were being offered and she decided to concentrate on childminding instead. The other stopped because he "didn't see eye to eye with social services". As a single male he was only approved to care for boys aged eight or over but would have liked to care for younger children too. He also wanted to be seen as a parent but felt that social workers expected more of a playworker role (this was his paid employment).

Two of the family support workers had also left despite having described their work in the Postal Survey as long term. Both had gone on to do training and intended to return to work with children when this was completed. However, while one was being sponsored by her employer to undertake a social work degree, the other (working in a different authority) had not been able to obtain such sponsorship and had had to leave in order to undertake a diploma in social work.

The community childminders who had stopped doing this work ranged in age from 27 to 54. Five had stopped childminding altogether. In three cases this represented a move to develop their work careers (to complete a teacher training degree, become a childminding network coordinator and become a nursery officer in a private day nursery). However, the other two had given up because of dissatisfaction with the work. In one case this was due to the difficulty of obtaining a regular income from community childminding, and in the other a mixture of health problems and the long hours that kept her away from her own young children (this was an atypical case of a 27-year-old woman who assisted another childminder in her home, and had been doing this for under a year at the time of the Postal Survey. She went on to become a school meals assistant, working an hour at lunchtimes only).

Three childminders were continuing to care for children privately but were not accepting sponsored placements. One of these had moved to a new area and was hoping to find a similar scheme to join. Another was a grandmother who had provided overnight care for social services but found that this interfered with babysitting her grandchildren, and a third had disliked the way she was treated by social workers placing children in her care and the fact that payments were often late.

Leavers (from the Postal Survey) who had thought they would stay

Seven of the childcare workers who left had indicated in their responses to the Postal Survey a year earlier that they saw their future in this work as long term, with most thinking they would continue for five years or more. What had happened to change their minds? Of the three residential social workers in this situation, one was a 38-year-old woman without children who had worked in children's homes for 13 years. She had moved on for positive reasons, to further her career, having just gained a social work qualification and applied for a job (as a service user participation officer), an opportunity that she had perhaps not foreseen at Time 1 or had not been focusing upon. As she said, the opportunity "came up at the right time" in the large voluntary company she worked for. The other two residential social workers had been in post with the same private company for less than a year when they completed the postal questionnaire, and although at that time they were enthusiastic and considered it the only kind of work they wanted to do, both had soon become disillusioned. They were at different stages in the lifecourse, although neither had children.

In one of these cases a care worker left aged 52 because of a critical incident – a physical attack on her by a young person in the home, which left her feeling that the job was "not worth personal injury and abuse", especially when she received little support in this situation from her manager and colleagues. She had gone on to work instead in a residential home for older people, although would consider returning to residential work with children who were younger or had less challenging behaviour. In the other case a better opportunity in terms of pay and autonomy seemed to have presented itself, although this was in the context of concerns about the quality of the care. This young woman of 24 had left after a short time in the job because she felt that the private company put its financial interests above the children's welfare, for example not employing enough staff and accepting children beyond its remit, and found she had become emotionally involved with the children and worried about them when she was not there. She also perceived few opportunities in the private company for career development. She had left to become a community support officer in student halls of residence, which gave her more autonomy and better pay, although she reported missing "the closeness of the team and being there for the good times in children's lives".

The case studies: why they left previous jobs

The accounts given in the case study interviews support and extend the picture suggested so far concerning why care workers might feel dissatisfied with the work, in particular concerning why they had left previous jobs. The different kinds of understanding about what 'care' is are discussed in Chapter Six, but they are broadly encompassed by Tronto's 1993 notion of an ethic of care (Chapter One) involving moral dimensions of caring about others, being sensitive to the need for care, competences in giving care and taking responsibility for and the reciprocal nature of care. Care workers leaving jobs in care work typically felt frustrated in their efforts to give good care. Family support worker Susanne Grant, for example, had resigned from a family centre when she became disenchanted with the nature of the work, seeing it as a 'stop gap' rather than a long-term solution to children's problems. She moved to a day nursery run by a children's charity, and then took up a post as an early years officer for social services before becoming a family support worker.

Gillian Dunscombe had left her job in a private nursery to become a childminder because she felt that the company was not concerned about the quality of care the children received: "They just counted it as money coming in the door, it wasn't really a child. So that's why I became a childminder". Natalie James had left a private residential school for autistic children due to her unhappiness with the standards of care, and now worked in a local authority children's home. This concern with quality seemed to be linked to a search for care work that was more meaningful. As we have seen in several chapters (Three, Six and Seven), this was often defined by workers as being able to make a difference and to improve children's lives. They cared *about* the children as well as *for* them. Indeed, one of the reasons given by Susanne for why she was good at her current job was "because I care".

An ethic of care was also revealed in reasons given by workers who had considered leaving between the Time 1 and Time 2 surveys, but had not done so. When asked why they had stayed on, the most common reason was not wanting to let down the children they cared for. This was particularly the case for foster carers, who often had a strong commitment to caring for the child currently placed with them, even if they might consider refusing further placements.

Comparing intentions over time

The follow-up Telephone Survey enabled us to compare how far intentions about leaving or staying in the work at Time 1 were reflected in workers' situations a year later and also their intentions as perceived at different points in time. Not surprisingly, there was some correspondence between intentions and practice. Less than a third (7/23) of those who were no longer doing the same kind of work at the time of the follow-up had said they considered it long term when they responded to the Postal Survey a year earlier, compared to nearly three quarters of those who had stayed in the work. Those who had left were also more likely to have said a year earlier that they thought they would only continue for one to two years, or did not know how long they would stay, than those who had remained in the work. However, the figure of almost a third who had seen their future as long term but then left within 12 months is still higher than might be expected if intentions are considered to be a good predictor of future practices.

As we suggested earlier, interviewees recount the past and the future through the lens of the present and are likely to see the future as an extension or reflection of the present. The future is a vague concept and plans are but one type of future orientation. The longer the time horizon the more likely plans are to shade into ambitions, hopes and dreams, as specific plans are shaped or disrupted by context and intervening events (Nilsen, 1999; Brannen and Nilsen, 2002, 2007). As we have seen in Chapter Four, the factors that prompted care workers to move into this work were often contextual and situational even though workers may have considered themselves as having a predisposition to care (see Chapter Three).

The conceptual issues surrounding notions of the future are compounded by methodological issues. Issues raised by data concerning the disparity between intentions and practice are also highlighted in the different responses given by the same workers at Time 1 and Time 2 to a question about the frequency with which they thought about giving up the work. Almost half (48%) gave a different response a year later. It seems likely that this question is measuring *current* satisfaction or dissatisfaction with their work, rather than actual intention or plans to leave.

Drawing upon the case studies, it is possible to see how differentiated the concept of the future is, with plans being related to short-term time horizons, hopes to the medium term and dreams being much longer term. Pat Foster, a 49-year-old family support worker, ticked 'often thought about leaving' in response to the Time 1 Postal Survey and "did not know" how long she would stay in the work. However, when interviewed at length, Pat gave no indication that she had any plans to leave care work, and indeed was about to embark on a social work degree that would require her to continue working for the local authority for several years. Her immediate plan was to undertake the social work degree; her hope was to obtain a post involving more direct and therapeutic-type work with children after the degree was completed; and her dream, "if I could afford it", was to do volunteer work with street children in Africa. The dreams of several other case study interviewees involved acquiring sufficient money to afford to buy a large house where they would be able to care for large numbers of disadvantaged and vulnerable children.

While responses to questions about their futures in care work may not reflect actual plans, nor dreams for the future reflect likely reality, both contain important messages for recruitment and retention. The dissatisfaction of childcare workers who often think about leaving may well have an impact on the quality of care that children receive, so the sources of this dissatisfaction need to be addressed. On the other hand, childcare workers' visions for the future often reveal a strong desire to continue helping vulnerable children, and this commitment to children's welfare is a powerful motivating force on which recruitment and retention strategies need to build.

Improving recruitment and retention

We turn next to consider the evidence from our study on recruitment and retention difficulties within the four types of childcare work, and the views of both managers and workers about the factors that might help to attract and keep more people in this kind of work.

The managers' perspectives

There were both similarities and differences in the staffing issues reported by managers of the four types of childcare worker. A problem for both independent and local authority fostering services was the high age profile of their current foster carers. Many foster carers were approaching retirement, and services faced difficulties in attracting sufficient numbers of new carers. Apart from loss to retirement and some movement of foster carers in both directions between independent and local authority fostering services, retention was generally described as less of a problem with this group than was recruitment.

Managers of residential services, by contrast, typically reported few difficulties in recruiting unqualified staff, but greater problems in keeping them especially once trained, and in filling managerial positions in children's homes. Similarly with family support workers, there appeared to be a relatively large pool of people from whom local authorities could appoint unqualified staff, including those who had moved into family support work after the closure of family centres, but more of a problem with retaining qualified workers. Neither of the two service managers with an oversight of community childminding schemes had experienced particular difficulties in finding childminders willing to do this work, except in one or two areas where private childminding attracted a higher rate of pay than the local authority was willing to pay. However, as our telephone interviews with care providers a year after initial contact suggested, the assumption that these carers would continue to be available for community placements was not always warranted.

The strategies adopted by managers to improve recruitment and retention included widening the pool of potential recruits (for example targeting older people or women returners), offering bonuses for qualified staff, and providing better support and training opportunities (see Chapter Two). Some attempts had been made to introduce family-friendly working practices, but as we show in Chapter Nine, these were rarely extensive.

The workers' perspectives

Information from the workers' perspectives on what might help with recruitment and retention was obtained from two sources. First, childcare workers who were no longer doing the same type of work at the time of the follow-up survey (the 'leavers') were asked if there was anything that might have encouraged them to stay. Second, case study workers were asked for their views on what could be done to assist with recruitment and retention into their type of work.

When the leavers were asked whether there was anything that would have encouraged them to continue in the work, half (11/21) said that there was and seven that there was not, while three were unsure. Childminders were most likely to say they would have continued (6/8) and most commonly mentioned the need for a more secure income. This was difficult to achieve with community childminding either because of lack of children being placed with them by the local authority or the need to provide one-to-one care for children with high levels of need, which meant they could not augment their income with private placements. Both of the foster carers who had stopped fostering would also have continued had the authority placed suitable children with them. Residential social workers were the group most likely to say they would not have wanted to continue (5/9). Factors that might have influenced their decision included better support from external agencies such as Youth Offending Teams and the police, access to counselling for the children, and care standards being rewritten "to show children there are boundaries to be maintained".

The case study workers were all still doing the same type of work as when they had responded to the Time 1 Postal Survey, although one (Carol Jones, described in Chapter Five) had left a private children's home and taken up a post in the public sector because of her dissatisfaction with the way the private home was run, the lack of support from management and the difficulty in providing the kind of care the children needed.

All the case study workers were asked what could be done to encourage others to do their kind of work. A common response from all four groups, which replicated findings in studies in Scotland of foster carers (Triseliotis et al, 2000) and residential childcare workers (Milligan et al, 2005), was a need for more accurate and accessible information about the nature of the work. This ranged from advertisements using easily understood language (one residential social worker described how she had not initially realised that 'residential units' referred to children's homes) to spelling out the range of options within a particular kind of work, for example that foster care could be provided on a short-term or weekend basis as well as full time, and that people from a range of backgrounds and ages were needed. Foster carer Brenda Reeves said that:

> "I think people need to know that they're needed ... some people could probably [pause] if they realise that some people just want a respite carer, would probably think 'oh yeah, I could do that. No I don't want to be a foster carer full time, but yes I could do that and offer something positive'. But I don't think people realise the full sort of umbrella of it."

Accurate information included challenging the negative public stereotype of social services as an agency that removed children from their families (Central Office of Information Communications, 2001). This was mentioned particularly by home-based carers (childminders and foster carers), who thought that potential applicants were put off by a fear that their lives would be under scrutiny "once social services gets inside their little front door".

Other suggestions for improving recruitment included an emphasis on opportunities for obtaining qualifications and career progression, and better rates of pay especially starting grades in residential care work. Although foster carers in our study had mixed views about whether fostering should be a paid profession, there was little disagreement that better compensation for the expenses involved in providing foster placements was needed in order to attract more people into this work.

The factors that case study workers thought would improve retention reflected their own experiences of what had encouraged them to continue with the work. Better pay alone was seen as insufficient to motivate people to continue in difficult and demanding work. Intrinsic factors such as the satisfaction of helping vulnerable children, and having their work appreciated by managers and others, were judged to be equally important in preventing people from leaving. As one residential social worker commented: "What's encouraged me has been seeing for myself some of the good work that you can do". Tom Jenkins, a manager in a children's home, said that his staff team would all say the same thing: "It's not the pay, it's that we're seen. It's how we're valued less than colleagues in the field". Recognition of their achievements and a sense that their work was valued was judged very important in retaining staff, particularly by family support workers.

Workforce flexibility: moving between types of childcare work

One way of addressing recruitment and retention problems could be by promoting greater flexibility within and between childcare workforces. In a large-scale survey carried out for the DfES in 2005 to test how far the *Every Child Matters* (HM Government, 2003) agenda was affecting ideas and practice, a wide range of workers with children and young people were asked if they agreed or disagreed with a statement that "it is difficult to move between different types of jobs across different children's and young people's services" (Deakin and Kelly, 2006). Respondents, who included foster carers, residential care workers and childminders, were more likely to disagree (45%) than agree (38%) that it was difficult, which suggests that there is a perception of flexibility within work with children.

In the current study, we asked managers with responsibility for the four different groups of workers about policy and practice within their organisation concerning movement between types of work with children and young people. Overall there was very little evidence from these interviews that managers had yet developed strategies for encouraging flexibility across the children's workforce as a whole. Some initiatives were being developed for family support workers, to enable them to work in different settings and to progress to children's social work by obtaining additional qualifications. A number of managers were positive in principle about greater transferability between types of work with children and could see its relevance in the light of more integrated children's services. Reasons given for encouraging flexibility included its benefits to recruitment, and an improved and more efficient service. One manager, when describing how several experienced community childminders had recently moved on to other childcare work, described this as a 'good loss' that would promote the community childminding scheme in a wider field. However, other managers cited factors that they thought discouraged a policy of flexibility, including a reluctance to lose carers to other care work sectors given the difficulties in recruitment, and disparities in pay and conditions across the different types of work.

Preference for working with particular groups

Although survey evidence may suggest that workers think it *possible* to move between different kinds of childcare work, this does not address the question of whether such workers would actually *want* to do so. In the case studies, we were able to examine in more depth the factors that had led people to choose a particular type of childcare work, and to explore how their choices were influenced by their stage in the lifecourse and personal histories (see Chapter Four).

On the one hand, we found that many workers expressed a strong preference for working with a particular client group, such as children of a certain age, gender or level of need, and it seemed that this would restrict their willingness to move between types of care work. For example, residential social worker Jenny Masters had started her care work in an army crèche but had found after volunteering in a youth club that she much preferred the challenge of working with teenagers. This had led her into working in a children's home. "The little 'uns are good, it's nice to see them, but there's only so much you can do with the little ones and that. Where with the older ones there's a lot more you can do with them." Community childminders, on the other hand, frequently referred to their enjoyment of working with babies and young children. Childminder Kate Humphries, who had an 18-year-old son as well as a five-year-old daughter, definitely did not want to work with teenagers: "They become difficult then and [pause] and just, they're so headstrong".

Mary Haywood, a foster carer, preferred placements of boys to girls, partly because of her concerns about the impact of self-harming or sexually active behaviour on her own 15-year-old daughter, but also because she had experienced more success with boys and thought that her rural location was less suitable for girls "who have got to be in town every five minutes". She felt that she had "done my baby bit. I would rather have the older child. And that's where my success rate has been".

Family support worker Justine Naisbitt was likewise drawn to working with difficult male adolescents, whom she regarded as "my forte". She said that she was especially able to relate to this group because of her experiences with her own sons, and relished the challenge that this particular client group provided.

Other care workers had started off providing a particular kind of care, such as short-term foster placements for teenagers, but then realised that this did not suit their family circumstances. Brenda Reeves and her husband had begun their fostering career with an independent agency providing emergency placements when their own children were young, but after four such placements had failed, they decided instead to foster a 12-year-old girl with an autistic spectrum disorder on a long-term basis. They had found it difficult to look after volatile teenagers while bringing up their own small children: "If you're looking after little children who get up at 6 o'clock in the morning and you've got grown-up children that are sort of being very angry and running away and doing stupid things, it just actually puts too much pressure".

The above examples suggest that government policy to encourage greater movement within the children's workforce may have limited success, when particular types of work are chosen due to personal circumstances and preferences. This was further supported by analysis of case study workers' responses to vignettes depicting movement between types of childcare work, and to a question about the notion of a 'core worker' able to work in a variety of settings with vulnerable children and young people. While there was general acceptance of the value of a common core of knowledge for all those working with children, and support for the idea of greater flexibility across different types of childcare work, many of those interviewed did not themselves want to be doing a different type of childcare work. Their responses when presented with specific situations tended to emphasise the differences rather than the similarities between the four types of work, such as the commitment needed to take on a foster child or the different knowledge needed by someone caring for babies and young children compared to someone supporting young people or care leavers. Although the normative view that a more flexible childcare workforce is a good thing received support, this does not necessarily mean that workers would take advantage of this flexibility for themselves.

Jenny Masters, for example, thought that the age differences of the children cared for would make it difficult to move between residential care (her current job) and community childminding, since residential care was mostly with older children and "early years is a totally different category". She had thought about fostering, but would not want to provide continuous care since "with residential work you leave it and you come home, your work's done, it's one of those [jobs] you can turn off from". Three of the six community childminders had also considered fostering, but had not pursued this because they feared that the emotional stress of parting from a child that had become a part of their life would be too difficult.

Flexibility within childcare work

On the other hand, the current study does provide evidence of considerable flexibility and movement *over time* between types of work with children, especially in work with children within a similar age range. Among respondents to the Postal Survey, over half (52%) had moved to their current post from another type of care work, sometimes with adults but more often with children and young people. More than three quarters (78%) had previous childcare experience in a different setting, such as preschool playgroup worker, classroom assistant, nursery nurse or youth worker. Family support workers appeared to have the greatest variety of experience with half having worked in three or more different childcare roles. Some of this flexibility is lifecourse related and reflects progression of care workers' careers as mothers or as workers.

In other evidence from our study a strong commitment to working with children and families supports the notion of a 'career' in work with children, although what career means varies considerably (see Chapter Five). When asked what they would do if they did leave their current job, the majority of respondents in the Postal Survey either did not want to stop what they were doing (21%) or would take another job working directly with children (40%). Most of the rest thought that they would retire, or did not know (Table 8.3).

Given that the majority of those who had moved to a different type of work in the year after the Postal Survey had remained in care work, it is not surprising that most (13/16) thought their previous job had provided them with skills that were useful in their current work. Patience, understanding children with difficult or challenging behaviour, communication and relationship skills were all mentioned as transferable between the different types of work.

The actual destinations of leavers a year later also provided support for the notion of flexibility within the children's workforce although the reasons for flexibility are various. As described above, two thirds were still working with children or families. When the leavers were asked about their future work plans, there was also some evidence of movement between different types of care work with children. For

Table 8.3: Intentions if left residential care, family support, foster care or childminding: Postal Survey

	Type of worker				
	Residential social worker (*n=82*)	Family support worker (*n=84*)	Foster carer (*n=72*)	Community childminder (*n=64*)	All (*n=302*)
	%	%	%	%	%
Don't want to stop	27	13	25	19	21
Another job with children	45	43	28	44	40
Care work with adults	6	2	11	6	6
A job not related to care and/or children	2	4	10	6	5
Take a break from paid work	2	2	3	3	3
Retire	6	20	14	9	13
Don't know	20	13	17	20	17

Note: Percentages do not always total 100 due to rounding.

example, a young woman who had left residential social work after a year to work in a private day nursery, was motivated by a sense of professional development and saw this work as a stepping stone to work in a primary school as a classroom assistant. A family support worker who had just begun a social work degree hoped to work for a charity providing direct play therapy with abused children after she qualified. A childminder who had stopped accepting sponsored placements intended to return to social work when her youngest child started school. Another had stopped community childminding to train to be a teacher, and a third was exploring the idea of fostering now that she had a larger house and her own children would soon leave home.

It was apparent from the stories told by case study workers that opportunities for practical experience of other types of work with children, such as placements undertaken as part of a social work degree or diploma, could play a significant role in encouraging workers to consider branching out into other types of work with children. Residential social worker Marleen Bennett, for instance, was nearing the end of her social work diploma during which she had shadowed a social worker in a school setting and worked with children with learning disabilities. She had 'really enjoyed' both placements and was now weighing up her options, which she was certain would still involve working with children and families. Debra Henry, a foster carer in the final year of her self-funded psychology degree, had spent time as part of the course in a school supporting children with learning difficulties and was now considering training to be a teacher. Such first-hand experience had opened up possibilities that might not have been previously considered.

Conclusion

In this chapter we have drawn upon three types of data, each with their own strengths and weaknesses. The Postal Survey gives an extensive view across childcare groups but is framed in terms of predetermined meanings that respondents interpret not only in terms of their own frames of reference, but in relation to their present timeframes. This latter aspect of present timeframes makes any interpretation about future work intentions highly problematic. This is not an issue of reliability as normally understood in the methodological literature, but to do with the way in which present time infuses our perceptions of the future, so that what people experience in their present jobs – such as dissatisfaction with constraints on the kind of care they can provide – shapes how they present their future work intentions. This in turn may or may not predict their future practice.

In addition, the Telephone Survey, even more so than the Postal Survey, is likely to suffer from issues of non-response, so that inclusion of those who have left childcare work may be underrepresented. Moreover, the case study interviews, while providing considerable insights into care workers' lives and their understandings of the work, 'represent' only themselves rather than the different worker groups. On the other hand, this rich data source can provide insights at a theoretical level showing, as we have done, how plans for the future may shade into hopes and dreams.

So what does this chapter suggest about issues of recruitment and retention in childcare work, issues that policy makers have highlighted as highly problematic? The reasons why people move on from particular types of childcare work reflect a variety of factors, including their life stage, personal or family situation, dissatisfaction with the work and better opportunities being available elsewhere. Given the often difficult and demanding nature of the work, and the conditions under which it is undertaken (see Chapters Six and Seven), the surprise is perhaps not that people leave, but that so many stay. When workers did move on, it was usually to another type of care work with children and young people. While frequent staff changes are likely to have a negative impact on continuity of care for individual children, the fact that this movement is mostly within — rather than out of — the childcare workforce should perhaps be regarded as a strength rather than a problem. It suggests the need for recruitment and retention strategies to move beyond concepts of entry and loss within a particular type of childcare work, to considering the needs of the childcare workforce as a whole and developing career paths between different types of work (as was beginning to happen for family support workers in our study, but less so for other groups).

This chapter reinforces findings presented in previous chapters, and also in other research. Those who care for vulnerable children often have a strong commitment to their work. They care *about* the work they do and the quality of care as well as caring *for* children. Such commitment is something that policy makers and recruitment/retention strategies need to build upon in order to prevent the highly committed from becoming disillusioned and discouraged and leaving the work. Residential social workers, especially those working in private homes, reported frustration and disillusionment at the inability of residential care to help many children, the frequent turnover of staff, the number of placement changes children experience and the inadequate resources for providing additional support such as counselling.

We set out on this study with a lifecourse perspective in mind: the idea that childcare work and other care work may have a close connection with where people are in their lives. In this chapter we present some evidence of transferable skills and movement between types of work with children — but also reasons why people choose certain types of work (for example, their life stage, location, preferred age of child, own personality/needs). Where this is the case, as when people with older or grown-up children decide to foster children and to look after older age groups, or when a community childminder wants to look after young children when she has her own at home, recruitment needs to be targeted, matching people to type of work. As suggested earlier, increased flexibility and encouragement to develop 'careers' in work with children, for example by offering professional training, can increase opportunities and make the work more attractive and financially rewarded. However, care needs to be taken not to lose the existing strengths of the workforce. For example, we found cases of family support workers who felt undervalued because they did not choose to train in social work (a possibility for some) yet felt they were doing equally important and demanding work.

To improve recruitment and retention, good support and supervision are also vital. In response to consultation on the Children's Workforce Strategy, government has recognised a need to 'examine urgently' the promotion of better front-line supervision for the workforce dealing with the most vulnerable children, and has noted that 'one of the reasons social workers leave is because they do not feel sufficiently protected and supported in difficult situations by good supervisors' (HM Government, 2006, p 29). Although this refers specifically to social work with children, where recruitment difficulties have received particular attention, our study shows the same need for good supervision and support to be available for all those who work with vulnerable children. Yet it is at this level — well-qualified staff to fill management and supervisory positions — that managers reported the greatest difficulties in attracting suitable staff, especially in residential childcare.

Notes

[1] Case studies were excluded from the Telephone Survey as they were conducted over the intervening year.

[2] Numbers add to more than 21 as some leavers gave more than one reason.

NINE

Managing care work and family life

Introduction

An important part of the jigsaw in understanding childcare workers' lives remains, namely how as parents and family members childcare workers managed to combine their work and other care responsibilities – how they connected their public and private worlds, not only over time but also on a daily basis. For these workers, caring was an intrinsic part of both work and family life, a condition with the potential to add to tensions and overload typically experienced by those juggling work and family responsibilities. If more people are to be attracted to and retained in this type of work, a consideration of work–family policies and practice may point to some of the issues that need to be addressed.

Much of the recent British literature has focused upon notions of work–life balance, a concept which implies that creating some balance between work and family life is feasible and that the power to do this is vested in the individual worker. In practice, most people manage their lives as best they can by deploying whatever resources are available to them in different contexts (workplace, home, wider social networks and public policy). Whether they achieve or seek to achieve balance is arguably less important than managing to get by on a day-to-day basis. Work and family are not mutually exclusive domains. Rather, work and family life may be conceptualised as sets of 'practices' that actors engage in. Thereby each set of practices may cross different domains, allowing the individual to create their own ways of doing things (Morgan, 1996). Thus the conceptual emphasis moves from actors operating in discrete social domains (workplace or family setting) to how they manage their different responsibilities and life modes *across* domains and in the context of differential access to resources of various kinds – cultural, structural and personal.

In this endeavour, work–family boundary theory has been helpful. This explores how people negotiate the boundary between work practices and family practices and the 'spill-over' between these

(Nippert-Eng, 1996; Campbell-Clark, 2000; Sullivan and Lewis, 2000; Brannen et al, 2001; Mauthner et al, 2001; Perrons, 2003; Reynolds et al, 2003; Brannen, 2005). Ways of negotiating work–family boundaries are not static but change over time, for example over the lifecourse as children grow up and parents and children have different needs and responsibilities. They are also likely to be affected by changes that have occurred in British social policy from the late 1990s, for example the increased importance placed by employers on work–life balance, the growth in childcare facilities, and greater entitlement to statutory forms of leave such as parental leave.

Moreover, the kind of work people do is likely to affect ways of managing the work–family interface. Studies of call centre workers and software workers have shown that these different types of work pose very different challenges and that workers adopt different coping strategies (see, for example, Hyman et al, 2005 on call centre workers). Childcare work with vulnerable children poses particular issues especially for those who are current parents. The challenges include the emotional intensity of the work, which means workers may require higher than usual levels of support. There is also the need to ensure that the children they care for have continuity of care while taking account of carers' own responsibilities to their families, together with issues to do with managing relationships between two sets of children. Yet other work–family issues arise in the contexts in which the work is done (at home or in institutional settings). For those who are home based, work–family boundaries are blurred compared to those working in institutional settings.

This chapter explores childcare workers' work–family practices and draws upon three sets of data. First, drawing upon the interviews with managers, it outlines work–family policies and practices in the local authorities upon which we focused. Second, drawing upon data from the Postal Survey, it compares the responses of the four types of childcare workers to direct questions about the effects of care work on family life and about the effects of family life on care work. This method was not intended to understand what this meant in practice for individuals. Third, the chapter draws upon the biographical interviews in order to understand how, at the micro level, individual care workers of different kinds negotiated their work–family lives and the nature of the issues they confronted.

The manager interviews

The issues that arise for, and hence the workplace support needed by, childcare workers are different for each group and relate to the type of work, workplace and location of the work. The story given by managers was, however, largely about the constraints upon family-friendly policy and practice, factors that they acknowledged made it particularly difficult to recruit workers – that is, *mothers* – who had younger children.

Local authorities employ some care workers directly, namely residential social workers and family support workers. These workers were covered by the employment conditions that are applicable to all council workers. However, local authority managers said that, while they tried to be flexible and to adhere to good council practice, this was difficult where the needs of the service took precedence. They cited obstacles to flexible working such as the requirement to offer full-time and often statutory cover, the right of young people in their care to expect stability of staff presence (as in residential care), and timetables that dictated staff attendance at, for example, child protection conferences. Many managers saw these constraints as largely insuperable in their own responses to their staff's needs for flexible conditions of work.

None of the local authorities or services we studied provided childcare facilities for their staff. No manager (or care worker) mentioned leave for dependants, leave that exists in some local authorities but is poorly publicised and taken up (Mooney and Statham, 2002; Brannen and Pattman, 2005). Rather, family friendliness had to be negotiated individually with managers and was granted at managers' discretion. Some service managers worried about the danger of 'setting precedents among staff' on the grounds of infringing equal opportunities. On the other hand, managers hinted that things might be arranged differently. Some managers (and care workers) suggested, however, that workers were able to juggle their shift working through informal agreements with their colleagues, and attributed any difficulties with these issues to 'poor managers'.

In the independent and private sector residential homes, managers said they lacked the financial capacity to respond to employees' family needs unless the local authority had stipulated in their contracts these entitlements and built them into the associated costs. Local authority managers did not seem to know whether these issues were addressed in such contracts. Yet, five of the nine home managers in the study (local authority, voluntary and private) said that family responsibilities were a factor in explaining why residential staff had left in the previous year and four mentioned problems with working hours.

There were particular constraints in family support work, especially in London where workers travelled around the community and were unable to use cars because of lack of parking. Such travel could extend workers' hours and create unpredictability in their lives even though on paper they were offered access to flexible employment contracts such as annualised hours, term-time working and extended unpaid leave.

Different work–family issues arose for home-based workers, in particular for foster carers. The issues here were to do with managing the lack of boundaries around their work. This could be especially difficult for those professional foster carers and those working on specialist schemes (although none were included in the study). Work–family support centred on reducing the stress of the work because of its 'spill-over' for home-based workers and their own children and families. Managers of foster carers and the carers themselves both said that out-of-hours support provided by social workers was generally poor. In some local authorities, there appeared to be no clear policies for the provision of respite care to give carers time away from the 'job'. Independent fostering agencies were better at offering support in general to carers. A solution mentioned in one such agency was to build up a team of outreach workers who would come into the home if a foster carer went on a course or needed a break, while another was to focus on the foster children by providing them with activities outside the foster home. Such solutions might also extend to the carers' own children. On the other hand, as demonstrated in particular cases, wider kin constituted an important source of support for foster carers, either directly or indirectly.

However, in general, the provision of support to foster carers prioritised the needs of the children, so that many managers stressed the importance of carers' full-time presence in the home. This often precluded (female) carers from doing paid work outside the home and thus rendered work–family balance an unrealisable goal. Yet managers did not regard compensation for lost waged work as a priority. On the other hand, because of the increasing shortage of carers, they were prepared to envisage foster carers, that is *women*, taking some part-time work as long as they were available in the school holidays. However, as a couple of managers mentioned, support for carers in paid work was sometimes on offer but could not be prioritised over support for carers prepared to offer cover on a 24-hours basis. As one senior manager noted: "So far we have been reluctant to pay [foster carers] to enable them to be available...." Mention was also made of the constraints of keeping foster children in their own schools, placing more demands on carers, together with the issue of school holiday cover. By contrast, managers were more disposed to help create work–life balance for community childminders by accommodating the length of children's day to carers' timetables, while one said that they were prepared for two childminders to share the care of a child. Community childminders were also reported to be well supported in being enabled to take the children out of the home to drop-in centres, as well as having access to home visits from scheme coordinators and out-of-hours support.

The effects of work on family life: the Postal Survey evidence

In the Postal Survey we asked care workers whether they found 'it difficult to manage their work and family life responsibilities'. Only 19% agreed that it was difficult, falling to 13% among community childminders.[1] Over half (58%) disagreed, with the rest 'sitting on the fence'. In short, most care workers seemed to feel that they managed in practice.

Another survey question concerning the effects of work upon family life produced more negative responses (Table 9.1). Overall just over a third agreed with the statement 'This work can make family life difficult'. Residential social workers and foster carers were significantly more likely to say so (47% and 48% respectively) compared to around one in five family support workers and community childminders.

The high proportion of foster carers suggesting that the work makes family life difficult is unsurprising given that they have 24-hour

Table 9.1:Agreement with the statement 'This work can make family life difficult'

	Type of worker				
	Residential social worker (*n*=83)	Family support worker (*n*=83)	Foster carer (*n*=71)	Community childminder (*n*=64)	All (*n*=301)
	%	%	%	%	%
Agree	47	18	48	22	34
Neither agree nor disagree	28	29	24	42	30
Disagree	25	53	28	38	36

Notes: 4 missing cases.
Percentages do not always total 100 due to rounding.

responsibility for children of a variety of ages whose behaviour is often challenging and difficult, as well as often caring for their own children at the same time (80% of the foster carers in our study were parents, with over half having a child aged 0-17). The residential social workers were more likely to have reported negative effects of work on family life for different reasons, since being younger than foster carers only half were parents. Thus it seems *unlikely* that current family responsibilities underpinned their negative view of the impact of work on family life. Some may have been thinking ahead to the time when they might become parents and feared that the non-standard hours and 'sleepovers' would make family life difficult (83% did shift work, 78% worked weekends, 71% evenings and 61% nights, representing much higher proportions than community childminders and family support workers). Their working hours were also highest, with 80% employed on contracts of over 30 hours per week, in contrast to 74% of community childminders and 66% of family support workers, a finding reflected in their higher levels of dissatisfaction with working hours. (Foster carers were not asked questions on working hours.) In addition, as we found in the biographical interviews and manager interviews, some residential social workers and family support workers were studying for higher qualifications, adding to the workloads they had to juggle.

Supporting Postal Survey evidence concerning the negative impact of work on family life included questions about work conditions, in particular possible reasons for considering leaving their current work (see Chapter Eight). Around two in five (41%) ticked 'the effects of my work on my family' as a reason to consider giving it up, particularly foster carers. Forty per cent of family support workers ticked 'workload' as a reason to leave; and 55% of residential social workers ticked 'the hours'. Around 30% of residential social workers and family support workers indicated that unsupportive management could be a reason to leave, while 34% of foster carers and community childminders ticked 'other work conditions' (Table 8.1).

By contrast, the survey evidence suggests a rather positive picture concerning feelings of support from their employers concerning work–family matters (Table 9.2). Overall 77% of the sample found their employer very or fairly supportive, with residential social workers and family support workers more likely to give a positive rating to their employers than other groups but not significantly so. This question is not without problems, however. It may be that care workers who were self-employed (foster carers and community childminders) felt that their 'employers' did not have a role to play in this respect: they may well

Table 9.2: Respondents' ratings of support given to them by 'employers' in helping to manage work and family responsibilities

	Type of worker				
	Residential social worker (*n*=83)	Family support worker (*n*=84)	Foster carer (*n*=73)	Community childminder (*n*=63)	All (*n*=303)
	%	%	%	%	%
Very supportive	39	50	32	49	42
Fairly supportive	40	38	27	35	35
Rarely supportive	13	6	25	10	13
Don't know	8	6	16	6	9

Notes: 2 missing cases.
Percentages do not always total 100 due to rounding.

have been thinking of the parents who paid them to provide childcare rather than the local authority who purchased places for children in need. Foster carers were the least satisfied with work–family support from 'employers': a quarter rated their employer as 'rarely supportive' compared to around 10% of other groups. This reflects the findings of other studies (for example, Wilson et al, 2003).

A limited range of family-friendly practices were reported to be available across the groups (Table 9.3). Almost all residential social workers ticked the box about being able to swap shifts and just under three quarters of foster carers ticked respite care for foster children. However, working term-time only was rarely mentioned as available to residential social workers or family support workers, in contrast to just over a fifth of community childminders (23%). Help with childcare from employers was again rarely reported to be available for the children of institutionally based carers (9% of residential social workers and 3% of family support workers mentioned this, no matter whether they had children or had children of the relevant age), compared to 24% of community childminders. (Foster carers had older children on average.) It may have been that some home-based workers included the childcare provided by others in the family such as their partners. Foster carers were less likely to have access to time off for family emergencies or leave for family reasons and community childminders and residential social workers were less likely to say they were able to reduce or change their hours.

A further source of evidence for this rather positive picture of the impact of care work on family life is indicated in the question: 'Work

Table 9.3: Help from employer with managing family responsibilities

	Type of worker							
	Residential social worker		Family support worker		Foster carer		Community childminder	
	%	n[a]	%	n	%	n	%	n
Can reduce/ change hours at short notice	54	45/83	61	51/84	n/a[b]		43	28/62
Able to swap shifts	96	80/83	n/a		n/a		n/a	
Help with childcare for own children[c]	9	7/81	3	2/78	22	15/69	24	15/63
Can take time off for family emergencies	84	70/83	88	73/83	58	41/71	95	61/64
Can take leave for family reasons	65	53/82	54	44/81	45	32/71	73	45/62
Respite care available for foster children	n/a		n/a		71	50/70	n/a	
Can work term-time only	5	4/81	3	2/80	n/a		23	14/62

Notes:
[a] The number responding positively out of the total number responding to the question.
[b] Not applicable to this group of workers.
[c] Possibly defined by some home-based workers as unpaid help with childcare, for example partner/spouse.
Percentages do not always total 100 due to rounding.

gives me skills I can use in family life'. Over half of the sample (51%) agreed with this statement, with only 15% disagreeing.

The effects of family life on care work

The converse question was posed in the Postal Survey concerning the spill-over from family to work – 'Family life can make work life difficult'. This question produced an even more positive picture than the effects of work on family: only 19% of residential social workers, 16% of family support workers, 19% of foster carers and 11% of community childminders agreed that family life could make work difficult, with over half the total sample disagreeing (Table 9.4). The group that stands out here is the community childminder group, rather fewer of whom thought their family life made their work difficult perhaps because they had chosen the work to enable them to care for their own children at home (see Chapter Four, and Mooney, 2003).

Other survey evidence supports the positive effects of family life on work. When respondents were asked to indicate if they agreed with the statement 'Caring for my own family helps me in my work', over half (58%) agreed and only 15% disagreed (27% neither agreed nor disagreed). Most likely to agree were community childminders followed by foster carers and least likely were the residential social workers. Again, unsurprisingly, those who were parents were twice as likely to agree as non-parents (66%). (See also Chapter Six on tacit forms of childcare knowledge.)

Relevant to this issue are responses to the survey question about the supportiveness of their own families towards their care work: 79% of the whole sample agreed that their families were supportive. Interestingly, those whose own families were most likely to be affected by their work were the most positive about their families' support – 85% of foster carers and 83% of community childminders – suggesting perhaps that this type of work was only sustainable *with* their families' support.

Thus, the survey evidence suggests that rather few care workers found it difficult to manage work and family responsibilities although more said work could make family life difficult, foster carers and residential social workers in particular. Work–family support from employers on some issues was reported to be high. However, managers' accounts

Table 9.4: Agreement with the statement 'Family life can make it difficult to do my work'

	Type of worker				
	Residential social worker (n=80)	Family support worker (n=83)	Foster carer (n=70)	Community childminder (n=64)	All (n=297)
	%	%	%	%	%
Agree	19	16	19	11	16
Neither agree nor disagree	31	25	29	30	29
Disagree	50	59	53	59	55

Notes: 8 missing cases.
Percentages do not always total 100 due to rounding

suggest that they felt that they could provide rather little support given the constraints under which they had to work. Such a finding is fairly common in British studies and is explained by a low sense of entitlement to work–family measures in the workplace, with most relying on manager discretion and informal arrangements (Lewis et al, 2002). By contrast, few care workers considered that their family lives could make their work lives difficult.

Managing work–family boundaries: the biographical case studies

The study was designed to enable us to contrast different kinds of conditions for managing work–family responsibilities: home-based and institutionally based. Thus, we sought to understand how different contexts shaped the ways that childcare workers managed their work–family lives. While the separation of the workplace from the household gave less opportunity for the integration of family life routines and rhythms with their work schedules and responsibilities, it did allow workers to leave their work stresses behind them in the workplace. Conversely, being a carer in one's own home offered practical benefits, allowing carers to look after their children at home but provided little escape from the demands of paid care. However, as we shall see, the picture is less clear cut with some institutional care workers bringing work home with them and some home-based workers making some distinctions between work and family life (Table 9.5). One worker may strive to make connections between their work and family worlds while another in a similar situation may try to keep the two worlds apart.

In the interviews, care workers were asked whether they thought it best to connect their work and family lives or to keep them separate. They responded to the question differently, with some referring to preferences, others to their practices and strategies. Several indicated that they found it difficult to put their preferences into practice.

Table 9.5: Ways of managing work–family boundaries

	Residential social worker	Family support worker	Foster carer	Community childminder
Connection	1	–	3	–
Connection and separation	–	2	2	5
Separation	5	4	–	–
Other	–	–	1	–

Tom Jenkins, a male manager of a residential home, expressed both a preference and a strategy:

> "The two really shouldn't be mixed. The bottom line is I should be leaving my work at home. And the stresses and strains – I mean at work – the stresses and strains I should be leaving at work as well. And when I go home I should be fresh for my family. That's the bottom line. If you want to look at the problem-solving role that I'm in then I shouldn't be taking those problems home with me because I shouldn't be sort of forcing them on my family, because they're not in my job, those issues aren't their responsibility etc etc and it just confuses the whole thing. Where I find ... it's not so much blurring, it's the impact that it has. If I've had a real hell day at work, I've got a throbbing headache, when I walk through the front door sometimes I don't particularly feel very family-ish. *(No)* And all I want to do is be left alone, maybe have a mug of coffee and just unwind for half an hour in peace and quiet. You can imagine with a five-year-old in there that's not very often."

Natalie James, a female residential social worker, answered the question in terms of practice, namely that she was able to switch off from work:

> "I do manage to switch off and I think I do quite well at keeping the two separate. It's quite easy really in the sense that a lot of things that happen up there are confidential anyway. So I'm not supposed to talk, about it all. You know, so in that sense it gives you that much [pause] Well it's confidential anyway, so I'm not going to sit here and discuss it, so I might as well forget about it till I go in next time. There's nothing I can do about it. *(No)* I find it much easier to switch off from there than I did."

Pat Foster, a family support worker, had a more connected view of her life and identity and felt that she was, and wanted to be, much the same person inside and outside work.

> "I don't have a great kind of huge divide. I mean I don't need one in my work. But, you know, I'm not somebody who kind of [pause] it's like, for example, you know, I have

a colleague who won't ever work at home on the computer, whereas I'll do that. Do you know what I mean? … I'm much the same person in my principles. I would say I tone down who I am when I'm at work. For my colleagues rather than for the work. Do you know what [pause] does that make sense? You know, I'm perhaps a bit more controversial in my personal life than I am at work.… I'm not [pause] I don't like keep everything private, you know. And in fact if you looked in my diary you would see I have [pause] I mean I don't have them on the wall but you know I've got a photograph of my unborn grandson in my diary at the minute."

Foster carers and community childminders by contrast accepted that work–family boundaries were blurred. Most foster carers expected, and were expected, not to have outside paid work (see earlier).

Negotiating work–family boundaries depends, however, upon the resources and conditions available from the household, kin and friends, together with formal sources of support and knowledge[2] (Jarvis, 1999). In typifying the issues for childcare workers and the ways they dealt with them, we have tried to avoid the concept of 'strategy' to convey a sense of conscious purpose or end in sight (Crow, 1989). Strategy is also a concept that, as Edwards and Ribbens (1991) have noted, carries the baggage of social science language that may not reflect the perspectives of those adopting particular ways of living their everyday lives. It is also difficult to maintain a conceptual distinction between long-term strategic choices and short term adaptations (Hyman et al, 2005). Rather we prefer the term 'practices' (Morgan, 1996), as discussed at the start of the chapter, to denote ways of managing or living with work–family responsibilities. Some of these practices are to do with negotiating a particular type of work, others are to do with the way care workers think about the children they care for. Others relate to the relational context, in particular how care workers cope with the stresses of the job by drawing upon support of significant others. Other practices relate to ways of working and organising working time and workers' ability to control this, whether they had access to family-friendly practices in the workplace, and whether they also integrated further training around work and family responsibilities.

Human service work: switching off from work and taking a break

The boundary between work and family life is about negotiating time. Time is not only about task allocation but about 'spill-over' time in which people may not be able to cut off from thinking about work or family life. Many referred to the importance of compartmentalising human service work because it was so stressful. This separation was seen as necessary both for the clients and for their own and their family's welfare. Sarah Butler, a family support worker, said she first realised the importance of switching off when she began working with older people:

> "When I was working for the elderly I had to learn to switch off. Because I was going so fast between people, you know, bang bang bang. You had to learn to switch off from that one in order to provide the service for the next one. And, you know, so that's where I learnt to switch off. And I can do that, I can switch off. And I've had to teach some of my support workers how to do that actually. 'Cos it's very difficult for a lot of people to switch off. I mean some of them had experiences, for example they were looking after an autistic child while the parents went out with the neglected sibling. They would come back and everybody would go to bed except for the mum, who would then insist on talking and dumping everything on my support worker. Who would then end up staying there till 11 o'clock at night or something. It's like 'Hello?' So I had to put a stop to that. But done in such a way that nobody felt offended. *(No)* You know, you have to work [pause] these people all have their own needs, and they're all seeking to have those needs met, and you've got to manage it somehow. And it is a difficult thing to manage. Well I think it can be."

Community childminders, although looking after children at home, were keen to switch off when the children they minded left at the end of the day. This was not so much because the work was stressful but because they wanted to reclaim their homes for themselves and their families. In her capacity as a private childminder, Eileen Wheeler resented the children's parents arriving late to pick up their children – seen as refusing to recognise that 'we have families too'. Several said they did not think about the children once they had gone home. Eileen noted that once a child on a sponsored placement had left her care permanently, she did not think about them but got on with 'everyday living': "I know they're outsiders and there's support there". Kathleen was adamant that she would not take children at night or weekends (respite childminding) and resented the way her home got into a mess. Moreover, three community childminders interviewed had older children who were at school or had grown up. Thus, for some, their childcare work was separate from their family lives.

Foster carers by definition had chosen to connect their work and family lives through fostering. For foster carers the whole point of the work was *not* to think of fostering as separate but to integrate it into family life timetables and routines. For them the children were there all the time; they were not visitors but family members. Brenda Reeves made a comparison between fostering and childminding:

> "If you've got a child living in your house you're all living under the same timetable. When you've got another child coming in and going out and coming in and going out, they're living under a different timetable."

However, some foster carers spoke about the importance of having time away from the foster setting – involving respite care for the foster child – whereby they could have a break and so be better able to cope. For some, however, the very concept of respite care for foster children was antithetical to their notions of fostering. Debra, a foster carer, said:

> "I couldn't phone up and say 'Oh I think you should have [foster child] for a week, 'cos I need a rest'. It's not just [her], I need a rest from them, I need a rest from my children, from children full stop. So I can't say 'Oh I need a rest from X, but I don't need a rest from my *own* children.... You can't just say 'Oh yeah well let them come and let her go off'. 'Cos then you're emotionally damaging her because she's seeing it 'Well you're saying that you need a rest, but you don't need a rest from them, but you need a rest from me.'"

The ability to find someone to come into the home to enable *foster carers* to take time away was not readily available. Most managed by drawing upon their own families. Obafemi Williams, a foster carer, drew upon the support of his (now adult) children who had all been assessed (by social services) and also his wife who was working but occasionally took a day off to look after the foster children:

"[T]hey can babysit, they can come here. Depending on who is free. Our youngest is 18. So if they are normal, no problem. They come back from school, you help them, do whatever you like – we can socialise, we can go out. Yes. Leaving them with grown-ups in the house."

Similarly, Margaret Henderson, another foster carer, drew upon the help of her adult daughters and her disabled parents, although she did not describe the time she and her husband went away without the foster child in terms of needing time off.

Connecting to or disconnecting from the workplace

Travel to work time was only available to institutionally based workers and was potentially an important resource in putting boundaries around different responsibilities and worlds. Those who had to and could afford to travel by car could use this as an opportunity to extend their working day by using the time to think about work. Tom Jenkins, a residential social worker with management responsibilities, described thinking through work problems during his drive to and from work. By contrast, another care worker used their travel to work time to switch off from work. Clare Glover, a family support worker, described using the drive home in the evening to wind down:

"Any anger I might have had from anything or any frustrations I might have had or anything would be gone by the time I get home. So, you know, working quite a way away from where you live is a good thing, to me … that's time for me in the car, 'cos I love driving, so it's not [pause], you know, that's my time."

Due to the confidential nature of the work with vulnerable children and young people, in some instances care workers had to keep the location of their workplace secret from their family and friends, a constraint that meant they had to separate work and family life. Carol Jones, a residential worker in a private home, described how her husband could not take or collect her from her workplace but had to drop her off several streets away. In the latter case the secret location of her workplace served to reinforce the divide between Carol's working life and her life outside work, while in Tom Jenkins' case, travel to work constituted an extension of his working day. By contrast, a family support worker (Justine Naisbitt) was unable to separate these spheres of her life, whether or not she wanted to, since she lived in the same neighbourhood as the young people with whom she worked, and some of them were acquaintances of her son who still lived at home. This had on occasion proved very difficult for her in her professional role. On the other hand, Justine had gone into this type of work because of her own personal experience of trying to sort out her son's problems and wanted to help young people in similar situations.

Those whose childcare work was done at home might resent the upheaval caused by caring in their own homes. Several childminders resented 'the mess' and wanted to stick to clear timetables for minding the children, views that none of the foster carers expressed.

Integrating looked-after children into family life

Some childcare workers saw caring for vulnerable children as a job. Foster carers were least likely to do so. Foster carers are expected to integrate foster children into their family lives and they were at pains to demonstrate this, explaining how house rules applied to all the children equally, how there were no locks on the doors and so on. The centrality of this to 'good fostering' is revealed in the following representation of the 'bad' foster carer:

> "But then there are foster carers out there which I think how the hell did they become foster carers, because they've got locks on the doors and you're not allowed in here. You're only allowed to do this at such and such. That's not family life is it? *(No)* So, you know, there's good and bad in everything I suppose, but [pause] not in this house." (Mary Haywood)

Debra Henry talked about the importance of not seeing a foster child as different or 'special' in relation to her own four children:

> "[Treating them as special is] what makes them tend to go off the rails as well really sometimes. And sometimes it is the things that gets said to them, you know. Like they're made to feel special. Well what's special about you? You're just a child, just like mine."

The view that foster children should be completely integrated into family life was not universally endorsed by foster carers in terms of their practices, however. Some foster carers made distinctions between foster children and their own. Indeed Debra was aware that she could not treat a foster child the same as her own in terms of discipline, giving the example of how she would lock her own in their bedroom if they misbehaved. She felt there were constraints on intimacy because of the social work emphasis on 'safe caring'. And she was aware that she lacked the taken-for-granted family knowledge she had about her own children, for example their childhood illnesses.

Celia Anderson, another foster carer, expressed ambivalence about treating foster children as part of the family or as separate from it. On the one hand she thought that a foster child should fit in with her own family's rituals and obligations (notably family visiting), on the other hand she was conscious of the foster child's allegiances to their own family. This led her to exclude the foster child from family rituals on some occasions.

By contrast, in Brenda Reeves' account it was the competition between her own children and the foster child that shaped her management of work–family boundaries so that on occasion she kept the two apart. The issue, as she saw it, was how to cope with the competing time demands upon *herself* rather than a question of whether foster children and her own children should be differently treated. Brenda explained how the foster child had begun to provoke her own children and this had led to some resentment. Similarly, the foster child was jealous of her own children when she cuddled them. Thus, on some occasions she had excluded the foster child from some family activities. She explained that when she had begun fostering there were no such issues, but that the situation had begun to change. Now that her elder daughter was older she wanted her own space and more time with her mother.

Institutionally based workers also had to contend with competition between their own children and those they cared for. For example, Brian Stratford, a residential care worker, reported that his son resented the fact that he looked after other children in the evening when he might have been at home with him. This made Brian very careful not to mention his work at home and so reinforced the impetus to keep work and family life separate. Similarly, another residential care worker, was afraid of the effects on her own children if they knew about the 'bad behaviour' of children in the residential home and that they were 'getting away with it':"[My children would think] how come they can do those things?" This again reinforced a conscious attempt to keep the two worlds apart.

By contrast, this appeared to be less of a problem for community childminders, at least for those four cases who had no children at home in the day. In the case of a childminder with a young child at home, she perceived her daughter's jealousy as having positive effects "because she has to learn to share".

Offloading to significant others

As noted already, a particular feature of working with vulnerable children is its sensitive and confidential nature. Moreover, childcare workers are in a difficult position: they do not have a great deal of authority over them. Child protection dictates that carers have to observe the rules carefully. These extend to not discussing children and their problems and situations outside the professional work context.

Nonetheless, because of the challenges and stress of the work, many childcare workers felt a strong need to unburden their worries and concerns and to offload to others, thereby bridging the boundaries between work and family life to some degree. Moreover, the opportunities to do this in a professional context are more limited for some workers than others. Some foster carers explained that while they were happy with the social work support they received it was often difficult to get hold of them when they needed it (Triseliotis et al, 1999). Several residential social workers mentioned lacking proper supervision or professional support in managing difficult young people. Community childminders said they obtained most support from other childminders, with the coordinators of community childminding schemes also providing a useful source of help and advice. Accounts from family support workers varied, with some mentioning a lack of support from their managers.

Those to whom workers felt most inclined to unburden themselves about the stresses of work were often those closest to them, persons whom they felt they could trust, in particular their partners (although not all care workers had a partner). Where partners worked in a similar human service occupation, they were better equipped to understand work with vulnerable children and were likely to have developed considerable interpersonal and support skills themselves. On the other hand, too much reliance by care workers upon the support of a partner could place a burden upon their relationships. Several care workers mentioned that their desire to talk through the stresses and strains of working in a challenging work environment was thwarted by their partners' lack of interest and unwillingness to listen. Some turned to friends, especially those working in a similar environment.

Carol Jones, a residential care worker, had few people to turn to. Her husband had a long-term illness, making him unable to work. Carol did not want to worry or upset him by talking about her stressful job. Indeed she reported that her partner could 'not understand' her desire to work with young people who could be so disruptive. After an incident in the residential home where she was threatened with broken glass by one of the young people, Carol reported keeping the matter to herself. Her only support seems to have been a brief discussion with the person who shared her shift during the particular incident. She clearly felt a loss in this regard:

> "You can't always discuss things with people that you want to, you need to offload sometimes, and that is a big thing. Because I can't come home and say to [husband] [pause] (a) because he's not well, but I can't say 'Oh that flipping kid....' da da da because you have to be careful what you say."

Similarly, Susanne Grant, a family support worker, said that her husband (working in a very different occupation) was not sympathetic to her work and she rang her friends instead, which her husband resented. She said she was therefore careful never to take work home but since she was studying for a diploma in social work, she had to do coursework at home.

> "He [husband] thinks my work is more important than the family. He thinks I see it that way. So [pause] he never listens to me moan about work or anything. I can't come home and tell him about work.... I'd phone up my friends *(Right)* and speak to them. Then he'll always say 'You're always on the phone'. So I can't win. *(No)* So, yeah it causes conflict yeah."

Teresa Thomas, a community childminder married to an ex-teacher, was more fortunate in having not only a sympathetic husband but one who was around to help with the children in the day.

But not all care workers felt such an urge to unburden themselves and considered that it was crucial to keep work and family life as separate as possible. It is surely not coincidental that the only male manager in the study was the most clear-cut instance of a care worker using a compartmentalising strategy. Tom Jenkins, a manager of a residential home for young people, was married. His wife was also in a human service occupation but Tom did not talk to her about his work. His way of coping with stress was to keep his thoughts to himself even though this practice seemed to have cost him dear. He described his normal way of coping with the stresses of the working day in terms of 'multitasking'. As can be seen in the following extract taken from his account of a day in his life, this way of managing his life was not without costs.

> "[After my son has gone to bed] I find myself sitting there and usually what I do, I'm a news freak, I like keeping abreast of current affairs, so I'll turn *News 24* on and start absorbing that. And at the same time I start multitasking then, and I'll be thinking about issues, management issues or client issues.... *(Did you mention this to your wife?)* Um [pause] at the end of the evening, probably about 10.30, I did actually make her a cup of coffee and apologise for my manner earlier in the evening. Because when she'd settled the little 'un to sleep she came down and um [pause] I can't remember what it was [pause] she asked me if I'd sorted a letter out to something.... It was a minor task but it involved me actually switching my computer on ... and I quite bit her head off, you know, reminding her that I'd been at work all day. And as soon as [pause] it was one of those situations where the words come out of your mouth and you think [clapping sound]. But I do remember that night sitting there and thinking, you know, I'm going to apologise. Anyway, I plucked up courage, because usually if I try and apologise I get it back 10 times worse [laughter from interviewer and interviewee]. So I plucked up courage and I made her a drink because I thought that might sweeten the situation a little bit. And I said 'Look, I'm really sorry about the mood I've clearly been in tonight, it has occurred to me it's because....' and I explained about the report. Which I'm sure she understood but I still got told off, which is fair enough, I deserved it."

Throughout the course of a long and highly reflective interview, it became clear that Tom was acutely aware that his total dedication to work had negative implications for his family life, something he had reflected upon since the breakdown of his first marriage. However, in keeping with his belief in separating work and family life, Tom had developed 'conscious strategies' (sic) in which he devoted himself exclusively either to work or to family life but never combined them. Thus, his work only extended silently into his family life while during holidays he sought to banish work entirely. To achieve the latter he described how every so often he took his family to some remote place away from people where they could spend time together:

> "I chop the year up so that we get [pause] as a family we go away camping in a mountain environment, because my wife and the little 'un they love it. And we'll actually go somewhere really sort of obscure where there isn't anybody for miles. And we'll camp for five or six or seven days. Or do a bit of fishing and talking [?] and [inaudible] and stuff like that. But it's just the three of us. And some families might find that extremely intense, but that's how we get back together and touch base, and it works. Because then I really do sort of put work totally out of my head."

Controlling working hours and having access to leave for family reasons

As discussed earlier, managers' perspectives on providing flexibility for family responsibilities suggested limited availability. In the interviews, care workers noted that control over working hours was dependent upon their employment contract. Residential social workers were obliged to do shift work and part-time work was less available. As noted earlier, discussing the survey results, the majority of residential social workers worked unsocial hours. Community childminders had some control over their working hours offering them a shorter working day than private childminding. However, they could not afford to turn their backs on private childminding as community childminding was not guaranteed. Family support workers, on the other hand, were attracted to the job in the first instance because on paper it offered flexibility but they often found that the hours were unpredictable, for example the expectation to work late to finish a job or to cover for someone else. The work typically meant travelling around the community, leading to long travel time. Pat Foster, a female family support worker, said that she had found centre-based family support work much easier to manage compared to her present community-based work and felt she could not have managed this work when her children were at home.

Some workplace practices enabled workers to use their work time flexibly or to change their hours. For example, working shifts was seen by some residential social workers as a way of enabling them to spend time with their own children. However, this was rarely seen as a satisfactory solution as shift patterns were not regular and isolated them from family and community routines. Brian, a male residential social worker, said that shift work allowed him to be at home with his young son at different times of the day and to spend a lot of time with him:

> "More than enough, yeah. More than most dads do I think. Well no because, you know, if they're at work nine to five, nine to six, whatever, I'm here in the afternoon when he gets home from school, go and play tennis. You know, most dads don't do that."

However, he found shift working difficult. When he was off in the week he was often on his own and when he did have time off at weekends he felt at a loose end since he was not part of a regular social circle.

> "And that's the problem you have I find at weekends, other people have got things to do.... And you're like 'Yeah' you're raring to do something and there's no one there to do it. 'Cos that's the bit I find hard. And you do spend a lot of time by yourself at home. 'Cos you're home and everyone else is out. I'm here now today and they won't come in till four o'clock. And at the time I'll be like 'Yeah, come on then'. They'll be 'Oh no I'm tired'. So that can be a bit of a stress, but you have to manage that."

Night working was seen as a particular constraint upon managing work–family boundaries. Jenny Masters, a residential social worker, described her mind as 'racing' after a long shift and she worried if she had done everything before handing over to the new shift. Her work–family 'strategy' was to work part time. She described coming home after a 24-hour shift thus:

> "It was like dozing in and out of sleep, so I was, and getting the kids to bed. Then the next thing I know, what you call [pause] 'cos I find after a sleep-in as well I get tired around 7 o'clock at night. And you will, you'll be sat there like dozing. But come 10 o'clock you're like ping! ... Which is a nightmare because it takes you a while to sort of get out of that. And then maybe just got over it, the next thing you know you're back in on a sleep-in again. That's why I've said I'm glad I'm not full time. 'Cos the full-timers can do up to four in a week."

However, as the Postal Survey evidence suggests, less than a fifth of residential social workers worked part time, that is under 30 hours per week (20%) compared to 26% of community childminders and 34% of family support workers. Clare Glover, a family support worker, had downsized her hours to a four-day 30-hour week when she became concerned about one of her children 'mixing with the wrong types'. Previously she had worked full time and felt unable to manage with a reduced income since her husband was on long-term sick leave. Similarly, Sarah Butler, a family support worker who was a lone parent, also reduced her hours. She was disillusioned with management and felt deskilled when family support work was transferred out of family centres into the community. She explained that her new approach to work part time was also driven by her desire to keep her teenage daughter focused upon her education. However, she found even part-time work difficult to combine with family life:

> "[A lot of the work is] crisis intervention. Suddenly you might find, you know, you're having to help take a child to a foster home on the first occasion and you might not get home till half seven. Fair enough it didn't happen every week, but on those occasions I felt X [daughter] was, you know, becoming unfocused and needed me around, so I decided to go part time. So I work three very long days and I have two days off.... 'Crises' don't wait until I'm at work [laughs] *(No)* You can hardly say 'Please don't try and commit suicide, I'm not at work until Monday'. So um, it's very difficult in my field to work part time. More so in the family support team. Part-time ... workers don't make it, I've watched it, they just can't make it in that field, the family support field that is.... It is difficult for the manager, our manager, to I suppose manage a team with part-timers. And I can see that now as a part-timer myself.... So, yeah. The part-timers are all leaving in droves."

The ability to take emergency time off for family reasons could affect all childcare workers but no service seemed to have such support in place. Carol Jones, a residential social worker whose children were now grown up, was employed in a private home where the rule was that staff gave two weeks' notice before taking leave. When her mother had a heart attack, she phoned head office and was told that she could not go to the hospital because "there weren't enough staff. I phoned and they said 'Well ... I expect she'll be all right, it's not really an emergency', and I was 'What?'" Carol had to wait until the next day when she was off duty to visit her mother.

Fitting in studies

There is considerable pressure on the care workforce to upgrade their skills with targets set for the attainment of NVQs (Levels 2 and 3). As the manager interviews suggested, in view of a shortage of qualified social workers, family support workers and residential social workers were being encouraged to study for a diploma in social work. Several care workers we interviewed had done or were doing diplomas in social work while others were doing NVQ qualifications, while yet others were waiting to start a course. Key to managing work–family boundaries was whether the employer allowed paid or unpaid time off for study. Jenny Masters, a residential social worker, had done NVQ Level 2 and was on a waiting list to do NVQ Level 3. She said she had been well supported in this by her manager and work colleagues.

> "I mean again the staff again have been fantastic. They've offered the support and all and anything I get stuck with they'll help me out and so on and that. They have been good and that. But like I say, it's normally when I'm on a shift that we're talking about it. And they have said phone home, what you call, and we'll arrange to meet up and, you know, you know, either you come to mine or I go to yours or we go out somewhere and we could sit and go through it all and that. But it's getting round to doing it, because that person could be on shift and you're off shift."

However, the key to her ability to fit her course around her two school-age children was her decision to work half time, enabling her to study on her days off when her children were at school.

Fitting in studies was very difficult for full-timers especially when they had young or school-age children. Marleen Bennett, a residential social worker, was trying to juggle three lives: a full-time job – doing waking nights in order to fit around her family; part-time study for a diploma in social work on her day off; and bringing up two school-age children. She did not attempt to keep these worlds separate since she had no space of her own in which to study and had to use the family living room. On the other hand, she studied late at night well after her children were in bed. She reported complaints about her studying both from her husband and children and said she was unable to talk to her husband (who worked in a very different occupation and had grown up in a culture in which men were totally spoilt by mothers and wives) about her course. Most support came from a friend on the course.

> "It's difficult. Because [husband] doesn't know what I am talking about and things. But then I've got college friends *(Right)* who we're very supportive to each other and we sort of like encourage each other. Which is a very big help to me ... if I'm finding like problems in whatever thing [pause] I usually like make her proofread my work also. So I sort of like do attachments and then email it to her. And then she'll do vice versa to me also. We'll ask each other whatever difficulties we're facing. If she's having problems with her partner we'll discuss it and I have problems with my husband I'll discuss it with her. It's really like working as a [pause] working together.... I think why we get on so well is also she has gone through the same thing I've been through. She was a single parent and all that and she's met her partner now. I mean right now with this course, everybody [pause] I mean they actually told us on the course 'You're going to have a lot of problems with family life'."

Yet despite all this, she considered her studies as having positive effects on family life:

> "And I thought maybe I would also set a good example to them [her children] to say 'If I can do it why can't you do it?' ... And with the twins that's what I always keep saying to them. I said 'Look, you know if you want to achieve something, if you want a better job and things like that, and if you really....'"

Conclusion

In this chapter we have brought together data from three sources based upon different research methods: data from semi-structured interviews with managers, evidence from the Postal Survey, and material from the biographical interviews. The first analysis articulates managers' perspectives while the latter two focus on those of care workers. The intention in the study design was to use different methods for different purposes (see Chapter Two).

The analysis and integration of mixed methods do not necessarily work out in the way that researchers plan in setting out on their research (Bryman, 2006) since in analysis it is necessary to consider the data in relation to the method chosen (see Chapter Ten) and the study's underlying ontological and epistemological positions. Given that different methods address different but related research questions, we would expect the data analysis to generate a degree of complementarity. On the other hand, there are some overlapping concerns as in the ways in which each method addressed similar issues in care workers' lives, as has been noted in this chapter. The survey data provide a general picture of work–family management practices and satisfaction in which home-based care workers found that care work made their family lives more difficult than institutionally based care workers. There was also some internal contradiction within the Postal Survey evidence, with fewer care workers reporting difficulties in *managing* their work and family lives than reporting negative *effects* of work upon family life. Such a finding is unsurprising when we turn to the qualitative evidence where people explained how they managed the difficulties in practice.

Survey evidence on its own is therefore not very illuminating. The biographical case studies show how childcare workers made the best of their situations and negotiated work–family boundaries in practice, typically working out their solutions on an individual basis with their manager (see a case study of social services by Brannen et al, 2004b). However, it was the managers who articulated most clearly the constraints against responding to their employees' requests for support: pressure on services in terms of lack of personnel to draw upon to cover staff shortfalls and lack of financial resources; the need to provide children in need with a long-term time commitment to ensure stability and continuity of care; the lack of any family-friendly policies and practices in some services. Paid time off from work to study was also an issue that some care workers did mention, suggesting considerable variability between and within services about what was on offer. For those unable to obtain paid leave and unable to afford to take unpaid leave, fitting studies around work and family life, going part time and extending the working day were the only options.

Working with vulnerable children, like human service work in general, is demanding, challenging and often relentless, requiring the engagement of the whole person including physical, intellectual, emotional and moral capacities. It requires considerable effort to leave the work behind at the end of a working day, while for some carers in the study the working day never ended. In this type of work, work–family boundaries are not delineated by time. People took their responsibilities and feelings home with them. The moral and emotional *commitment* of childcare workers to the children they look after was considerable and, as we described in Chapter Seven, provided considerable intrinsic rewards. The commitment required was especially great for foster carers who looked after vulnerable children in their own homes on a 24-hour basis, often over long periods of time. Foster carers who had their own children at home could face dilemmas about treating foster children as 'their own' and treating them differently from their own children. They lacked authority over foster children and had to be mindful at all times of issues of child protection, especially concerning discipline and showing affection. These issues made the ideal of total integration of work and family life difficult in practice.

The nature of childcare work and the way it flows into family life gives a particular twist to the issue of negotiating work–family boundaries, suggesting that children's services need to give greater recognition to this and to invest the necessary resources to support workers not only in terms of policies and practice to address carers' work–family responsibilities but also professional support for the work. On the other hand, the need to provide continuity of care and high-quality care for vulnerable children and young people may not always mean that employers can be as flexible as care workers might wish them to be in meeting their family needs. This is particularly the case in terms of the organisation of care workers' time so that some types of care have to be 24-hour cover and long term.

Notes

[1] The community childminders were predominantly drawn from two schemes that aimed to take account of childminders' work–family responsibilities, for example hours were fitted to the requirement of the childminder.

[2] This analysis is drawn from the whole interview and not just from their responses to questions concerning work–family boundaries.

TEN

Conclusions and policy implications

Main conclusions from the study

The study sought to examine four particular groups of childcare workers. The four groups have in common that they care for some of the most disadvantaged children in society. The children's situations are on a continuum of disadvantage and include children of different ages (young children to young adults) with different levels of need.

The study is unusual in having adopted a *time* perspective in its multi-phase, multi-method research design and in its use of a biographical perspective. In the book we have stressed how accounts of motivations and explanations for doing care work with vulnerable young people are given in the present. They are thus framed in relation to the interests of the study and how the study was presented to informants – what they thought we as researchers were interested in. Stories and interview accounts are also framed through the lens of hindsight in the context of events that took place in the past and to which a range of meanings have subsequently been attached. Thus, present explanations are offered by individuals in the knowledge of the persons they have become and the experiences they have currently. They are framed too in the context of how they think about the future: their plans, hopes and dreams.

In its focus on the past the study sought to understand care workers' past lives: how the inclination to care for others developed, their pathways into childcare work and caring for vulnerable children in particular. It also focused upon their current experiences: the ways in which childcare workers interpreted the nature of the work they do and the resources and knowledge bases they drew upon and their experiences of the different work contexts and work conditions. It also took a future perspective in terms of looking at care workers' expectations of their futures in childcare work and through its prospective design examined how far intentions matched practices, the reasons why care workers stayed or left the work and what they went on to do. The study therefore fills a significant gap in our understanding of care workers' lives over time, through its focus upon childcare workers' biographies and in its prospective design.

The study is unusual for a second reason, namely in focusing upon how carers' working lives intersect with their family lives, in particular with responsibilities for their own children and the extent to which they set boundaries around the work they do. Such a focus is important given that care workers who are currently bringing up their own children have to manage others' children alongside their own, a feat especially demanding for those who are home based (foster carers and childminders). In addition, the experience of parenthood constitutes a resource for childcare workers, especially in the context of the rather limited training (in comparison with other European countries) available for this work (Boddy et al, 2006).

The origin of a care ethic

Chapter Three explored how care workers, in telling the story of their lives, recounted the origins of a care ethic. In telling their stories in the biographical case studies, most care workers referred to their childhoods or early lives, with some suggesting a direct link between their childhoods and an ethic of care. Some spoke of strong similarities between their own and the childhoods of those children they currently cared for. Others recalled doing a significant amount of caring work, for example caring for their siblings in childhood. Yet others recounted childhoods characterised by loving parents, an experience that they now felt able to offer others' children. Thus, a supportive or caring childhood may become a powerful personal resource that translates into a concern to work with vulnerable children and one that childcare workers were able to capitalise upon in offering good care. On the other hand, having a difficult childhood in which care was lacking could also be transformed: the experience of feeling unloved as a child could become a resource enabling childcare workers to identify and empathise with similarly unloved children.

The contexts in which care workers entered childcare occupations

Chapter Four focused on the point of entry into childcare work. It showed that this occupational decision was often part of a complex chain of events and experiences – that occupational choices are part of the context in which people live their lives. It identified a number of themes that encompass the main routes into childcare work. First, some childcare workers entered this type of work at particular lifecourse phases although some worked in the care sector before this. Some young women chose this gender-typical work on leaving school while mothers with young children sought the work because it fitted in with their family responsibilities. There was some correspondence between lifecourse phase of the carer and the age of children they wished to care for. Thus, those with older or grown-up children tended to be less attracted to caring for young children. Second, childcare workers were often drawn to this work after they had problems in their own lives or after their own children had experienced developmental, mental health or behavioural problems. Third, entry into care work at a particular moment was often serendipitous, dependent on being at the right place at the right time, as when a person worked in a non-care occupation but was located in a social services context and was attracted to childcare work. For female care workers voluntary work often constituted a route out of full-time motherhood and into childcare work while for men entry into care work was another occupation decision. Fourth, entry into childcare work could hinge upon a professional, family member or friend having experience of or recommending the work. Such a recommendation by another may result in self-validation – the feeling that the individual's qualities and potential have been recognised and can be used for the well-being of vulnerable young people.

A 'career' in childcare work?

Chapter Five examined whether childcare workers considered they had 'careers'. It suggested that the notion of 'career' has a range of meanings, and that even those who lack training and promotion opportunities consider they have careers as much as those who have such resources. In the four case studies analysed, a more complex picture emerged of the identities that care workers forged over the lifecourse.

A male care worker aged fifty told two stories that were in tension with one another, reflecting the dilemma he faced as he moved up the tiers of management in residential social work. One was a story of personal change in which he underwent professional training, became an educated person with a high respect for knowledge, and rose up the organisational hierarchy. The other story he told was about the person he had always felt himself to be, someone who was committed to being 'hands on' and driven by the challenges of working with others.

Another story, by a female residential social worker who was only slightly older than the latter, was a story about feelings of missed opportunities in which she glimpsed the person she might have become as she realised that the moment for developing a career in childcare had passed. This story was one of thwarted ambition realised after considerable disappointment and dissatisfaction while working in a private residential children's home. Yet another story was told by a female foster carer in her late fifties whose life was described in terms of a succession of other professional identities; these she regarded as resources for fostering in the claims that she made for its proper recognition and remuneration as professional work. The last story concerned a female foster carer whose story suggested an identity that appeared to have undergone little change in adulthood, in which motherhood sat at its centre and flowed into the other spheres of her life. It is significant that the three cases of women childcare workers involved women who had embarked on childcare work when they and their children were older.

These cases indicate the flexibility and variation in the routes taken by *women* in childcare work, while the trajectories of men are more linear. They also show the different processes by which identities in care work develop (or not) and their impact upon the types of knowledge accumulated (see Chapter Six). Care identities are created and develop over time: often beginning in childhood, and interwoven with other identities and formal and informal commitments.

Understandings of care work

In Chapter Six we looked at how carers understood their work, the goals they sought to achieve and the knowledge that they drew upon in meeting these goals. The survey evidence suggested that people were often motivated to become childcare workers because they believed they could make a positive difference to young people's lives. Although making a difference was interpreted in a number of ways, care workers generally defined their roles in terms of compensation and change. Care workers spoke about compensating for the deficits in the lives of children and young people, in particular providing the opportunity for a 'normal' family life and about bringing a change in the young people themselves through, for example, raising their self-esteem and confidence. Often compensating for what was missing in the young person's life was seen as providing the necessary conditions to bring about a positive change.

The analysis showed that the compensation model was more likely to be expressed by foster carers and community childminders while residential social workers and family support workers tended to place more emphasis on the change model. These differences among childcare workers are attributable to a number of factors including the context in which they work, their personal qualities and life experiences, training and qualifications and the needs of the children they cared for.

The chapter highlighted the salience of good relationships between children and their carers: relationships built on trust. Such relationships take time to develop and require continuity of care, which are themselves an integral part of good-quality care. Yet, short-term placements, high staff turnover and the use of agency staff can mitigate the chances of good relationships occurring. Although social workers made every attempt to reduce the number of placements that children experience, lack of resources such as suitable provision, placements for assessment and emergencies made this difficult to achieve.

The relational model that some carers hoped for was often one based on friendship and sharing personal information. Disappointment was therefore voiced when this was not achieved. However, adult– child relationships are not equitable and professional–client relationships can never be the same as relationships between friends. Care workers in their training may need help with understanding the development of good relationships within 'professional' boundaries. For foster carers, the development of good relationships may be further complicated by the ambiguous role they find themselves in with respect to acting like parents, but, being subject to regulation, they did not have the same responsibilities and powers to set their own boundaries. While wanting to integrate foster children into their families, in their role as 'corporate parents' they also felt ambivalent in having to restrain themselves in showing children the affection they would show to their own children. Integrating a 'strange' child into one's own family, particularly a child who may be 'acting out' or distressed, should not be underestimated. The fact that the six foster carers in our case studies had experienced successful placements is a testament to their skills in being able to do this. The preparation and support for foster carers and foster children before and immediately after a new placement did not always seem to be in place, although emergency placements often meant this was not possible before the placement occurred.

How care was understood affected views about training and qualifications in relation to their own experiences. Three types of knowledge were identified. In stressing tacit knowledge, carers referred predominantly to their own experiences, particularly parenting, and personal qualities (see Chapter Three). Those stressing functional knowledge also considered tacit knowledge important, but emphasised the need for training and qualifications that helped carers to understand the tasks they had to fulfil and the rules they had to follow. Those referring to the importance of professional knowledge, although acknowledging the importance of tacit and functional knowledge, spoke about the importance of training and qualifications in providing a theoretical base, which enabled better understanding of children's behaviour and different approaches.

The experience of childcare work

In Chapter Seven we examined the high level of commitment workers brought to caring for vulnerable children and their considerable enjoyment of the work. The majority of survey respondents reported satisfaction with most aspects of their work, apart from pay and status. Yet the case studies revealed a more complex picture. They showed that intrinsic rewards were counterbalanced by considerable dissatisfaction, especially with particular aspects of carers' work situations so that for some the frustrations and difficulties were beginning to outweigh the rewards. The high level of commitment to caring was often undermined by the low status accorded to the work and lack of resources to provide good-quality care. Moreover, positive and negative aspects of the work were often two sides of the same coin. So, for example, the variety and challenge of the work could also be a source of stress and danger; satisfaction in seeing children improve and achieve was set against a sense of failure and disillusionment if children did not improve or a placement broke down; the pleasure care workers took in children becoming close to them was counterposed by the sense of loss they experienced when children moved on.

Different types of childcare worker reported different issues. Residential social workers, especially those working in private homes, reported frustration and disillusionment at the inability of residential care to help many children, the frequent turnover of staff, the number of placement changes children experience and the inadequate resources for providing additional support such as counselling. For family support workers, pay and status were particular issues, and although opportunities for career development (such as obtaining social work qualifications) were welcomed by some, this could create tensions for those who did not want to 'progress' in this way. For home-based care workers, creating a home-like environment was an explicit goal but could create tensions when carers were unable to enforce rules or were not permitted to show children explicit affection. Community childminders enjoyed the autonomy and control they had over their working environment, but often experienced isolation and lack of adult company.

Recruitment and retention issues

The great majority (82%) of childcare workers were still in the same type of work some 12 months after the original survey; residential social workers being most likely to move on. This apparent stability masked the fact that a surprisingly high proportion of home-based carers did not have a child placed with them at the time of the follow-up (a third of the community childminders and one in six of the foster carers), although they remained available for this work.

The reasons why people moved reflected a variety of factors, including their lifecourse phase, personal and family situations, dissatisfaction with the work and better opportunities being available elsewhere. Given the often difficult and demanding nature of the work, and the conditions under which it is undertaken, the surprise is perhaps not that people left, but that so many stayed. When workers did move on, it was usually to another type of care work with children and young people. While frequent staff changes are likely to have a negative impact on continuity of care for individual children, the fact that this movement was mostly within − rather than out of − the childcare workforce should perhaps be regarded as a strength rather than a problem. It suggests the need for recruitment and retention strategies to move beyond concepts of entry and loss within a particular type of childcare work, to considering the needs of the childcare workforce as a whole and developing career paths between different types of work (as seemed to be beginning to happen for family support workers in our study, but less so for the other groups).

Managing work and family life

The survey evidence suggests that rather few care workers found it difficult to *manage* work and family responsibilities, although more said work could make family life difficult, foster carers and residential social workers in particular. By contrast, few care workers considered that their family lives could make their work lives difficult. Most reported some family-friendly provisions from their employers. Levels of felt support were high (reflecting a low sense of entitlement to such support) while the interviews with managers suggested that management provided rather little support to care workers to help them with their informal care work. Explanations from managers focused on the constraints under which managers had to operate: pressure on services leading to a lack of personnel to draw upon to cover staff shortfalls; lack of financial resources; the need to provide continuity of care for children;

the difficulty of implementing family-friendly policies for 'front-line' workers.

The case studies provided a more refined picture of how care workers negotiated the boundaries between work and family life in practice. They revealed the way in which the particular nature of childcare work could make the idea of work–life balance particularly difficult, in particular its demanding and stressful character. Care workers reported the considerable effort needed to leave the work behind at the end of a working day, so much so that many felt they took their responsibilities and feelings home with them. For foster carers the working day never ended: work–family boundaries for them were not, nor could be, delineated by time. In addition, foster carers who had their own children at home faced dilemmas about treating foster children as 'their own' or treating them differently from their own children. Legally they lacked authority over foster children and had to be mindful at all times of issues of child protection, especially concerning discipline and the showing of physical affection. These issues made what for many was an ideal – the total integration of work and family life – difficult in practice. The need to provide continuity of care and high-quality care for vulnerable children and young people may not always mean that employers can be as flexible as care workers may wish them to be in meeting their workers' family needs. Particular challenges present themselves in the organisation of care workers' time.

Methodological issues

Since the study adopted a mixed methods design, some comments are in order about the processes of analysis for the different data sources and their integration, the ways in which the data analyses matched our intentions in designing the research, and the claims we can make for the study's results.

The first point is that this mixed methods study was based on team research (four persons) with different types of expertise and disciplinary background (sociology, psychology and social policy). Its different methods involved a degree of method specialisation within the team but also some overlap so that different team members took responsibility for the two surveys and their analysis, while several team members carried out and analysed the biographical interviews. The whole team participated in reflecting upon the case study material and discussing the overall analysis.

The different methods broadly addressed different timeframes, with the two surveys focusing upon care workers in present 'researcher time' and the biographical case studies providing insight into workers' perspectives over time and their own lifecourse. As suggested in Chapter Two, the different methods had different purposes. A strength of the Postal Survey was its potential as a sampling source for the biographical case studies and for a follow-up Telephone Survey a year later to determine the work destinations of childcare workers over time, given the policy interest in issues of the recruitment and retention among the childcare workforce. In addition, the Postal Survey and manager interviews sought to provide contextual information on larger groups of childcare workers and the local authorities and services in which they were located. The surveys provided extensive data on *group* characteristics, childcare workers' experiences of the work and their management of their work–family responsibilities. While the survey questions were in general designed to address different research questions from the biographical interviews, inevitably there was some overlap. However, the contexts in which the particular data were collected have been taken into account in their interpretation, in particular the timeframes adopted by informants and the particular form in which responses were elicited.

The data sources have been integrated largely in two ways, as suggested in the methodological literature (Greene et al, 1989; Brannen, 1992, 2004). The main mode of integration has been one of complementarity in which each data source and data analysis has addressed a rather differently framed research question. It is, however, the case that different methods reflect interpretivist epistemological assumptions albeit that some methods were regarded as more fit for purpose. A second mode of integration has also been relevant, namely the use of the survey evidence as a basis for further exploration and to initiate new questions to be explored in the biographical case study interviews.

The analysis of the biographical interviews involved a focus upon the *whole case* in contrast to the analysis of the surveys, which involves variable-based analysis. Drawing upon the transcript and the extended summary of each case, each team member took two cases from each of the four care worker groups and compared and contrasted them along a number of dimensions: care ethic orientations and origins, family life and care work patterns, experiences and perspectives on care work, the notion of care work as a career, and managing work–family responsibilities. Chapters Three, Four and Five draw mainly on the biographical material as cases. These analyses involved a number of strategies: the use of 'sensitising concepts' (Blumer, 1954) such as an ethic of care and forging a care work career and care worker identity; the application of concepts and substantive findings from the literature that informed the design of the study; and the drawing out of new themes generated by a close reading of the interviews. We were also attentive to the *form* that care workers' narratives took – in particular how people started their life stories and at which points in the lifecourse and in their narratives they articulated an ethic of care. Interviewees moved in and out of the narrative mode (as discussed in Chapter Two).

In other parts of the book, our approach has been more thematic, using the biographical cases as brief exemplars and juxtaposing this material with the survey evidence and manager interview analysis (Chapters Six, Seven, Eight and Nine). In Chapters Eight and Nine we alerted the reader to some of the deficiencies of relying upon only one type of evidence. For example, in Chapter Nine, which addressed how childcare workers managed their work–family responsibilities, the survey analysis offered little illumination on its own. A deeper understanding of the ways in which care work was experienced in workers' everyday lives and the constraints that impacted upon them was provided by the case study interviews and manager interviews.

Some contradictions arose between different types of evidence, notably between the survey evidence and the biographical interviews, for example in Chapter Eight, which examined the follow-up Telephone Survey evidence concerning who left and who stayed in their childcare occupations a year after the original Postal Survey. While the Postal Survey was designed to generate extensive data on each childcare group and across the groups, the responses to the set questions were pre-coded. This made it difficult to take account in the analysis of the context and timeframes in which care workers were considering the questions. Thus, Postal Survey data concerning care workers' future employment intentions were difficult to interpret and in some cases proved unreliable predictors of later actions, as reported in the Telephone Survey evidence. This is not an issue of reliability as normally understood in the methodological literature, but to do with the way in which present time infuses our perceptions of the future, so that people's experiences of their present jobs shaped how they presented their future work intentions at a particular moment.

The case material was also used to generate new themes and analysis not envisaged in the design of the project (Greene et al 1989), and therefore not reflected in the survey evidence. For example in Chapter Nine on childcare workers' coping with work and family responsibilities, the following issues emerged: the importance of the particular nature of childcare work (which varied by occupation), the emotional stress of the work, which workers often found difficult to manage because of issues of confidentiality in relation to child protection, and the need to create some boundaries around their work while seeking to be committed to the children in their care – both their own and those they cared for.

A key way in which claims are made for a study relates to issues of sample representativeness and generalisability. The Postal Survey was not based on a representative sample of childcare workers, either for the UK or for particular communities, although we did attempt to reach all the workers within the targeted areas. To do so we were reliant upon gatekeepers who were generally very cooperative and efficient in distributing the questionnaires. Although the overall response rate of 56% was higher than is often achieved in postal surveys, possible sample bias has to be borne in mind. For example, with respect to the Telephone Survey results, those who have left childcare work may have been underrepresented. The distinctiveness of the areas where we found the care workers also has to be recognised. However, the characteristics of our participants are broadly similar to those found in other larger studies, with some exceptions. Foster carers with higher qualifications were overrepresented together with a greater number of carers from minority ethnic backgrounds and lone-adult households. These differences reflect one of the areas in which the study was located.

The case study material involves a logic of extrapolation from one case to other similar cases, rather than the logic of statistical generalisability based on probability theory. The case studies were intended to provide insights into individual care workers' lives *as a whole* and *in context*. In that sense they 'represent' only themselves rather than the different worker groups. However, they also provide insights at a theoretical level about how childcare workers' commitment to caring developed over the lifecourse, how their working lives unfolded and the kinds of identities they crafted, and the processes by which they made sense of and experienced their work. Such theoretical insights speak to more than the particular case albeit that the complex of conditions, experiences and perspectives remain peculiar to each individual.

Policy implications

The findings of this study support the attention being given in current government policy in England to developing the care workforce in children's services, including the need to improve pay and conditions, provide better training and support, and develop an overarching framework for the Children's Workforce. At the same time, the study suggests the need for a more radical re-evaluation of the nature and purpose of care work with 'vulnerable' children, and illustrates the complexity of taking forward many of the workforce policy aims. In this final section of the book, we highlight a number of issues to which those who plan and run children's services may wish to pay attention.

The first relates to a concern with *childhood* – of the workers as well as those of the children they care for. The importance of childhood experience and its subsequent impact on adult life is the sine qua non for policies directed to providing good care for vulnerable children and young people. As this study has shown, most care workers located the care ethic in their own childhood. Some had experienced traumatic childhoods, which enabled them to identify and empathise with the children they care for, while others explicitly brought to bear on their work good childhood experiences or early experiences of caring. These resources need to be recognised in recruitment campaigns and developed through training, supervision and support. Individuals' own life experiences may substantially influence the way they understand care work and their care practice. High-quality childcare thus requires not only training and support for care workers, but time for reflection and self-understanding.

A second issue relates to policy concerns about *recruitment and retention* of what is increasingly a scarce labour force. The study found that childcare workers entered childcare at different lifecourse phases although some worked in the care sector earlier. It also found some correspondence between lifecourse phase of the carer and the age of children carers wished to care for. Thus, those with older or grown-up children were often less attracted to caring for young children. Recruitment strategies, national and local, need to be lifecourse specific, and provide the necessary work–family policies and supports at different lifecourse phases in order to retain staff.

For many female care workers, voluntary work constituted a route out of full-time motherhood into childcare work. Recruitment strategies may be able to capitalise on this especially among those with few qualifications and who may not return to their former occupations after maternity leave. Children's centres and extended schools could play an important role here through providing practical opportunities to engage with a range of family support and childcare services. Short hands-on 'taster' courses, or the possibility of shadowing or spending time with established carers, could provide a powerful recruitment tool. Certainly, practice placements as part of a social work diploma or degree appeared to have been a key factor in encouraging workers in our study to consider different types of care work.

The study also found that entry into care work at a particular moment is not always an active choice but is often serendipitous and dependent on a care worker being at the right place at the right time, for example working in a non-care occupation but located in a social services context and being attracted to childcare work. It may hinge upon a professional, family member or friend having experience of, or recommending, childcare work. The Children's Workforce Strategy needs to ensure that professionals be made more aware of their possible influence on the recruitment of other workers and clients that they meet in the course of their work. Recruitment agencies need therefore to be alerted to the range of routes by which care workers come into the work.

Gender is likely to remain a crucial issue affecting the different routes that men and women take in care work including the rewards they seek and competences they bring. Pathways into management need to become *less* gendered. The gendered pursuit by many women of caring work needs to be encouraged through the increased provision of opportunities for professional training leading to positions that are appropriately financially rewarded.

In relation to retention of care workers, our study found that childcare workers who left a particular occupation were not necessarily lost to the care workforce. Movement across care sectors could therefore be regarded as progression and an asset to be built upon rather than necessarily a problem, and provisions put in place to facilitate the movement and progression of childcare workers, as recommended in the Children's Workforce Strategy. On the other hand, this needs to be balanced against issues concerning the continuity of care of individual children.

Some loss of carers could be addressed by improving the rewards and employment conditions of care work, which we consider in more detail below. Better utilisation of the resource offered by home-based carers who are not directly employed by the local authority or care agency (foster carers and community childminders) could also help to address retention problems. The study found that a surprisingly high proportion (a third of community childminders and one in six of foster carers) did not have a child placed with them at the 12-month follow-up, and some were considering ceasing to offer the service for this reason. While local authorities clearly need to have a large pool of potential carers in order to facilitate matching placements to children's needs, this suggests a need to keep existing carers informed and 'on board', for example through regular newsletters or other forms of contact. Feedback that helps carers to feel they are treated as partners in the child's care should also help to retain workers. For example, the disappointment expressed by care workers in this study about lacking information on how children progressed after leaving their care could be remedied by finding appropriate ways of sharing this information, while taking into account the need for confidentiality.

A third concern is with *improving training and support*. The study found that childcare workers are often drawn to this work after they have experienced problems in their own lives, including traumatic personal and family experiences; having children with developmental, mental health or behavioural problems; needing to take on the care of stepchildren; having been in care themselves or taken on the care of siblings. This reinforces the importance of providing good supervision and support for carers. Childcare requires self-validation – workers feeling they have the potential to contribute to the well-being of vulnerable young people. Such self-validation depends not only on what individuals bring to the work, but upon ongoing training and mentoring support.

The study highlights how much childcare workers care *about* the quality of the care work they do as well as caring *for* children. Across different types of workers the study found an attraction to the idea of therapeutic or longer-term work with children. Interestingly, in countries such as Denmark, heads of residential establishments have reported relatively few difficulties with staff recruitment and retention compared to their counterparts in England (Petrie et al, 2007). One reason could be the emphasis in such establishments on actively working with young people to help them solve their problems, rather than the emphasis on containing children and keeping them safe that has characterised residential care in the UK. The expectation in countries with a social pedagogic approach to care work with children is that staff will be highly skilled in developing relationships with children in their care. This may well increase the rewards of such work for those who care for disadvantaged children in the hope of being able to 'make a difference'.

Proper professional training opportunities are needed to encourage and sustain the strong commitment that care workers bring to care work, in order to prevent the highly committed from becoming disillusioned and discouraged. However, the evidence from this study also points to the importance of recognising and building upon the experience and personal qualities that care workers bring to their work in developing an understanding of what it means to be a 'professional' care worker.

The study raises a number of issues concerned with professionalisation of the childcare workforce through qualifications and training. If the care of vulnerable young children is equated with being a 'good' mother, as it clearly was for some of our case study care workers, suggesting the need for training or a qualification may imply to them, if not intentionally, that their parenting skills are inadequate or lacking. How the work is understood influences attitudes towards the need for, and importance of, training and qualifications. Those workers, mainly foster carers and community childminders, who drew predominantly on tacit knowledge were more likely to say that training and qualifications were unnecessary. Having a work-based vocational qualification did not guarantee a shift in this view, although it did lead to a view that training and qualifications were important in providing functional knowledge. Those who had taken or were undertaking a higher qualification, such as a diploma in social work, all referred to the way such training and qualifications provided a theoretical base for their work. This has implications for training policies, suggesting a possible hierarchy of training opportunities that allow for a variety of different routes into and through the variety of work with children. Moreover, as research on adult literacy suggests (Barton and Hamilton, 1998), basic skills, when combined with other resources and opportunities, such as values and life experiences, may have a bearing on the functioning of skills and enable actors to build upon them.

The fourth issue concerns *financial rewards and working conditions*. The study suggests that childcare work is a pathway of the self as well as an occupation for some workers. Care workers forged identities for themselves as well as being shaped by the opportunities available to them. Seeing it in these terms poses challenges for policy – in terms of targeting and supporting workers with different trajectories and resources. One group with particular needs are older female childcare workers with few qualifications and little work experience who may think it too late to do further training even though they are disposed to make the effort. Another group are those care workers with greater cultural capital and resources and hence higher expectations in terms of monetary rewards and employment conditions compared to those who lack such resources. Issues arise as to whether and what kinds of experience and expertise can attract greater remuneration, and the consequences of such differential treatment for recruitment and retention.

The study has highlighted both the tensions in care work and the rewards. Management and social workers need to build upon the rewards and address the issues raised by childcare workers. Care workers felt undervalued and unappreciated: "Just a little bit of appreciation every now and then doesn't come amiss". Ways need to be found to improve the low status of childcare work through management practices and financial rewards. On the other hand, the study found that even care workers who had experienced little progression in the work, such as community childminders, saw themselves in some cases as 'having a career'. Policies need to provide childcare workers with increased flexibility and encouragement in order to make the notion of 'careers' meaningful.

Home-based workers often experienced isolation in their work, while some institution-based workers complained about lack of management or back-up support. Independent fostering agencies seemed better able than local authorities to offer the kind of support that foster carers wanted, partly as a result of having fewer carers allocated to each link worker and thus a more personalised response. Resources are needed to create good workplace environments in which there is support for dealing with challenging and stressful situations. For home-based care workers, fostering link workers and childminding scheme coordinators have an important role to play in organising support groups and in being available themselves for advice and support.

Family support workers felt that they were often used as social workers without the responsibility or status. Greater attention needs to be paid to teamwork for family support workers, in the context of their changing role and relocation in some authorities to social work teams. As other research with family support workers has also found (Carpenter and Dutton, 2003), working more closely alongside social work colleagues has not always led to greater teamwork, and in some cases has created a degree of role confusion and resentment among family support workers at their implied inferior status.

Finally, the issue of *family-friendly policies and practice*. Earlier we highlighted the importance of lifecourse phase and how it is necessary to take account of this in order to attract and retain different groups. Managers reported that the support on offer to help workers manage the interface of work and family life was limited, especially leave for family reasons. The study found that childcare workers managed their work–family responsibilities as best they could but this could be difficult, especially for home-based childcare workers. A consistent approach across types of care and local authorities is needed, with time off for family reasons. Paid time off from work to study would also provide useful support, since many care workers have to fit studies around family responsibilities as well as work. Such practices would provide key challenges since they have to be counterbalanced against the time needs of care of vulnerable children.

In managing the boundaries between work and family life, childcare workers reported two issues in particular that were difficult: the stressfulness of the work, which they could find difficult to cut off from, and the need to 'offload' their concerns to others in the context of the necessary conditions of confidentiality. Policy needs to find better ways of mentoring, including utilising those with professional skills in human service work and perhaps pairing workers to support one another, with well-qualified persons to support such arrangements.

Although such strategies may improve the situation in the short term, policy makers and services will, however, need to review their strategies for finding childcare workers in the *future* more radically. Reliance on the recruitment of home-based childcare workers from women who stay at home with their own young children is likely to become increasingly problematic. The norm today is for mothers to resume employment after parental leave. As the workforce in general, and the female workforce in particular, becomes more skilled and better remunerated, so childcare work faces greater competition. The result will be fewer low-qualified women (and men) of the kind found in our study available and prepared to do childcare work unless the financial rewards are increased and training needs are addressed accordingly.

Beyond this, however, the challenges are more profound, raising issues about how we as a society of both adults and children view children and childhood and the kinds of conditions that we create for full participation and citizenship in that society. How the least well-endowed – the 'vulnerable children' in this study – are provided for is a key indicator of that success or failure. The challenges for developing opportunities for the care workforce are no less great. As this book testifies, care not only links formal and informal contexts spatially, it also resonates and is interwoven with workers' lives over time and the lifecourse, raising important questions for policy and practice.

Appendix

Box A1: Contextual information about the organisations from which postal survey sample was drawn

Authority A

London local authority. *Foster care:* around a 100 foster carers with an older age profile. High proportion of single parents. Fees lower than independent sector. *Residential care:* no units. *Family support:* 23 based in nursery/centres, fostering team and leaving care teams. Mixed age group. No difficulty with recruitment and retention. *Community childminding:* approximately 45 childminders in the scheme. Hourly rate less than for private work. Entitled to 5 days sick/dependency leave and 4 weeks paid holiday. Support includes regular home visits and helpline. Good support for training. Low turnover.

Authority B

Shire authority in South of England. *Foster care:* approximately 500 foster carers, mostly couples with an older age profile and White British. Neighbouring authorities and independent fostering agencies paying higher fees. Problems with recruitment rather than retention. *Residential care:* 12 residential units, which tend to be 6-bed and with approximately 14 staff. Running homes 1-3 (see Box A2). *Family support:* service reorganised and family support workers joined social work teams and became known as social services assistants. New post of social work assistant created, which many family support workers moved into. *Community childminding:* no organised scheme although one planned.

Authority C

Shire authority in South of England. *Family support:* around 100 family support workers, although now known as social work assistants. Predominately female with a mix of full-time and part-time workers, but variable working patterns. Originally all based in family centres, but some teams now work independently. Introduced a career structure with different grades and pay related to competence and qualifications. Diversification of role: for example offering support to foster carers, taking on 'duty' officer duties, working in crisis and asylum teams, although some resistance to diversification among workforce.

Authority D
Metropolitan authority in North of England. *Community childminding:* 32 childminders in scheme who tend to be older with older children. Experience taken into account when recruiting childminders to the scheme, but can and do recruit new childminders. Little difference between hourly rate for private and community placements. About half are registered for overnight care and can care for a child for 28 nights without registering as a foster carer. Turnover has been low. Regular visits to support childminders.

Independent foster agency
Approximately 120 carers in South of England. Within southern region employs 7-8 social workers to provide support to about 70 foster carers. Higher proportion of single carers and carers from minority ethnic backgrounds. Recruitment more difficult than retention. Low turnover. Range of support including social events, supplying equipment and outreach workers.

Voluntary sector organisation (a)
Providing care and accommodation for children and young people. Running 6 children's homes, one of which is home number 4 (see Box A2). Approximately 15 staff per home, predominately female and full time.

Voluntary sector organisation (b)
Providing services for young people with disabilities across 3 authorities in one part of the country (including Authority B) and responsible for home number 6 (see Box A2).

Private childcare company (a)
10 homes and 130 staff. Most staff are female. Have 2 homes of 3 beds in each town where the company operates. Pay just over minimum wage for unqualified staff when they start. No sick pay if absence less than 4 days. No time off allowed for training. High turnover among care staff although not managers. Running home 7 (see Box A2).

Private childcare company (b)
3 homes and 50 staff. 40% of staff are male and 12% have a minority ethnic background. Male staff are older (aged 30+) and often pursuing a second career, while female staff are younger, most of them without children. Most (80%) are full time. Staff well qualified compared to national average. Training usually in staff's own time. Day staff not expected to do 'waking nights'. No sick pay. Running homes 8 and 9 (see Box A2).

Box A2: Characteristics of the residential homes for the postal survey

Public

1 6-bed long-term care unit for 12+ age group. 10.5 staff (fte) and 3.5 vacancies. 6 male staff.
2 5-bed respite care unit for 5-18+ age group. 12 staff (fte). No male staff.
3 6-bed respite care unit for 12+ age group. 12.5 staff (fte). 4 male staff.

Voluntary

4 8-bed assessment unit for 12-15 age group. 9 fte staff and 3 vacancies. 3 male staff.
5 9-bed respite care unit for all ages. 12 staff (fte). No male staff.
6 3-bed respite care unit for children with severe learning difficulties. Open weekends and school holidays. 5 staff (fte). 2 male staff.

Private

7 3-bed long-term care unit for 11-17 age group. 11 staff (fte). 2 male staff. Open a year.
8 3-bed unit offering long-term and respite care, and assessment. 8 staff (fte). 2 male staff. Open less than a year and run by same company as home number 9.
9 5-bed long-term care unit for 10-19 age group. 16.5 (fte) staff. 6 male staff. Open less than a year.

Box A3: Managers interviewed for the study

Authority A
Assistant director for children and families
Manager for foster care in Authority A (responsibility for short-term foster care)
Coordinator of sponsored childminding scheme in Authority A
Human resources manager (male)

Authority B
Assistant director for children and families (foster care, residential care and family support services) (male)
Operations manager (foster care, residential care and family support services)
Service manager for family placement (including retention of foster carers)
Strategic manager for family placement (foster care)
Area service manager for family support and children (services for children with disabilities including respite care and family support)
Human resources manager (male)

Authority C
Policy and standards manager (responsibility includes family support workers)

Authority D
Coordinator of sponsored childminding scheme

Independent foster agency
Regional manager

Voluntary sector
Service manager for charity with homes in Authority A (male)

Private sector
Human resources manager for company with residential homes in Authority B and across the country
Manager with responsibility for one home and services for children with disabilities for company with residential homes only in Authority B

Table A1: Demographic and employment details for the 24 case studies

Foster carers	Debra Henry	Mary Haywood	Brenda Reeves	Obufemi Williams	Margaret Henderson	Celia Anderson
Name	Debra Henry	Mary Haywood	Brenda Reeves	Obufemi Williams	Margaret Henderson	Celia Anderson
Age	44	47	40	55	51	57
Gender	Female	Female	Female	Male	Female	Female
Ethnicity	Black Caribbean	White British	White British	Nigerian	White British	White British
Marital status	Single parent	Recently married (previously a widow)	Married (2nd)	Married	Married	Single parent
Spouse's occupation		Builder		Social worker	HGV driver	
Children:						
Number	4	1	3	4	3	4
Ages (yrs)	11 to 23	15	3-7	18-23	25-30	20-35
At home	2	1	3	1?	0	1
Qualifications	NVQ Level 3	Art qualification	Dance qualifications	Masters degree	None	Qualified teacher
Years in job	8 with LA	16 with LA (includes fostering kin)	4 with IFA	8 initially with LA, now with IFA	5 with LA	9 with LA

continued .../

Foster carers cont						
Other work	Full-time student	Teaches art to young people	Dance teacher 6 hours a week	Volunteer work 3 days a week	Care assistant (self-employed) hours not known	None
Current placement(s):						
Number	1	2	1		2	1
Age(s)	13	14 and unclear	14		3 and 10	16
Type	Long-term	Long- and short-term	Long-term	No current placement	Long-term and respite	Long-term
Community childminders						
Name	Brenda Nelson	Gillian Dunscombe	Kate Humphries	Kathleen Robertson	Eileen Wheeler	Teresa Thomas
Age	50	40	37	47	41	56
Gender	Female	Female	Female	Female	Female	Female
Ethnicity	White British	White British	White British	White British and Black African	White British	White British
Marital status	Married	Single parent	Married	Married	Single parent	Married (2nd)

continued .../

Community childminders cont						
Spouse's occupation	Builder	Builder	Builder	Builder		Retired teacher, but working part time
Children:						
Number	2	3	2	2	3	2
Ages (yrs)	24 and 30	2, 12 and 14	5 and 18	16 and 21	16, 19 and 21	32 and 34
At home	1	3	2	1	2	0
Qualifications	None	NNEB	CSEs	GCSEs		NVQ Level3
Years in job	24	6	4	17 (although not continuously)	9, but fostering for 20 years (including kin)	30
Other work	Part-time voluntary work at school					Crèche worker 1.5 hours a week
Current community placement(s):						
Number	1	1	1	1	1	1
Age(s)	Preschool age	Toddler	Toddler	Toddler	4 months	2

continued .../

Community childminders cont					
Type	Weekend care. Private placement	Respite care at weekends. Also 1 private placement	2 days. Also 1 private placement	Long term. Also 9 private placements – part time and after school	2 nights a week. Also fosters 4 and has 3 private childminding placements	4 days a week
Residential social workers						
Name	Jenny Masters	Carol Jones	Natalie James	Marleen Bennett	Brian Stratford	Tom Jenkins
Age	33	48	36	45	39	50
Gender	Female	Female	Female	Female	Male	Male
Ethnicity	White British	White British	White British	White British and Black African		White British
Marital status	Married	Cohabiting	Married	Married (2nd)	Married	Married (2nd)
Spouse's occupation	Armed forces	Unemployed	Car service manager	Mechanic	Student (full time)	CAB advisor (part time)
Children: Number	2	2 from 1st marriage	1	3 adult ch from 1st marriage; 2 from 2nd	1	2 adult ch from 1st marriage; 1 from 2nd

continued .../

Residential social workers cont						
Ages (yrs)	7 and 10	24 and 26	4	19-23 and 9	13	5
At home	2	5	2	3	14	18
Qualifications	NVQ Level 2	NVQ Level 3	None	NVQ Level 3,	NVQ Level 3	Dip SW, NVQ Level 4
Years in job	2	5	2	3	14	18
Hours per week Other work/ studying	18.5	Full time	18.5	2 shifts a week	Full time	Full time
Family support workers						
Name	Clare Glover	Susanne Grant	Justine Naisbitt	Michelle O'Connor	Pat Foster	Sarah Butler
Age	41	39	47	36	49	47
Gender	Female	Female	Female	Female	Female	Female
Ethnicity	White British	Black Caribbean	White British	White British	White British	White British
Marital status	Married	Married	Single parent	Married	Cohabiting	Single parent
Spouse's occupation	Psychiatric nurse	Telephone Engineer		?	Musician?	
Children:						

continued .../

Family support workers *cont*						
Number	2	3	3	2	2	1
Ages (yrs)	11 and 14	8, 15 and 21	19, 20 and 26	2 and 6	23 and 33	15
At home	2	2 and 1 at university	2	2	1	1
Qualifications	NNEB	NNEB	GCSE	None	GCSE	BA
Years in job	8	3	4	10	14	3
Hours per week	4 days (30 hours)	Full time	Full time	16 hours	Full time	3 days
Other work/ studying	Dip SW (part time)	Dip SW (part time)		Part-time evening bar work and NVQ Level 3	About to start SW degree (part time)	

Notes: BA is Bachelor of Arts; CSE is Certificate of Secondary Education; Dip SW is Diploma in Social Work; GCSE is General Certificate of Education; IFA is independent fostering agency; NNEB is a qualification to be a Nursery Nurse; NVQ is National Vocational Qualification; LA is local authority; SW is Social Work.

References

Aldgate, J. and Bradley, M. (1999) *Supporting Families through Short-term Fostering*, London: The Stationery Office.

Antze, P. (1996) 'Telling stories, making selves: memory and identity in multiple personality disorder', in P. Antze and M. Lambek (eds) *Tense Past: Cultural Essays in Trauma and Memory*, New York: Routledge, pp 3–23.

Audit Commission (2002) *Recruitment and Retention: A Public Sector Workforce for the Twenty-first Century*, London: Audit Commission.

Balloch, S., Pahl, J. and McLean, J. (1998) 'Working in the social services: job satisfaction, stress and violence', *British Journal of Social Work*, vol 28, no 3, pp 329–50.

Barton, D. and Hamilton, M. (1998) *Local Literacies: Reading and Writing in One Community*, London: Routledge.

Bebbington, A. and Miles, J. (1990) 'The supply of foster families for children in care', *British Journal of Social Work*, vol 20, no 4, pp 283–307.

Becker, S., Aldridge, J. and Dearden, C. (1998) *Young Carers and their Families*, Oxford: Blackwell Science.

Bernstein, B. (2000) *Pedagogy, Symbolic Control and Identity:* Theory, Research, Critique, Lanham, MD: Rowman and Littlefield.

Blumer, H. (1954) 'What is wrong with sociological theory?', *American Sociological Review*, 19, pp 3–10.

Boddy, J., Cameron, C. and Petrie, P. (2006) 'The professional care worker: the social pedagogue in Northern Europe', in J. Boddy, C. Cameron and P. Moss (eds) *Care Work Present and Future*, Abingdon: Routledge, pp 93–110.

Brannen, J. (1992) *Mixing Methods: Qualitative and Quantitative Research*, Aldershot: Ashgate.

Brannen, J. (2004) 'Working qualitatively and quantitatively', in C. Seale, G. Gobo, J. Gubrium and D. Silverman (eds) *Qualitative Research Practice*, London: Sage Publications.

Brannen, J. (2005) 'Time and the negotiation of work–family boundaries: autonomy or illusion?', *Time and Society*, vol 14, no 1, pp 113–31.

Brannen, J. and Moss, P. (2003) 'Concepts, relationships and policies', in J. Brannen and P. Moss (eds) *Rethinking Children's Care*, Buckingham: Open University Press, pp 1–22.

Brannen, J. and Nilsen, A. (2002) 'Young people's time perspectives: from youth to adulthood', *Sociology*, vol 36, no 3, pp 513–37.

Brannen, J. and Nilsen, A. (2003) 'Adult development: changing definitions and concepts', in M. Pitt-Catsouphes and E. Kossek (eds) *The Work and Family Encyclopedia*, Chestnut Hill, MA: Sloan Work and Family Research Network, Boston College, available at: www.bc.edu/wfnetwork

Brannen, J. and Nilsen, A. (2007) 'Young people, time horizons and planning: a response to Anderson et al', *Sociology*, vol 41, no 1, pp 153-160 [

Brannen, J. and Pattman, R. (2005) 'Work–family matters in the workplace: the use of focus groups in a study of a UK social services department', *Qualitative Research*, vol 5, no 4, pp 523-42.

Brannen, J., Heptinstall, E. and Bhopal, K. (2000) *Connecting Children: Care and Family Life in Later Childhood*, London: Routledge Falmer.

Brannen, J., Moss, P. and Mooney, A. (2004a) *Working and Caring over the Twentieth Century: Change and Continuity in Four-generation Families*, Basingstoke: Palgrave.

Brannen, J., Pattmann, R. and Brockmann, M. (unpublished 2004b) *UK Social Services Organisational Case Study: A Cross National Study Funded by the EU*

Brannen, J., Lewis, S., Moss, P., Smithson, J. and McCarraher, L. (2001) *Workplace Change and Family Life: Report of Two Case Studies*, Manchester: Manchester Work–life Research Centre.

Bryman, A. (2006) 'Paradigm peace and implications for quality', *International Journal of Social Research Methodology: Theory and Practice*, vol 9, no 2, pp 111-26.

Cameron, C. (2003) 'An historical perspective on changing child care policy', in J. Brannen and P. Moss (eds) *Rethinking Children's Care*, Buckingham: Open University Press, pp 80-97.

Cameron, C. and Boddy, J. (2006) 'Knowledge and education for care workers: what do they need to know', in J. Boddy, C. Cameron and P. Moss (eds) *Care Work Present and Future*, London: Routledge.

Cameron, C., Mooney, A. and Moss, P. (2002) 'The child care workforce: current conditions and future directions', *Critical Social Policy*, vol 22, no 4, pp 572-95.

Cameron, C., Owen, C. and Moss, P. (2001) *Entry, Retention and Loss: A Study of Childcare Students and Workers*, London: DfEE.

Campbell-Clark, S. (2000) 'Work/family border theory: a new theory of work/family balance', *Human Relations*, vol 53, no 6, pp 747-70.

Cancian, F. and Oliker, S. (2000) *Caring and Gender*, Thousand Oaks, CA: Sage Publications.

Carey, M. (2003) 'Anatomy of a care manager', *Work, Employment and Society*, vol 17, no 1, pp 121-37.

Carpenter, B. and Dutton, J. (2003) *Outcomes and Costs of Therapeutic Family Support Services for Vulnerable Families with Young Children*, Report to the Department of Health, Durham: University of Durham.

Central Office of Information Communications (2001) *Perceptions of Social Work and Social Care: Report of Findings*, www.dh.gov.uk/assetRoot/04/07/43/21/04074321.pdf

Crow, G. (1989) 'The use of the concept of 'strategy' in recent sociological literature', *Sociology*, 23, pp 1-24.

CSCI (Commission for Social Care Inspection) (2005a) *The State of Social Care in England 2004-2005*, London: CSCI.

CSCI (2005b) *Making Every Child Matter: Messages from Inspections of Children's Services*, London: CSCI.

CSCI (2006) *The Right People for Me – Helping Children to Do Well in Long-term Foster Care*, www.csci.org.uk

Dahlberg, G., Moss, P. and Pence, A. (1999) *Beyond Quality in Early Childhood Education and Care: Postmodern Perspectives*, London: Falmer.

Daly, M. and Lewis, J. (1999) 'Introduction: conceptualizing social care in the context of welfare state restructuring', in J. Lewis (ed) *Gender, Social Care and State Restructuring in Europe*, Aldershot: Aldgate, pp 1-23.

Deakin, G. and Kelly, G. (2006) *Children's Workforce Research*, DfES Research Report No. 716, www.dfes.gov.uk/research

Dex, S. and Scheibl, F. (2002) *SMEs and Flexible Working Arrangements*, Bristol/York: The Policy Press/Joseph Rowntree Foundation.

DfES (2004) 2002/03 *Childcare and Early Years Workforce Survey: Childminders*. London: Department for Education and Skills.

DH (Department of Health) (1998) *Living Away from Home: Studies in Residential Care*, Chichester: John Wiley.

DH (2001) *Children's Homes at 31 March 2000, England*, Statistical Bulletin. London: Department of Health.

DH (2002) *National Minimum Standards for Children's Homes*, London: The Stationery Office.

Duncan, S. and Edwards, R. (1999) *Lone Mothers, Paid Employment and Gendered Moral Rationalities*, Basingstoke: Macmillan.

Eborall, C. (2003) *The State of the Social Care Workforce in England*, First Annual Report of the Topss England Workforce Intelligence Unit, Leeds: Topss England.

Eborall, C. (2005) *The State of the Social Care Workforce 2004*, The second skills research and intelligence annual report, Leeds: Skills for Care.

Edwards, R. and Ribbens, J. (1991) 'Meanderings around 'strategy': a research note on strategic discourse in the lives of women', *Sociology*, vol 25, no 3, pp 477-91.

Elder, G. (1978) 'Family history and the life course', in T. K. Hareven (ed) *Transitions: The Family Life Course in Historical Perspective*, New York: Academic Press.

Elder, G. H. (1985) 'Perspectives on the life course', in G. H. Elder Jr (ed) *Life Course Dynamics: Trajectories and Transitions 1968-1980*, Ithaca, NY: Cornell University Press, pp 23-49.

Erikson, E. (1950) *Childhood and Society*, New York: Norton.

Everett Hughes, C. (1958 [1984]) 'Cycles, turning points and careers', in *The Sociological Eye: Selected Papers*, Somerset, NJ: Transaction Publishers.

Farmer, E., Moyers, S. and Lipscombe, J. (2004) *Fostering Adolescents*, London: Jessica Kingsley Publishers.

Felstead, A. and Jewson, N. (2000) *In Work at Home: Towards an Understanding of Homeworking*, London: Routledge.

Finch, J. and Mason, J. (1993) *Negotiating Family Responsibilities*, London: Routledge.

Fostering Network (2004) *Shortage of Foster Carers Reaches Critical Levels*, Press release, 24 August, www.fostering.net/news

Fostering Network (2006) *Statement on the Government's Announcement of National Minimum Fostering Allowances*, Press release, 27 July, www.fostering.net/news

Freud, S. (1949) *An Outline of Psychoanalysis*, New York: Norton.

Greene, J., Caracelli, V. J. and Graham, W. F. (1989) 'Towards a conceptual framework for mixed-method evaluation designs', *Education, Evaluation and Policy Analysis*, vol 11, no 3, pp 255-74.

Greenfields, M. and Statham, J. (2004) *Support Foster Care: Developing a Short-break Service for Children in Need*, Understanding Children's Social Care Series No 8, London: Institute of Education.

Hareven, T. K. and Masaoka, K. (1988) 'Turning points and transitions: perceptions of the life course', *Journal of Family History*, 13, pp 271-89.

Harrison, A. (2006) *The Children's Workforce Development Council and Residential Child Care Staff*, National Centre for Excellence in Residential Child Care Conference proceedings, Issue 21, pp 17-19, www.ncb.org.uk/ncercc/20060428ncerccnewsletter.pdf

Hill, M. (2005) 'Children's boundaries: within and beyond families' in L. McKie and S. Cunningham-Burley (eds) *Families in Society*, Bristol: The Policy Press.

HM Government (2003) *Every Child Matters*, London: The Stationery Office.

HM Government (2005a) *Children's Workforce Strategy*, Nottingham: DfES.

HM Government (2005b) *Common Core of Skills and Knowledge for the Children's Workforce*, Nottingham: DfES.

HM Government (2006) *Children's Workforce Strategy: The Government's Response to the Consultation*, Nottingham: DfES.

Hollway, W. (2006) *The Capacity to Care: Gender and Ethical Subjectivity*, London: Routledge.

Hollway, W. and Jefferson, T. (2000) *Doing Qualitative Research Differently: Free Association, Narrative and the Interview Method*, London: Sage Publications.

Hyman, J., Scholarios, D. and Baldry, C. (2005) 'Getting on or getting by? Employee flexibility and coping strategies for home and work', *Work, Employment and Society*, vol 19, no 4, pp 705-27.

Jarvis, H. (1999) 'The tangled web we weave: household strategies to co-ordinate home and work', *Work, Employment and Organisation*, vol 13, no 2, pp 225-47.

Johansson, S. and Cameron, C. (2002) *Review of Literature since 1990: Job Satisfaction, Quality of Care and Gender Equality*, Consolidated Report, available from http://144.82.31.4/carework/reports/WP5finalConsolidatedReport.pdf

Johnson, S., Dunn, K. and Coldron, J. (2005) *Mapping Qualifications and Training for the Children and Young People's Workforce. Short Report 6: Research Review*, www.dfes.gov.uk/research/

Kellerhals, J., Ferreira, C. and Perrenoud, D. (2002) 'Kinship cultures and identity transmissions', in B. Bawins-Legros (ed) 'Filiation and identity: towards a sociology of intergenerational relations', *Current Sociology*, vol 50, no 2: Monograph 1, March.

Kirton, D., Beecham, J. and Ogilvie, K. (2003) *Remuneration and Performance in Foster Care: Report to Department for Education and Skills*, Canterbury: University of Kent.

Laming, Lord (2003) *The Victoria Climbié Inquiry Report*, London: The Stationery Office.

Levy, R. (2005) 'Phases of individual and family life, and sex-specific master statuses: two necessary lenses for getting depth of view about family interactions', Keynote paper at the Lisbon Workshop on Contemporary Families of the ESA Research Network, Sociology of Families and Intimate Lives, Lisbon, March.

Lewis, S., Smithson, J. and das Dores Guerreiro, M. (2002) 'Into parenthood: young people's sense of entitlement to support for the reconciliation of employment and family life', in J. Brannen, A. Nilsen, A. Lewis and J. Smithson (eds) *Young Europeans, Work and Family Life: Futures in Transition*, London: Routledge.

McKie, L., Gregory, S. and Bowlby, S. (2002) 'Shadow times: the temporal and spatial frameworks and experiences of caring and working', *Sociology*, 36, pp 897-924.

McLean, J. (1999) 'Satisfaction, stress and control over work', in S. Balloch, J. McLean and M. Fisher (1999) *Social Services Under Pressure*, Bristol: The Policy Press.

Mainey, A. (2003) *Better Than You Think: Staff Morale, Qualifications and Retention in Residential Childcare*, London: National Children's Bureau.

Mason, J (1996) 'Gender, care and sensitivity in family and kin relationships', in J. Holland and L. Atkins (eds) *Sex, Sensibility and the Gendered Body*, London: Macmillan.

Mauthner, N., McKee, L. and Strell, L. (2001) *Work and Family Life in Rural Communities*, York: Joseph Rowntree Foundation.

Mayall, B. (1996) *Children, Health and Social Order*, London: Routledge.

Milligan, I., Kendrick, A. and Avan, G. (2005) 'Nae too Bad': job satisfaction and staff morale', *Scottish Journal of Residential Child Care*, vol 4, no 1, pp 22-32.

Mills, C.W. (1959 [1980]) *The Sociological Imagination*, London: Penguin Books.

Mooney, A. (2003) 'Mother, teacher, nurse? How childminders define their role', in J. Brannen and P. Moss (eds) *Rethinking Children's Care*, Buckingham: Open University Press, pp 131-46.

Mooney, A. and Statham, J. (2002) *The Pivot Generation: Informal Care and Work After Fifty*, Bristol: The Policy Press

Mooney, A., Knight, A., Moss, P. and Owen, C. (2001) *Who Cares? Childminding in the 1990s*, Bristol: The Policy Press.

Morgan, D.H.J. (1996) *Family Connections*, Cambridge: Cambridge University Press.

Morgan, R. (2005) *Being Fostered: A National Survey of Foster Children, Foster Carers and Birth Parents*, London: CSCI.

Moss, P. (1999) 'Renewed hopes and lost opportunities: early childhood in the early years of the Labour government', *Cambridge Journal of Education*, vol 29, no 2, pp 229-39.

Moss, P. and Petrie, P. (2002) *From Children's Services to Children's Spaces*, London: Routledge and Falmer.

Moss, P., Boddy, J. and Cameron, C. (2006) 'Introduction', in J. Boddy, C. Cameron and P. Moss (eds) *Care Work, Present and Future*, Abingdon: Routledge.

Moss, P., Dillon, J. and Statham, J. (2000) 'The 'child in need' and 'the rich child': discourses, constructions and practice', *Critical Social Policy*, vol 20, no 2, pp 233-54.

Nilsen, A. (1996) 'Stories of life – stories of living: women's narratives and feminist biography', in *NORA: Nordic Journal of Women's Studies*, vol 4, no 1, pp 15-31.

Nilsen, A. (1997) 'Great expectations? Exploring men's biographies in late modernity', in S. Grønmo and B. Henrichsen (eds) *Society, University and World Community: Essays for Ørjar Øyen*, Oslo: Scandinavian University Press, pp 111-35.

Nilsen, A. (1999) 'Where is the future? Time and space as categories in the analysis of young people's images of the future', *Innovation: European Journal for the Social Sciences*, vol 12, no 2, pp 175-94.

Nippert-Eng, C. E. (1996) *Home and Work*, Chicago, IL: University of Chicago Press.

Nutt, L. (2006) *The Lives of Foster Carers: Private Sacrifices, Public Restrictions*, London: Routledge.

Penna, S., Taylor, I. and Soothill, K. (1995) *Job Satisfaction and Dissatisfaction among Residential Childcare Workers*, York: Joseph Rowntree Foundation.

Perrons, D. (2003) 'The new economy and the work–life balance: conceptual explorations and a case study of new media', *Gender, Work and Organisation*, vol 10, no 1, pp 65-93.

Petrie, P. (2003) 'Social pedagogy: an historical account of care and education as social control', in J. Brannen and P. Moss (eds) *Rethinking Children's Care*, Buckingham: Open University Press, pp 61-80.

Petrie, P., Boddy, J., Cameron, C., Simon, A. and Wigfall, V. (2007) *Working with Children in Residential Care: European Perspectives*, Buckingham: Open University Press.

Prout, A. and James, A. (1997) 'A new paradigm for the sociology of childhood', in A. James and A. Prout (eds) *Constructing and Deconstructing Childhoods: Contemporary Issues in the Sociological Study of Childhood*, London: Falmer Books.

Pugh, G., De'Ath, E. and Smith, C. (1994) *Confident Parents, Confident Children: Policy and Practice in Parent Education and Support*, London: National Children's Bureau.

Ragin, C. (1989) *The Comparative Method: Moving Beyond Qualitative and Quantitative Strategies*, Berkeley, CA: University of California Press.

Reynolds, T., Callendar, C. and Edwards, R. (2003) *Caring and Counting: The Impact of Mothers' Employment on Family Relations*, Bristol/York: The Policy Press/Joseph Rowntree Foundation.

Ricoeur, P. (1992) *Oneself as Another*, Chicago, IL: University of Chicago Press.

Rolfe, H., Metcalf, H., Anderson, T. and Meadows, P. (2003) *Recruitment and Retention of Childcare, Early Years and Play Workers*, London: National Institute of Economic and Social Research.

Rose, M. (2004) *Career Perceptions and Career Pursuits in the UK 1986-2002*, Bath: University of Bath.

Rousseau, J-J (1762) Emile

Sellick, C. and Connolly, J. (2002) 'Independent fostering agencies uncovered: the findings of a national study', *Child and Family Social Work*, 2, pp 107-20.

Sellick, C. and Howell, D. (2004) 'A description and analysis of multi-sectoral fostering practice in the United Kingdom', *British Journal of Social Work*, 34, pp 481-99.

Simon, A., Owen, C., Moss, P. and Cameron, C. (2003) *Mapping the Care Workforce: Supporting Joined-up Thinking: Secondary Analysis of the Labour Force Survey for Childcare and Social Care Work*, London: Institute of Education.

Sinclair, I. (2005) *Fostering Now: Messages from Research*, London: Jessica Kingsley Publishers.

Sinclair, I., Gibbs, I. and Wilson, K. (2004) *Foster Carers: Why They Stay and Why They Leave*, London: Jessica Kingsley Publishers.

SSI (Social Services Inspectorate) (2001) *Modern Social Services: A Commitment to deliver*, The 10th Annual Report of the Chief Inspector of Social Services, 2000/2001, London: Department of Health Publications.

Statham, J. and Mooney, A. (2006) 'Location, location, location: the importance of place in care work with children', in J. Boddy, C. Cameron and P. Moss (eds) *Care Work: Present and Future*, London: Routledge, pp 71-89.

Statham, J., Dillon, J. and Moss, P. (2000) *Placed and Paid for: Supporting Families through Sponsored Day Care*, London: The Stationery Office.

Sullivan, C. and Lewis, S. (2000) 'Space and the intersection of work and family in homeworking households', *Community, Work and Family*, vol 3, no 2, pp 185-204.

Triseliotis, J., Borland, M. and Hill, M. (1999) *Fostering Good Relations: A Study of Foster Care and Foster Carers in Scotland*, Edinburgh: The Stationery Office.

Triseliotis, J., Borland, M. and Hill, M. (2000) *Delivering Foster Care*, London: British Agencies for Adoption and Fostering.

Tronto, J. (1993) *Moral Boundaries: A Political Argument for the Ethics of Care*, London: Routledge.

Tronto, J. (2004) 'Care as the work of citizens', in K. Waerness (ed) *Dialogue on Care*, Bergen: Centre for Women's and Gender Research, University of Bergen, pp 91–119.

Walker, M., Hill, M. and Triseliotis, J. (2002) *Testing the Limits of Foster Care*, London: BAAF.

Wengraf, T. (2001) *Qualitative Research Interviewing: Biographic Narrative and Semi-structured Methods*, London: Sage Publications.

Whitaker, D., Archer, L. and Hicks, L. (1998) *Working in Children's Homes: Challenges and Complexities*, Chichester: John Wiley.

White, M., Hill, S. and Smeaton, D. (2004) *Managing to Change: British Workplaces and the Future of Work*, Basingstoke: Palgrave.

Wilson, K., Sinclair, I., Taylor, C., Pithouse, A. and Sillick, C (2003) *Fostering Success: An Exploration of the Research Literature in Foster Care*, London: Social Care Institute for Excellence.

Winchester, R. (2003) 'Stay or go?', *Community Care*, 16–22 October, pp 32–4.

Index